Haslam's Journey

About the Author

Chris Wright is the author of over twenty books, including *Billy Bray In His Own Words,* published by Highland Books in 2004. Chris served as an aerial reconnaissance photographer with Royal Air Force squadrons in Germany and Malta. This was at the height of the cold war, with surveillance being done at high altitude over Middle East countries and along the Soviet border. Leaving the RAF to specialise in industrial photography, Chris has gone on to develop remotely operated cameras and equipment to inspect components deep within nuclear reactors.

The Timpitters' Mine was the first of seven children's adventure titles with Victory Press (now Kingsway), many of which were sold as Sunday School prizes. In the 1980s Chris rewrote seven Christian Classics for young readers published by Bridge in the United States, and later an updated edition of FW Bourne's *The King's Son.* Five of his thrillers have recently been published by Hard Shell (www.hardshell.com) in the USA.

The parents of three grown up children - Jonathan, Simon and Emma - Chris and his wife Liz live in the West Country, where Chris has been a home group leader in his local church for many years.

The website www.williamhaslam.com is maintained by the author.

About Highland Books

You can find out more about our publishing programme from our website www.highlandbks.com. If you see any mistakes, you can e-mail us on errata@highlandbks.com: there's also an error page on our website where we post corrections.

Haslam's Journey

'From Death Into Life'
and
'Yet Not I'

Autobiographical accounts of William Haslam's ministry, abridged and annotated by

Chris Wright

Highland

From Death Into Life first published 1880
Yet Not I first published 1882 by Morgan and Scott, London.

This combined abridged and annotated edition first published in 2005 by Highland Books, Two High Pines, Knoll Road, Godalming, Surrey GU7 2EP

Line illustrations © 2005 Simon Wright

All Scripture quotations are from the Authorised Version of 1611.

ISBN: 1-897913-78-8

Cover design by Steve Carroll

Printed in Finland by WS Bookwell

Contents

Dedication

For my wife Liz

Acknowledgments

Many people have encouraged me in this work, and I am really grateful for their interest and support. I would like especially to thank Angela Broome of the Courtney Library in Truro, Cornwall for her great patience in hunting through the archives on many occasions - even after I kept assuring her I would want nothing more! Also Richard, William Haslam's great great-grandson who has come up with many fascinating details, photographs and other memorabilia. In addition, Alasdair Denton, the www.williamhaslam.org website co-ordinator, who has provided the portrait of William Haslam used on the cover of this book, and contributors to his website, particularly Geraint Jones and David F Haslam (no relation), who have helped with several dates and written references.

Foreword

I was thrilled to hear that Chris Wright had made the writings of William Haslam available for modern readers. I first read *From Death Into Life* just before going to theological college – someone had recommended it on a conference and a number of us got hold of second-hand copies. Word about the book seemed to spread. It made a big impact on us all.

It was easy for us to be fooled into thinking that the key to bearing fruit in future ministry was to be well-trained and competent. *From Death Into Life* underlined that without the power of the Spirit all our labour is futile. What struck us all was that the effect of the Spirit's work in Haslam was not just to bless him, but to send him out into the hardest and neediest corners of the country, and to equip him for the sort of ministry which he would otherwise never have contemplated doing in a million years.

The church today desperately needs authentic ministry that is empowered by the Spirit. There is much talk of the Spirit's work at the moment, but so often His work is confined to the realm of personal blessing, rather than as empowering God's people for radical and costly ministry – of the sort that Haslam undertook.

I hope and pray that it will be possible to get this book into the hands of not just people already engaged in Christian ministry – as an inspiration to them – but also into the hands of the sort of everyday Christian who fears that they can't possibly be used by God, but might, by reading Haslam, see how God by His Spirit takes hold of the most unlikely people and uses them in extraordinary ways.

Mike Cain, Associate Vicar
Christ Church Clifton, Bristol

Prologue

BALDHU, CORNWALL AT SUNSET: the final glow of orange from the high clouds is reflected briefly from the slate roof of the church. Its first cleric, the Rev William Haslam, designed this building in 1847 to hold nearly six hundred people. But sadly the situation in 2005 is that the building is closed and boarded-up.

Where have the parishioners gone? Indeed, where are the dwellings? The answer lies with the tin industry. Nearly all the Cornish tin and copper mines closed at the end of the nineteenth century, forcing mining families to depart this area in droves to seek a more secure life in countries like Australia and Canada.

The smartest thing round here is Billy Bray's grave, topped with a granite obelisk. He was a legendary Cornish miner and preacher who saw the winds of revival visit this community and fill this church to overflowing – his house is just down the road, in an even worse state than this building. Billy Bray came here to Baldhu in 1848 to witness William Haslam's grand opening ceremony, watching in dismay as Bishop Phillpotts of Exeter carried out the consecration. Billy takes one look at William Haslam and leaves in disgust. Five years later Billy is back, lifting Haslam in the air and dancing round with him in celebration.

Something changed. This book is the story of a life taken over by God. We are going to travel with William Haslam on his journey from personal tragedy to joy as he faces the prospect of an early death, struggles with a lifeless faith, encounters an apathetic congregation – and deals with serious hostility from various bishops and fellow clergy. Not one to feel sorry for himself, Haslam tells his story with humour and honest self-deprecation.

William Haslam was a prolific writer, publishing books and articles on both archaeology and the Christian faith. He wrote the intriguing story of his ministry in two volumes, *From Death Into Life* and *Yet Not I*. In the first volume Haslam tells of his early years in the church, especially in Cornwall, and in the second of his middle years in Bath, Norfolk, Scotland, Buckingham and London.

To produce this single volume from Haslam's two books it has been necessary to cut words from some sentences, sentences from some paragraphs, paragraphs from some chapters, and even remove whole chapters. Very occasionally I have altered a word that has either completely dropped out of use or changed its meaning. Other than that, and a couple of simple words joining edited sections, all the words here are Haslam's.

With simplified punctuation, shorter paragraphs and a modern typeface the writing is now easier to digest. The occasional words in square brackets [like this] in quoted sections are mine, inserted to help the reader understand the meaning or appreciate the situation more readily. I have generally copied Haslam's over-use of capital letters for terms such as Vicar and Bishop, as this is in keeping with his obvious respect for these titles. Perhaps I should add that many of the chapter divisions and headings are not from the originals, a necessity caused by the exclusion of so much text.

From Death Into Life was first published in 1880 and reprinted many times up to the present. *Yet Not I* followed in 1882, and also went into several reprints in Haslam's lifetime. Their combined word count is nearly 214,000, compared to the 85,000 of Haslam's words in this book. Anyone wanting more details of Haslam's life can look for copies of the originals, one of the recent reprints, or OCR copies on the internet.

Rather like seeing the film of a book, readers who are familiar with the original writing will realise some of their favourite events are missing, but this abridged book is intended to introduce new readers to a great life of Christian faith, and I have endeavoured to choose a varied and unforgettable selection.

Will some of the events recounted here sound too far-fetched to be true? Haslam himself ran up against this problem after publishing *From Death Into Life* in 1880, and in the foreword to *Yet Not I* two years later he makes the following statement:

> Some people have considered the statements in my former volume [*From Death Into Life*] as exaggerated, not to say "untrue!" I will only say that persons who have been in such scenes, and have witnessed the mighty power of God, will think that they are somewhat guardedly and tamely put forth. Indeed, for fear of taxing the credulity of some of my readers too much, I have understated some things and left many others unsaid.

> Exception has been taken, especially in reference to the dreams, visions and revelations recorded which were given to people among whom I was working. I do not profess to account for these things, or even to explain them. I merely relate the facts as they came under my notice, and that not altogether so fully as I might have done.

> Again, the work of the Lord is attributed to "Cornish excitement". As to this, I cannot but think that it is not in Cornwall only that persons are excited, who have anything to be excited about. I am bound to say that people in other parts of England, under similar circumstances, demonstrate in the same way.

The sun may have set for now on Baldhu, but wherever the sun is going down, somewhere else it is rising. The witness of William Haslam continues through the world, for everyone seems to have heard of a parson who was converted while preaching his own sermon! William Haslam is that man. Later, another of his 'famous' sermons will cause a mass walkout of assembled clergy in St Paul's Cathedral.

You are in for a mixture of laughter, tears and wonder as William Haslam's calling takes him across Cornwall and thence to work in the long-gone slums of Bath, to be part of a major revival in Norfolk, and later to find both Disraeli and Gladstone attending a mission in his prestigious church in London's Mayfair.

From Death Into Life

CHAPTERS DO NOT CORRESPOND TO
ORIGINAL EDITION

CHAPTER 1

The Broken Nest – 1841

I HAD TAKEN my degree, was about to be ordained, and [at the age of twenty-three] had plans to settle down as an efficient country Parson. One evening after a hard and tiring day a letter was put into my hand, which had been following me for several days. 'Most urgent' was written on the outside. It told me of the alarming illness of the lady to whom I was engaged, and went on to say that if I wished to see her alive I must set off with all haste.

At eight o'clock I left London by the night mail for the journey of two hundred and eighty miles. All that night I sat outside the coach, and all the next day, and part of the following night. The fatigue of sitting up all night, together with the intense cold of the small hours of the morning, were almost beyond endurance.

With the morning came a warm and bright sunshine, which in some degree helped to cheer me. About thirty hours after starting I found myself staggering along to the well-known house. The door was softly opened by a relative who had been anxiously watching for my arrival. She conducted me upstairs to what I expected was a sick chamber. To my horror the first thing I saw in the middle of the room was a coffin, with candles burning on either side.

I nearly fell to the ground with this tremendous shock and surprise. Here was the face so dear to me. There was no smile, no voice, no welcome: nothing but the silence of death to greet me.

The happy nest that I thought was mine was now broken. Murmuring and complaining I spoke unadvisedly. A gentle voice upbraided me, adding that I had far better kneel down in submission to God, and say, "Thy will be done."

This, however, was not so easy. The demon of rebellion had seized me, filling my mind with hard thoughts against

God. For three hours I walked about the room in the most perturbed state of mind, so much so that I grieved my friends who came repeatedly to ask me to kneel down, and say, "Thy will be done."

"Kneel down. Just kneel down."

At length I did so, and while someone was praying my tears began to flow. I said the words, "Thy will be done." Immediately, the spell was broken and I was enabled to say from my heart, again and again, "Thy will be done."

I was conscious of a marvellous change in my mind. Rebellion was gone and resignation had come in its place. God had been, as it were, a stranger to me. Now I felt as though I knew and loved Him and could kiss His hand, though my tears flowed freely.

The funeral took place the same morning. It was a time of great emotion. Sorrow and joy met and flowed together. I thought of the dear one I had lost, but yet more of the God of love I had found. To remember that she was with Him was an additional comfort. The funeral service was soothing and elevating beyond expression. When it was all over, such a sense of desolation came upon me that I felt utterly forlorn and truly sad. Yet I was conscious that God was looking on, and that He had not forsaken me.

The strain I had undergone brought on an illness. I was seized with inflammation of the lungs and was dangerously ill. The doctor pronounced that I could not recover, and bade me prepare for eternity.

Judges and doctors, when they pass sentence of death, seem to regard religion as a necessary preparation for it. Having received this solemn warning, I took down the Prayer Book and religiously read over the office for the Visitation of the Sick. I became so interested that I determined to read it three times a day. The prayer for a sick child commended itself to my mind, so that by changing a few words I made it applicable to my own case. I used it not only three, but even seven times a day. In substance it petitioned that I might be taken to heaven if I died, or that if it should please God to restore my health, He would let me live to His glory.

One morning the thought came to me as I was sitting all alone by the fire, "What have I been praying for? That the Lord would take me to heaven if I die? Or if I live, that He would let me live to his glory?" Why, I thought, this is heaven both ways. Heaven in heaven, or heaven on earth, whichever way it pleases God to answer my prayer. Somehow I felt certain that He would answer it. I was exceedingly happy and could not help thanking Him.

From that day I began to feel better, and became impressed with the idea that I was to live and not die. The doctor smiled when I told him so, for he did not believe it. He and two other physicians told me that my lungs were diseased. Indeed, six months afterwards all three sounded me and declared that one lung was inoperative, and the other much affected.

My doctor also told me, "It is one of the fatal signs of consumption for the patient to feel or think he is getting better."

Yet I had a certain conviction that I was to recover. As soon as he had gone I put on my coat and hat and went out for a walk. I trembled much from weakness, and found it necessary to move very slowly and stop often. Under the shelter of a wall, courting the warmth of the bright shining sun, I managed to make my way to the churchyard.

While I was sitting there alone, the great bell struck out unexpectedly and caused me to shake all over. It was the sexton tolling to announce the departure of the soul of some villager from the world. Having done this he came out with his boards and tools to dig the grave. He did not observe me and went on diligently with his work. The ground had so often been broken before that it did not take him long to accomplish his task. He gradually got deeper and deeper into the ground till he disappeared altogether from my sight. I crept to the edge of the narrow pit in which he was, and looked into it.

I have even now a most vivid remembrance of this, and place it on record to show how delusive are our feelings. Because I did not feel my soul was in any danger, I took it for granted that there really was none. That day was an eventful one in my life. In the gladness of my heart I gave myself to

God, to live for him. I had given my will before, and now I gave my life, and was happy in the deed.

I did not know at that time that faith does not consist in believing that I have given myself, even if I meant it ever so sincerely, but in believing that God has accepted me.

When I was able to return south I did so by easy stages, till I got back to the neighbourhood of London where I was ordered to remain indoors for the remainder of the winter.

I spent my time most happily in reading and prayer. I used to have much pleasure every day in asking God to give me a deeper sense of his love, that I might thank Him and show forth His praise with my life as well as my lips.

God was good to me, and therefore I loved Him. I turned over a new leaf, and therewith covered up the blotted page of my past life. On this new path I endeavoured to walk as earnestly, in a religious way, as I had lived in a worldly one.

I did not see then, as I have since, that turning over a new leaf to cover the past is not by any means the same thing as turning back the old leaves and getting them washed in the blood of the Lamb. I thought my acceptance with God depended upon my works. This made me very diligent in prayer, fasting and alms deeds. I often sat and dreamed about the works of mercy and devotion I would do when I was permitted to go out again.

I took it for granted that I was a child of God, because I had been baptised and brought into the Church. And having been confirmed and admitted to the Lord's Table, I concluded that I was safely on the way to heaven.

All this, be it observed, was because God had saved not my soul, but my life; for as yet I had not felt any trouble about my soul. I had not been awakened by the Spirit to know the danger and sorrow of being separated from God – which is spiritual death. I was perfectly unconscious that between God and myself there was the "impassable gulf".

As a boy in India I remember being greatly struck with the calmness of the Hindus, as contrasted with the impatience and angry spirit of the English. On one occasion I observed one of the former at his devotions.

He, with others, had been carrying me about in a *palankeen* all day in the hot sun. In the evening he most reverently took from his girdle a piece of mud of the sacred river Ganges, and dissolving this in water he washed a piece of ground. Then having washed his feet and hands he stepped on this sacred spot and began to cook his food. While it was preparing he was bowed to the ground with his face between his knees, worshipping towards the setting sun.

A boy who was standing by me, said, "If you touch that man he will not eat his dinner."

In a thoughtless moment I did so with my hand, and immediately he rose from his devotions. Instead of threatening and swearing at me, as some might have done who belong to another religion, he only looked reproachfully, and said, "Ah, Master William!" Then emptying out the rice which was on the fire he began his ceremony all over again.

It was quite dark before he had finished his *poojah* or worship, and his meal. This man's religious self-possession made a greater impression on me than if he had abused or even struck me for hindering his dinner. I thought to myself, "I will be a Hindu when I grow up!"

And truly I kept my word, though not in the same form; for what else was I in my earnest, religious days!

It was a happy winter to me. I had no desire for the world and its pleasures. I was happier now than ever I had been before, so I am convinced from personal experience that even a religious life may be one of joy, though by no means so satisfying and abiding as a truly spiritual one.

I longed for the time when I could be ordained, and devote my energies to work for God in the ministry.

CHAPTER 2

Ordination and First Parish 1842/43

IN THE RETURNING SPRING, as I was feeling so much stronger, I thought I would go and see the physician who had sounded me some months before. After a careful examination he still adhered to his previous opinion, and gave me very little hope of recovery. He suggested that if I went to the north coast of Cornwall there might be a chance for me.

On my return home I took up an *Ecclesiastical Gazette*, though it was three months old, and looked over the advertisements. There I observed one which invited a Curate for a church in that very neighbourhood. It was a sole charge, but strange to say, a title for holy orders was offered also. I wrote a letter asking for particulars, in which I stated my Church views and that I was ordered to that part of the country for the benefit of my health.

The Vicar, who resided in another parish thirty miles off, was so eager to get help that he wrote back to say he had sent my letter to the Bishop with one from himself, and that I should hear from his lordship in a few days.

I was surprised at this precipitation of affairs, and even more so when I received a note from Bishop Phillpotts of Exeter[1] bidding me come to him immediately, that I might be in time for the Lent ordination. Accordingly I started westward.

Having passed my examination, I was sent a year afterwards to Bishop Denison of Salisbury for priest's orders. I was very weak and much exhausted with travelling, but still went on though I know not how.

1   Henry Phillpotts, Bishop of Exeter from 1830 to 1869.

THE MEN BEHIND THE COLLARS

In the nineteenth century, Anglican parish clergy were divided into Perpetual Curates, Vicars and Rectors in order of ascending status. All had security of tenure, but their mode of remuneration was different, giving rise to their individual titles. Church income came from so-called major and lesser tithes, glebe land, and fees for marriages and burials etc.

Perpetual Curates had no independent resources, being supported by the diocese or patron(s). They were full incumbents who would nowadays be called Vicars.

Vicars could keep the 'lesser' tithes but the patron(s) often topped up their income.

Rectors could keep both the 'major' and 'lesser' tithes and were expected to be financially self-sufficient.

Parson: a general term for the parish clergyman.

Priest (or Parish Priest): *Priest* was another word for an ordained clergyman, which Anglo-Catholics in Haslam's time preferred, as putting a strong emphasis on the Eucharist.

Bishop: A high-ranking cleric, usually in spiritual charge of a geographic diocese, and of all the above clergy and their parishes.

OTHER CHURCH WORKERS

Scripture-reader: A man employed by the local clergy, especially in large parishes, to go from house to house reading parts of the Bible to try and encourage people to attend church; also read Scripture during some services.

Bible-woman: This missionary-cum-social worker was a

working class woman drawn from the neighbourhood. She was usually trained in the Poor Law, hygiene, and Scripture, and sought to turn the outcast population into honest, Christian citizens.

The long-desired day arrived and I was duly ordained. Instead of being full of joy I became depressed in mind and body, and could not stop myself from dwelling upon the Bishop's address which was very solemn. He told us that we were going to take charge of the souls of our parishioners, and we must take heed how we tended the Lord's flock. What could I do with souls? My idea of ordination was to be a clergyman, read the prayers, preach sermons and do all I could to bring people to church. How could I answer for souls which had to live for ever? And what was I to do with them?

In the evening I roused myself to go amongst the other candidates, to ascertain their feelings with regard to the Bishop's solemn address. They merely thought that it was very beautiful and that he was a holy man. Then some of them proposed that we should all go in a riding party to see Stonehenge the next day. It was especially thought that a drive on the Wiltshire plains would do me a great deal of good, even if I did not feel strong enough to ride on horseback. I agreed to this, and went with them to see this famous temple of Druidical worship, and after that set off for Plymouth on my way to the far west.

Alas, the charm of ordination had fled, and I was more than half sorry that I had undertaken so much. It had been done so precipitately, for even now it was only ten days since I had last seen the physician.

After resting a day I proceeded to Truro, and there took a post-chaise and drove out to my first parish, called Perranzabuloe, which was situated about eight miles [13km] from Truro, on the north coast of Cornwall. I alighted at an old manor house where I was to have apartments with a farmer and his family. Being much fatigued I soon retired to bed, anything but happy or pleased with the bleak and rough-looking place to which I had come.

The present (third) parish church of Perranzabuloe today. The short tower and much of the main building were constructed in 1803/4 using stone and timber from the second church.

I slept well, and the next morning felt considerably better and revived in spirits. After making many inquiries about things in general, I obtained the keys and made my way to the parish church[2] which was about ten minutes' walk from the house. I was greatly grieved and disappointed to see such a neglected churchyard and dilapidated church. When I went inside my heart sank, for I had never seen a place of worship in such a miserable condition. Moreover, I was told that the parish was seven miles [11km] long and its large population of three thousand souls was scattered on all sides.

I had left my friends a long way off and was alone in a strange place, with an amount of work and responsibility for

2   The church had stood there for just forty years, built with much material from St Piran's Old Church that had been abandoned to the sands in 1803.

which I knew I was thoroughly unprepared and unfit. I returned to my lodgings and began to ruminate as to what was to be done.

I had now sole charge of this extensive parish, for the duties of which I was to receive the very moderate stipend of forty pounds a year. Of this I did not complain, for my board and lodging, with washing and the keep of a horse included, was only twelve shillings a week, leaving me a margin of nearly ten pounds [a year] for my personal expenses. But what was I to do with three thousand people? And how was I to reach them?

In due course Sunday morning arrived, and with the help of a neighbouring clergyman who kindly came over, as he said, "to put me in the way," I got through the service – there was only one for the day at that time – having about twenty listless people lounging in different parts of the church. This was my first Sunday in my first parish.

My ordination gave me an ecclesiastical position in the parish, the law maintained me in it, and the people expected me to do the duties of it. But how to carry all this out, except in a dry and formal way, I did not know.

I had to baptise the children, marry the young, visit the sick and bury the dead.[3] I had carried a kind of dreamland parish in my head, with daily service, beautiful music and an assembly of worshipping people. Instead of this I found a small, unsympathizing congregation who merely looked upon these sacred things as duties to be done, and upon me as the proper person to do them. When I went to visit the sick I had nothing to say to them. I read a few Collects, and sometimes gave them a little monetary relief for which they thanked me, but I came out dissatisfied with myself. I longed for something more, though I did not know what.

Notwithstanding all these trials and disappointments, my health was gradually improving. I found that the air of

3   The first burial by Haslam is recorded as March 23
     1843 and the first baptism March 26, the month of his
     ordination in Salisbury Cathedral.

this place gave me an appetite for something more substantial. I often frequented the beach with its beautiful cliffs, and was much exhilarated by the bracing sea air. Indeed I had, and still retain, a love for the place. As my strength and energy increased I rode about the parish all day, making the acquaintance of the people and inviting them to come to church.

During my visits I found out that the churchwarden was a good musician, and he knew others in the parish who were able to play various instruments. In order to improve the services and make them more attractive, I urged him to invite these musical people to his house to practise. In due course we had a clarinet, two fiddles and his bass viol, with a few singers to form a choir. We tried some metrical psalms, for there were no hymnbooks in those days, and soon succeeded in learning them. This musical performance drew many people to church. The singers were undeniably the great attraction, and they knew it. Consequently I was somewhat in their power, and had to submit to various anthems and pieces such as *Vital Spark* [Harwood], *Angels Ever Bright and Fair* [Händel] and others not altogether to my taste, but which they evidently performed to their own praise and satisfaction.

Finding that the people were beginning to frequent the church I thought it was time to consider what steps should be taken about its restoration, and made it the subject of conversation with the farmers. It awakened and alarmed many of them when I said that the church must be restored, and that we must have a church rate.

The chief farmer shook his head. "You cannot do that."

But I replied. "According to law you are bound to keep up the fabric, and it ought to be done. I will write to the Vicar at once about it."

The farmer smiled at that and said, laughing, "I will pledge myself that we will do as much as he does."

It so happened that the Vicar, equally incredulous about the farmers doing anything, promised that he would do one half if they would do the other.

I immediately sent for the mason of the village, who played the clarinet in the church, also his son who played one of the fiddles, and consulted with them as to how this matter was to be accomplished. They, being in want of work at the time, readily advised me in favour of restoration.

The churchwarden, the "bass viol", said he had no objection to this proceeding but that he would not be responsible [for any disputes]. "In two months," he added, "will be the annual vestry meeting."

"That will do," I said, interrupting him. I made up my mind that I would at once restore the church, and let the parishioners come and see it at that time.

Having made all necessary preparations, we commenced one fine Monday morning with repairing the roof and walls. While the men were employed outside, we took out the windows and opened all the doors to let the wind blow through, so that the interior of the building might be thoroughly dried. This done, we next coloured the walls, the stone arches and the pillars. Having cleaned the seats and front of the gallery, we stained and varnished them, matted the floor and carpeted the sacrarium. Then we procured a new cloth for the Communion Table, the pulpit and the reading desk.

All this being completed, I painted texts on the walls in old English characters. I had great joy in writing these, for I felt as if it was to the Lord himself and for His name, and finished with Nehemiah's prayer, "Remember me, O my God, concerning this; and wipe not out my good deeds that I have done for the house of my God, and for the offices thereof."[4]

Altogether it was a pretty church now, and a pretty sum was to be paid for it. I told the vestry that I alone was responsible, but that the Vicar had promised to pay one half if the vestry would pay the other. It seemed to be such a joy to them to get anything out of him that they made a rate at once, and upon the Vicar's letter raised the money and paid off the debt.

4   Nehemiah 13:14

The people were now much pleased with their church, and brought their friends and neighbours to see it. Besides this, I observed something which gratified me very much. When they entered the church they now did so with reverence, taking off their hats and walking softly, in place of stamping with their heels and coming in with their hats on, as they had previously done without any respect or concern whatever. A neglected place of worship does not command reverence.

My church now began to be the talk of the neighbourhood. Numbers of people came to see it, among them several clergymen who asked me to come and restore their churches. In many places the people could not afford to rebuild the structure, so I was invited to exercise my skill in repairing, as I had done with my own. In others I was asked to give designs for restoring portions of the edifice, and in some for rebuilding altogether. In this district, schools were not built, nor Parsonage houses enlarged without sending for me.

For several years I was looked upon as an authority in architectural matters. I rode all over the county from north to west, restoring churches and designing schools, and was accounted the busiest man alive! My horse, my dog and myself were the "three leanest things in creation." We were to be seen flying along the roads day and night in one part or another.

The Bishop of Exeter, who at that time presided over Cornwall, appointed me to make new Peel districts.[5] I designed nineteen and made all the maps myself, calling on the Vicars and Rectors for their approval. I was at this time a very popular man, and it was said that "the Bishop's best living" would be given to me in due time.

5   The Peel districts were the new ecclesiastical districts
     created under the Church Extension Act introduced
     by Sir Robert Peel.

CHAPTER 3

Exploration and Ministry — 1843/46

ANOTHER THING, which raised my name in and beyond the county, was the "Lost Church" at Perranzabuloe. There was an old-British church existing in some sand-hills in the parish, and it was said to be entire as far as the four walls. The hill under which it was buried was easily known by the bones and teeth which covered it. The legend said that the patron saint, St Piran, was buried under the altar, and that close by the little church was a cell in which he lived and died.

This was enough. I got men, and set to work to dig it up. After some days' labour we came to the floor, where we discovered the stone seats, and on the plaster of the wall the greasy marks of the heads and shoulders of persons who had sat there many centuries ago. We found the chancel step, and also the altar tomb which was built east and west, not north and south. It was fallen, but enough remained to show the original shape and height of it.[6]

I put a notice in the newspapers, inviting people to come and see the old church which had been buried for fifteen hundred years! In the presence of many visitors, clerical and lay, we removed the stones of the altar, and found the

---

6   The Oratory had been excavated eight years earlier by William Michell from Truro, but the interior had once more become filled with sand and water. Haslam discusses Michell's 1835 findings in a book he wrote in 1844. See Appendix 2 for an answer to the criticism Haslam has attracted over the years for this excavation. Strange as it sounds, I am assured by a professor of archaeology that grease stains like these can remain for much longer than would be necessary to date from the time of St Piran.

skeleton of St Piran, which was identified in three ways. The legend said that he was a man seven feet high; the skeleton measured six feet from the shoulder-bones to the heel.[7] Again, another legend said that his head was enshrined in a church forty miles away; the skeleton corresponded with this, for it was headless. Moreover, it was said that his mother and a friend were buried on either side of him; we also found skeletons of a male and female in these positions.

St Piran's cross.

Being satisfied on this point, we set the masons to work to rebuild the altar tomb in its original shape and size, using the same stones as far as they would go. We made up the deficiency with a heavy granite slab.

On this I traced with my finger, in rude Roman letters, "SANCTUS PIRANUS." The mason would not cut those crooked letters unless I consented for him to put his name in better ones in the corner. I could not agree to this, so his apprentice and I, between us, picked out the rude letters which have since – I have heard – been copied for a veritable Roman inscription!

7   Skeletons nearly always look taller than their real
    height. To get an accurate measurement,
    archaeologists today have to wire a skeleton together,
    since it is impossible to measure the height of a
    person with certainty in any other way. Nevertheless,
    relative heights are easier to judge without resorting
    to this procedure.

My name was now up as an antiquary, and I was asked to be the West of England secretary for the Archaeological Society. I was supposed to be an old gentleman, and heard myself quoted as the "venerable and respected Haslam" whose word was considered enough to settle a knotty point beyond doubt! I was invited to give a lecture on the old Perran Church at the Royal Institution Truro, which I did, illustrating it with sketches of the building and exhibiting some remains of carving which are now preserved in the museum there.

The audience requested me through their chairman to print my lecture. Being very young in literary enterprises, I added a great deal of other matter to the manuscript which I then prepared for the press. There was much in the book[8] about early Christianity and ecclesiastical antiquities. I imagined that this parish was in British and Druidic times a populous place and somewhat important. There was a Round, or amphitheatre, for public games, and four British castles. Also a great many sepulchral mounds on the hills, the burial place of chieftains.[9] I supposed that St Piran came here among these natives, perhaps painted savages, to preach the Gospel and then built himself a cell by the seashore near a spring or well where he baptised his

8   Haslam's early footnote says, *"The Church of St Piran,* first published by Van Voorst in 1850." In later editions the date is omitted. The book is *Perran-zabuloe, The Oratory of St Piran in the Sands,* 151 pages, published in 1844 by Van Voorst London. In the preface Haslam says "The substance of this little work was read at an evening meeting of the Cornwall Royal Institution…" In 1998 Oakmagic Publications published a partial reprint of this book, in a 58-page paperback using a selection of pages from the original.

9   Haslam and more than a few professional archaeologists at this time were mistaken in thinking that the burial mounds were contemporary with the early Christians. They are mostly Bronze Age, and so were at least 2,000 years old when St Piran saw them.

converts. Close by he built this little church in which he worshipped God and prayed for the people.

Here then, more than fourteen centuries ago, people called upon God. When their little sanctuary was overwhelmed with the sand they removed to the other side of the river, and built themselves another church. But they continued to bury their dead around and above the Oratory and resting place of St Piran.

The Oratory of St Piran after excavation in 1835, redrawn from an original engraving in the 1839 edition of *Perranzabuloe*, by Collins Trelawny. A similar view in Haslam's book of 1844 shows the doorway arch fallen.

When my book was published, there ensued a hot controversy about the subject of it, and some who came to see the Lost Church for themselves declared that it was nothing more than "a modern cow-shed." Others would not believe in the antiquity I claimed for it. One of these even ventured to assert his opinion in print that it was at least eight centuries later than the date I had fixed. Another asked in a newspaper letter, "How is it, if this is a church, that there are no others of the same period on record?"

This roused me to make further research, and I was soon rewarded by finding in the registry at Exeter a list of ninety-two churches existing in Cornwall alone in the time of Edward the Confessor, of which Lam-piran was one.

I used to entertain people with these wondrous subjects, and one evening I had the honour of agitating even the Bishop of Exeter himself. In his enthusiasm he bade me write a book and dedicate it to him. *The Cross and the Serpent* is the title, and it was duly inscribed to his lordship.

It excites me even now to think about it, though it is thirty-five years since I made these discoveries. The old librarian at Oxford declared that I was mad, and yet he could not keep away from the subject and was never weary of hearing something more about it.

This reverend doctor said, "If you are right, then all the great antiquaries are wrong."

I suggested that they had not had the advantage I possessed of placing their various theories side by side, or of making their observations from my point of view.[10]

Notwithstanding all these external labours, I did not neglect my parish. I felt, however, that my parishioners did not know anything about ecclesiastical antiquities or architectural science, and that they knew nothing and cared less about Church teaching. They did not believe that in order to be saved hereafter they ought to be in the Church and receive the Holy Communion – that there is no salvation out

10   In his book *The Cross and the Serpent,* H Parker, Oxford 1849, Haslam explains his theory that a cross and a serpent can be found in many ancient mythologies, both in words and images. He traces these back to what he believes to be a common Biblical source, where the cross of Christ was foreshadowed in the Old Testament by Moses' bronze serpent on a pole being a source of healing. Would this theory be supported today? Many of Haslam's views on the past, in common with various establishment opinions at that time, would no longer be accepted. See Appendix 2.

of the Church, and no Church without a Bishop.[11] They were utterly careless about these things, and from the first had been an unsympathetic and unteachable people.

From the commencement of my ministry I did not as a general rule preach my own sermons, but Newman's, which I abridged and simplified. As far as Church teaching went, they were to my mind perfect. They stated doctrines and drew manifest conclusions, but my people were not satisfied with them. I can see now, thank God, that with all their excellences they were utterly deficient in spiritual vitality.

My "bass viol" called on me one day, and said, "If you go on preaching that doctrine you will drive away the best part of your congregation."

"Excuse me," I answered, "not the best part. You mean the worst part."

"Well," he said, "you will see."

On the following Sunday I gave out my text, and had scarcely read three pages of my manuscript when I heard a voice say, "Now we *will* go!"

With this the bass viol, the other fiddles, the clarinet, the ophicleide[12] and the choir came stumping down the gallery stairs and marched out. Some of the congregation followed their example, with the determination never to come back to the Church again. I waited till the noise was over and then went on with my sermon meekly, and thought myself a martyr for Church principles.

From this time there was a constant feud between the parishioners and myself. One day a Dissenter called to pay a burial fee for the funeral of his child, which he had purposely omitted paying at the proper time because he wished to tell me a piece of his mind. I was absent for the funeral on some architectural or archaeological business, which was to me all important.

---

11   It is clear from Haslam's writing that this was his
     belief while at Perranzabuloe, not his later
     understanding of the Christian faith.

12   A type of keyed bugle.

"I know," he said, "why you went away and would not bury my child."

"Do you?"

"Yes, it is because I am a Dissenter."

"Oh." I said, "I would bury you all tomorrow if I could, for you are no good and can do none either!"

This went round the parish like wildfire, and did not advance my popularity or do my cause any good.

At this time I thought that separation from the Church of England was a most deadly sin – it was schism. Idolatry and murder were sins against the Mosaic Law, but separation was a sin against the Church. I little dreamt then that many of the people with whom I thus contended, and whom I grieved so much, were real spiritual members of Christ, and had only ceased to be members of the Church of England because I did not preach the Gospel – that I was the cause of their leaving the services.

Since the feuds and dissensions in my parish, the church was almost deserted. It was left chiefly to myself, my clerk and a few poor people who for the most part were in ill favour in the chapels.

One day I was absorbed in writing, or rather re-writing a text over the porch door of the church: THIS IS NONE OTHER BUT THE HOUSE OF GOD, AND THIS IS THE GATE OF HEAVEN.[13]

A man who was standing at the foot of the ladder, said, "Heaven is a long way from that gate, I reckon."

I pretended not to hear him, but his speech stuck to me. I knew only too well from this, and many other indications, that the people had no respect for the church under my ministrations.

13   Genesis 28:17

CHAPTER 4

Baldhu — 1846/47

ABOUT THIS TIME the news reached us that the Vicar was dead, and thus ended my connection with Perranzabuloe. As the dean and chapter would not appoint me to succeed, I had no alternative but to arrange for my departure.

In one sense I was not sorry to go, but for various other reasons I much regretted having to leave a place where my health had been so wonderfully restored and sustained, and in which I had received so many tokens of God's favour. I also regretted leaving the place before I had done any good to the people, for I had not succeeded in persuading them to receive my idea of salvation by churchmanship.

This crisis happened at the exact time of another important event in my life. I was just engaged to be married. I therefore had an additional interest in looking for a sphere of labour which would suit me and the partner of my choice, who was in every respect likely to be an effectual helpmeet. We agreed together to give ourselves to the Lord's work. [14]

One of the Peel districts in the neighbourhood of Truro which I had designed was called Baldhu, on the Earl of Falmouth's estate. It came to his lordship's mind to take an interest in this desolate spot, so he bought the patronage from the commissioners and offered it to me, to be made into a new parish. This I accepted with many thanks, and began immediately to dream out my plans for the future.

It was a time of great distress in that place amongst the tenants, because of the failure of the potato crop. So his

---

14 Haslam married Frances Ann Taunton of Totnes,
    Devon, in 1846. Her father, William Doidge Taunton,
    was a man of considerable influence in the area,
    related to the Earl of Falmouth

lordship employed some hundreds of the men in breaking up the barren croft for planting trees, and there he gave me a good central site for a church.

Now I made up my mind to have everything perfect, with my own rules and regulations. With my surpliced choir, churchwardens and frequent services, all after my own heart, it could scarcely fail to be otherwise. I thought that having free scope, mine should be a model place. The district was in a barren part of a large parish. Three thousand souls had been assigned to me, and I was to go and civilise them, build my church, schoolhouse, and indeed establish everything that was necessary.

To begin with I took a room, which I used for a village school in the week and for a service on Sunday. This succeeded so well that in a few months I determined to enlarge the building in which we assembled. Having made all necessary plans, and procured stones, timber and slate, we commenced operations at five o'clock one Monday morning. By Saturday night we had a chancel ready for Sunday use.

All the world came to see this temporary church which now held three hundred people. With the addition of a new choir, and a hearty service, it was a great success – or at least so I imagined, for in those days I did not look for more. I entered upon my work with renewed energy and hope, and preached on holy living, not conversion, for as yet I knew nothing about the latter.

In 1847 I went on a visit to a very remarkable man who had a great effect upon me. He was the Rev Robert Hawker of Morwenstow, a parish in the extreme north of Cornwall [near Bude].

This friend was a poet and a High Churchman, from whom I learned many practical lessons. He was a man who prayed – and expected an answer. He had a wonderful perception for realising unseen things, and took Scripture literally, with startling effect. He certainly was most eccentric in many of his ways, but there was a reality and straightforwardness about him which charmed me very much. I was the more drawn to him from the interest he took in me and my work.

He knew many legends of holy men of old, and said that the patron saints of West Cornwall were in the calendar of the Eastern Church, and those in the North of Cornwall belonged to the Western. Morwenna, his own patron saint was a Saxon, and his church a Saxon fane. He talked of these saints as if he knew all about them.

THE CLERGY HASLAM WOULD HAVE MET

ROMAN CATHOLIC: The largest religious denomination of Christianity, currently with over one billion members. For them, the nineteenth century was a time of growth in the UK, mainly due to Irish immigration. The liturgical language was Latin in all churches in all countries.

HIGH CHURCH (OR ANGLO CATHOLIC): A branch of the Anglican Church, with a style of worship that values ritual, and obedience to the hierarchy, without recognising the authority of the pope. Haslam would have called himself High Church in his early years in the ministry. After his conversion, he changed his views and later wrote critically about a neighbouring High Church: "We heard nothing but the theology of 'doing'. You were to do this, observe that and abstain from the other. Prayer was recommended, as if religion and devotion consisted in saying prayers so many times a day." We must remember that all the quoted comments here are Haslam's observations and reflect his personal views of particular churches.

BROAD CHURCH: Quite close the modern Liberal, often with an educated distrust of religious certainties. Haslam reported the following comment on a 'Broad Church' Vicar: "He made some startling statements which certainly kept us awake wondering what was coming next. 'The Bible is not inspired.' 'It is not a book to be relied upon.' 'There are many assertions in it which modern science has proved to be false.' 'Nothing should be believed which is not understood.' This was indeed bringing down the wisdom of God to the mind of man, instead of bringing up the mind of man to the wisdom of God. The fact is, we must believe the Word of God before we can understand it. We must do His will before we can know His doctrine." This is truly a church that is broad by nature, and many members today would disagree with Haslam's quick dismissal, saying for example that they want to be free to query the inspiration of Scripture, while not automatically dismissing it.

EVANGELICAL (OR LOW CHURCH): A grouping within the Anglican Church seeing the denomination as essentially rooted in reformed Bible-based theology, with a style of worship that emphasises the acts of the congregation in worship, ordinances and learning. Although identifying with the evangelicals, Haslam could write: "As to the low or evangelical preacher, he was very wordy and equally dead. He pleased his hearers and they pleased him – though they remained unconverted. There was a great deal of the word of the Spirit, but nothing about the work. His congregation might truthfully say, 'We have not so much as heard whether there be any Holy Ghost!'" So Haslam saw that one could be Low Church in style but lack an authentic personal testimony. The modern connotation of 'Evangelical' as implying the need for a 'born-again' moment of commitment would have been more associated with 'revival', which was a concept especially prized by the next group.

DISSENTERS AND NONCONFORMISTS: Dissenters were Protestants and free thinkers who refused to worship with the Established Church in England (the term did not apply in Presbyterian Scotland). Dissenters increased in numbers in 1662 when many Vicars (nonconformists) refused to adhere to the Act of Uniformity reimposing Bishops and the Book of Common Prayer. Thus were the born the Methodists whom Haslam mentions several times, and a variety of major and minor denominations, many of which are still very active today.

St Morwenna Church, Morwenstow, today.

He used to give most thrilling and grand descriptions of the storms of the Atlantic which broke upon the rocky coast with gigantic force, and tell thrilling stories of shipwrecks: how he saved the lives of some of the sailors, and how he recovered the bodies of others he could not save. In the churchyard he would show a broken boat turned over the resting place of some, two oars set up crosswise over others, and in another place the figurehead of a ship to mark the spot where the body of a captain was buried.

The Vicarage house was as original as himself. Over the door was inscribed: A house, a glebe, a pound a day; a pleasant place to watch and pray. Be true to Church, be kind to poor, O minister, for evermore.

The interior was furnished with old-fashioned heavy furniture, and the outside was conspicuous for its remarkable chimneys which were finished off as models of the towers of churches where he had served. [A design for] the kitchen chimney, which was oblong, had perplexed him very much till, as he said, "I bethought me of my mother's tomb, and there it is in its exact shape and dimensions."

He had daily service in his church, generally by himself, when he prayed for the people. "I did not want them there," he said. "God hears me, and they know when I am praying for them, for I ring the bell."

He had much influence in his parish, chiefly amongst the poor, and declared that his people did whatever he told them. They used to bring a bunch of flowers or evergreens every Sunday morning and set them up in their pew ends, where a proper place was made to hold them. The whole church was seated with carved oak benches which he had bought from time to time from other churches, when they were re-pewed with deal boxes.

On the Sunday I was asked to help him in the service, and for this purpose was arrayed in an alb, plain, which was like a cassock in white linen. As I walked about in this garb, I asked a friend, "How do you like it?"

In an instant I was pounced upon by the Vicar, and grasped sternly on the arm. "Like has nothing to do with it. Is it *right?*"

He wore a chasuble over his alb, which was amber on one side and green on the other, and was turned to suit the Church seasons; also a pair of crimson coloured gloves which he contended were the proper sacrificial colour for a priest.

I had very little to do in the service but to witness his proceedings, which I observed with great attention and even admiration. His preaching struck me very much. He used to select the subject of his sermon from the Gospel of the day. This happened to be Good Samaritan Sunday, so we had a discourse upon the "certain man who went down from Jerusalem to Jericho."[15]

He told us, "The poor wounded man was Adam's race; the priest who went by was the Patriarchal dispensation; the Levite, the Mosaic dispensation; the good Samaritan

15   Luke 10:30

represented Christ; the inn was the Church; and the two pence, the Sacraments."

He held up his manuscript before his face and read it out boldly because he hated, as he said, "Those fellows who read their sermons, and all the time pretend to preach them." He especially abhorred those who secreted notes in their Bibles: "Either have a book, sir, or none!"

He had a great aversion to Low Church clergymen and told me that his stag Robin, who roamed on the lawn, once pinned one of them to the ground between his horns. The poor man cried out in great fear. So he told Robin to let him go, which he did, but stood and looked at the obnoxious individual as if he would like to have him down again and frighten him, though he would not hurt him. "Robin was kind-hearted."

"This Evangelical," Hawker continued, "had a tail coat. He was dressed like an undertaker, sir. Once upon a time there was one like him travelling in Egypt with a similar coat and a tall hat, and the Arabs pursued him, calling him the 'father of saucepans with a slit tail.'"

This part of his speech was evidently meant for me, for I wore a hat and coat of this description, finding it more convenient for the saddle, and for dining out when I alighted.

He persuaded me to wear a priestly garb like his, and gave me one of his old cassocks for a pattern. After considerable difficulty I succeeded in getting it made to my satisfaction.

I came back to my work at Baldhu full of new thoughts and plans, determined to do what was "right".

I held up my manuscript and read my sermon like Mr Hawker, and I wore a square cap and cassock instead of the "saucepan" and the "tails". This costume I continued to wear for several years, though I was frequently laughed at and often pursued by boys, which was not agreeable to flesh and blood. But it helped separate me from the world, and make me feel that I was set apart as a priest to offer sacrifice for the people.

Baldhu. Left to right in background: the parsonage, church and school. Redrawn from an original engraving in *From Death Into Life*.

I now began to make preparations for my permanent church. I drew the designs, passed them, and obtained money enough to begin to build.[16] There was a grand

16   Haslam must mean he did the design, as might someone if they were getting a house built. They would draw up an overall plan, and a number of detailed ones, including size and position of bedrooms, bathrooms, staircase, downstairs layout and so on, sometimes right down to the type of taps and doorknobs. They then pass these over to an architect who makes full architectural drawings for the builders and covers any structural issues. The architect is recorded as William White (1825-1900), and his must be the final plans Haslam says he passed—note that White would only have been only twenty-two at the time. Haslam is credited with the design of St George's Church Truro in 1855 (See link on author's website).

ceremony at the stone-laying, and a long procession. We had banners, chanting and a number of surpliced clergy, besides a large congregation.

The Earl of Falmouth, who laid the stone, contributed a thousand pounds towards the edifice. His mother gave three hundred pounds for a peal of bells, and others of the gentry who were present contributed. Upwards of eighteen hundred pounds was promised that day. Just twelve months after, July 20 1848, Bishop Phillpotts of Exeter came to consecrate the "beautiful church."

In the meantime, between the stone-laying and the consecration, the Parsonage house had been built, papered, furnished and inhabited. Besides all this, there was a garden, and a doorway after an ecclesiastical mode leading into the churchyard, with this inscription over it:

BE TRUE TO CHURCH, BE KIND TO POOR, O MINISTER, FOR EVERMORE.

In this church there were super-altar, candles, triptych and a painted window; organ, choir and six bells. For those days it was considered a very complete thing. "The priest of Baldhu", as I was known with my cassock and square cap, was considered quite a character in his small way.

I preached in a surplice, of course, and propounded Church tactics, firmly contending for Church teaching. The Wesleyans and others had their distinctive tenets, and the Church must have hers. They had their members enrolled; the Church must have hers. Therefore I would have a guild with the view of keeping my people together. Outwardly there was an *esprit de corps*, and the parishioners came to church and took an interest in the proceedings. But it was easy to see that their hearts were elsewhere.

So I went on, hoping against hope, building from the top without any foundation, while teaching people to live before they were born.

CHAPTER 5

Only Unconverted People go to Church — 1848/51

THE BETTER I KNEW the people, the more I saw that mere attachment to the Church, punctual attendance at the services, or frequency of Communion, was not sufficient. I wanted something deeper. I wanted to reach their hearts in order to do them good.

I was told a story about a clergyman's dream in which he thought the Judgment Day was come. The clergy were mustering and appeared in their gowns, but instead of being alone they had part of their congregations with them. Some had a few followers, others had more, and some a great many. All these received a gracious smile from the Judge when their names were called.

The clergyman who dreamed was waiting, as he supposed, with a large number of people at his back. His turn came to go forward, but as he approached he saw that the Judge's countenance was sad and dark. In a sudden impulse of suspicion he looked back – and lo, there was no one behind him. He stopped, not daring to go any further, and turning to look at the Judge, saw that His countenance was full of wrath. This dream had such an effect on him that he began to attend to his parish, and care for the souls of his people.

I also was beginning to see that I ought to care for the souls of my people, at least as much as I did for the services of the Church. As a priest I had the power, so I thought, to give them absolution. Yet none availed themselves of the opportunity. How could they have forgiveness if they did not come to me? This absolution I believed to be needful before coming to Holy Communion, and that it was the true preparation for that sacred ordinance. I used to speak privately to the members of the Church Guild about this, and persuaded some of them to come to me for confession and absolution.

But I was restless, and felt that I was doing good by stealth. Besides this, those whom I thus absolved were not satisfied, for they said they could not rejoice in the forgiveness of their sins as the Methodists did, or say that they were pardoned. I did not know what else to do.

I used to spend hours and hours in my church alone in meditation and prayer. While thinking, I employed my hands in writing texts over the windows and on the walls, and in painting ornamental borders above the arches. I remember writing over the chancel arch, with much interest and exultation: NOW IS COME SALVATION, AND STRENGTH, AND THE KINGDOM OF OUR GOD, AND THE POWER OF HIS CHRIST.[17]

One day I saw a picture in a friend's house. It was nothing artistic, nor was it over-well drawn, but it engaged my attention in a way for which I could not account. Even after I left the house this picture haunted me. At night I lay awake thinking about it, so much so that I rose early the next morning and went to a bookseller's shop where I bought a large sheet of tracing paper and a pencil. I sent them out by the postman with a note to my friend begging him to give me a tracing of the picture in question.

I had to wait for more than a fortnight before it arrived, and then how great was my joy. I remember spreading a white cloth on my table and opening out the tracing paper upon it. There was the true picture of the Good Shepherd. His countenance was loving and kind. With one hand He was pushing aside the branch of a tree, though a great thorn went right through it, and with the other He was extricating a sheep which was entangled in the thorns.

The poor thing was looking up in helplessness, all spotted over with marks of its own blood, for it was wounded in struggling to escape. Another thing which struck me in this picture was that the tree was growing on

17   Revelation 12:10

the edge of a precipice, and had it not been for the tree, with all the cruel wounds it inflicted, the sheep would have gone over and perished.

After considering this picture for a long time I painted it in a larger size on the wall of my church, just opposite the entrance door. I cannot describe the interest with which I employed myself about this work. When it was done, finding that it wanted a good bold foreground, I selected a short text: "He came to seek and to save that which was lost."[18]

God was speaking to me all this time about the Good Shepherd who gave His life for me, but I did not hear Him, or suspect that I was lost, or caught in any thorns, or hanging over a precipice. Certainly I remember that my thoughts dwelt very much on forgiveness and salvation, but I preached that these were to be had in and by the Church, which was as the Ark in which Noah was saved. Baptism was the door of this Ark, and Holy Communion the token of abiding in it.

What would become of those outside the Church was a matter which greatly perplexed me. I could not dare to say that they would be lost for ever, but where could they be now? And what would become of them hereafter? One day I baptised myself conditionally in the Church for fear that I had not been properly baptised in infancy, and consequently should be lost hereafter.

I had many conversations with the earnest people in my parish, but they were evidently resting on something I did not know. One happy woman told me, "Ah, you went to college to learn the Latin. But though I don't know a letter in the Book, yet I can read my title clear to mansions in the skies."

Another woman, whenever I went to see her, made me read the story of her conversion which was written in a copy-book. Several others, men and women, talked to me continually about their "conversion". I often wondered

18   Luke 19:10

what that was. As I did not see much self-denial among these converted ones, and observed that they did not attend God's House or ever come to the Lord's Table, I thought conversion could not be of much consequence or anything to be desired.

I little knew that I was the cause of their remaining away from church and from the Lord's Table. One thoughtful man told me, "Cornish people are too enlightened to go to church. A man must give up religion to go there. Only unconverted people and backsliders go to such a place."

This was a prayerful man. What did he mean? At various clerical meetings I used to repeat these things, but still obtained no information or satisfaction.

I made it a rule to visit every house in my parish once a week, calling on from twelve to twenty each day, when I sought to enlighten the people by leaving Church tracts. I even wrote some myself, but they would not do. I found that the Religious Tract Society's publications were more acceptable. To my great disappointment I discovered that Evangelical sermons drew the people, while sacramental topics did not interest them. So in my ardent desire to reach and do them good I procured several volumes of Evangelical sermons and copied them, sometimes putting in a negative to their statements to make them, as I thought, right.

Now I began to see and feel that there was some good in preaching, and used the pulpit intentionally, in order to communicate with my people, carefully writing or compiling my sermons. But I must confess that I was very nervous in my delivery, and frequently lost my place – sometimes even myself; and this to the great confusion of the congregation.

I will tell how it pleased the Lord to deliver me from this bondage of nervousness, and enable me to open my lips so as to plainly speak out my meaning.

One day a friend with whom I was staying was very late in coming down to breakfast. So while I was waiting I employed myself in reading the *Life of Bishop Shirley of Sodor and Man*. My eyes happened to fall on a passage describing a difficulty into which he fell by losing his sermon on his way to a country church. When the prayers were over, and the psalm was nearly sung, he put his hand into his pocket for his manuscript, and to his dismay it was gone. There was no time to continue his search; so he gave out a text and preached, as he said, in dependence upon God – and never wrote a sermon afterwards.

When my friend came to breakfast he asked me what I had been doing all the morning. I told him.

"Ah!" he said, quietly. "Why do you not preach in dependence upon God and go without a book like that good man?"

"I, preach like that!" I said in amazement, terrified at the very thought.

"Yes," he answered, mischievously, "You. Who needs to depend upon God for this more than you do?"

Seeing that I was perturbed at his suggestion, he went on teasing me all breakfast time, and at last said, "Well, what is your decision? Do you mean to preach in future in dependence upon God?"

I said, "Yes, I have made up my mind to begin next Sunday."

Now it was his turn to be terrified, and he did all he could to dissuade me, saying, "You will make a fool of yourself!"

"No fear of that," I replied. "I do it already; I cannot be worse. No, I will begin next Sunday."

I came back with the determination to keep my promise, but must confess that I grew more and more uneasy as the time approached. However, on Sunday I went up into the pulpit and spoke as well as I could, without any notes, and found it far easier than I had feared.

In the evening it was still easier; and so I continued week by week, gaining more confidence, and have never written a sermon since that day – that is, to preach it. Once I was tempted to take a book up into the pulpit, feeling I had nothing to say, when something said to me, "Is that the way you depend upon God?" Immediately I put the volume on the floor, and standing on it, gave out my text and preached without hesitation. This going forward in dependence upon

God has been a deliverance to me from many a difficulty besides this one, and that through many years.

One day I went in my cassock and cap to the shop to a man whom I regarded as a dreadful schismatic. He sold the publications of the Religious Tract Society. On entering he appeared greatly pleased to see me, and took unusual interest and pains in selecting tracts, giving me a double portion for my money.

His kindness was very embarrassing, and when on leaving he followed me to the door, and said "God bless you," it gave me a great turn. A schismatic blessing a priest! This indeed was an anomaly.

I was ashamed to be seen coming out of the shop, and the more so because I had this large Evangelical parcel in my hand. I felt as though everybody was looking at me.

However, the tracts were very acceptable at home and in the parish. I even began to think there was something good in them. So I sent for more. Three men one after another told me that they had been converted through reading them. One of these said that the tract I had given him "ought to be written in letters of gold."

A few months later this same man died most happily, rejoicing in the Lord and leaving a bright testimony behind. I mentioned the conversion of these three men to many of my friends and asked them for some explanation, but got none. Still, the thought continually haunted me: what can this conversion be?

At that time my gardener, a good Churchman who was duly despised by his neighbours for attaching himself to me and my teaching, fell seriously ill. I sent him at once to the doctor, who pronounced him to be in a miner's consumption and gave no hope of his recovery. No sooner did my gardener realise his position and see eternity before him, than all the Church teaching I had given him failed to console or satisfy. His heart sank within him at the near prospect of death.

In his distress of mind he did not send for me to come and pray with him, but actually sent for a converted man who lived in the next row of cottages. This man, instead of building him up, as I had done, went to work in the opposite direction – to show my servant that he was a lost sinner and needed to come to Jesus, just as he was, for pardon and salvation. He was brought under deep conviction of sin, and eventually found peace through the precious blood of Jesus.

Immediately it spread all over the parish that, "the Parson's servant is converted!" The news soon reached me, but instead of giving joy it brought the most bitter disappointment and sorrow to my heart. I felt hurt to think that after all I had taught him against schism he should fall into so great an error. However, he sent for me again and again, till at last his entreaties prevailed and I went. Instead of lying on his bed, a dying man as I expected to find him, he was walking about the room in a most joyful and ecstatic state.

"Oh, dear master," he exclaimed, "I am glad you are come. I am so happy. My soul is saved. Glory be to God!"

"Come, John," I said. "Sit down and be quiet, and I will have a talk with you and tell you what I think."

But John knew my thoughts well enough, so he burst out, "Oh, master, I am sure you do not know about this, or you would have told me. I am quite sure you love me, and I love you, that I do. But, dear master, you do not know this. I am praying for the Lord to show it to you. I mean to pray till I die, and after that if I can, till you are converted."

He looked at me so lovingly, and seemed so truly happy, that it was more than I could stand. Almost involuntarily I made for the door and escaped before he could stop me.

I went home greatly disturbed in my mind, altogether disappointed and disgusted with my work among these Cornish people, thinking, "It is no use, they never will be Churchmen."

I was as hopeless and miserable as I could be. I felt that my superior teaching and practice had failed, and that the inferior and, as I believed, unscriptural dogmas had prevailed. My favourite and most promising Churchman had fallen – and was happy in his fall. More than that, he was actually praying that I might fall too!

Like the elder brother of the Prodigal Son I was grieved, and even angry, because he was restored to favour and joy. Nothing seemed to give me any rest in this crisis of my parochial work. I thought I would give up my parish and church, and go and work in some more congenial soil. Or else that I would preach a set of sermons on the subject of schism, for perhaps I had not sufficiently taught my people the danger of this great sin.

Every parishioner I passed seemed to look at me as if to say, "So much for your teaching. You will never convince us!"

CHAPTER 6

The Parson is Converted! — 1851

WHEN I WAS FIRST building my new church at Baldhu, and talking about the tower and spire we were going to erect, an elderly Christian lady who was sitting in her wheelchair calmly listening to our conversation, said, "Will you begin to build your spire from the top?"

It was a strange question, but she evidently meant something and looked for an answer. I gave it, saying, "No, madam, not from the top, but from the foundation."

She replied, "That is right. That is right," and went on with her knitting.[19]

This question was not asked in jest or ignorance. It was like a riddle. In a few years this lady passed away, but her enigmatic words remained. No doubt she thought to herself that I was beginning at the wrong end, while I went on talking of the choir, organ, happy worship and all the things we were going to attempt in the new church.

I can see now that she implied I was teaching people to be holy before they were saved and pardoned. No wonder my life was a failure and my labours ineffectual. My work was not done as a thank-offering, but rather as a meritorious effort to obtain favour from God

Repentance towards God, however earnest and sincere, is not complete or satisfying without faith towards our Lord Jesus Christ. It is like preparing the ground without sowing

---

19 Haslam subsequently put a much fuller version of
    this account into a long track, *Building From the Top*,
    which he reprinted with twenty-three others in a book
    of the same name.

seed, and then being disappointed when there is no harvest. We have to believe, not in the fact that we have given ourselves, but in the fact that God, who is more willing to take than we to give, has accepted us.

I will now tell how I was brought at this critical period in my life to real faith towards our Lord Jesus Christ, in a way I little expected. I had promised a visit to Mr Aitken of Pendeen, to advise him about his church which [he] was then building. In order to divert my thoughts I made up my mind to go to him at once.[20]

Soon after my arrival, as we were seated comfortably by the fire, he asked me how the parish prospered. He said, "I often take shame to myself when I think of all your work. But, my brother, are you satisfied?"

I said, "No, I am not satisfied."[21]

"Why not?"

"Because I am making a rope of sand, which looks very well till I pull; and then when I expect it to hold, it gives way."

"What do you mean?"

"Why," I replied, "these Cornish people are ingrained schismatics." I then told him of my gardener's conversion and my great disappointment

"Well," he said, "if I were taken ill I certainly would not send for you. I am sure you could not do me any good, for you are not converted yourself."

"Not converted!" I exclaimed. "How can you tell?"

20 The village of Pendeen is on the far north west coast of Cornwall halfway between Lands End and St Ives. In 1844 Robert Aitken (1799-1873) was appointed the first Vicar of what was then a new parish. There he and the parishioners built their own church. For a full biography of this outstanding preacher see link on my website.

21 Haslam published this episode as a tract, *Are you Satisfied?* It is not, however, included in his book of 24 tracts, *Building From the Top*.

He said quietly, "I am sure of it, or you would not have come here to complain of your gardener. If you had been converted you would have remained at home to rejoice with him. It is very clear you are not converted."

I was vexed with him for saying that, and attempted to dispute the point. But he was calm and confident. I, on the other hand, was uneasy and trying to justify myself.

In the course of our conversation, he said, "You do not seem to know the difference between the natural conscience and the work of the Spirit."

Here he had me, for I only knew of one thing, and he referred to two. However, we talked on till nearly two o'clock in the morning and then he showed me to my bedroom. Pointing to the bed, he said in a voice full of meaning, "Ah, a very holy man of God died there a short time since."

This did not add to my comfort, or induce sleep, for I was already much disturbed by the conversation we had had. I did not enjoy the idea of going to bed and sleeping where one had so lately died, even though he was a holy man. Resolving to sit up I looked round the room, and seeing some books on the table took up Hare's *Mission of the Comforter*.[22] Almost the first page I glanced at told of the difference between the natural conscience and the work of the Spirit. This I read and re-read till I understood its meaning.

The next morning, as soon as breakfast was finished, I resumed the conversation of the previous night with the additional light I had gained on the subject. We had not talked long before Mr Aitken said, "Ah, my brother, you have changed your ground since last night."

I at once confessed that I had been reading Hare's book, which he did not know was in my room, nor even in the house. He was curious to see it.

22 *Mission of the Comforter and Other Sermons* by Julius
Charles Hare, John W Parker, London, 1846.

He then challenged me on another point, and said, "Have you peace with God?"

For eight years or more I had regarded God as my Friend. I answered without hesitation, "Yes."

Mr Aitken went on to ask me, "How did you get peace?"

"Oh," I said, "I have it continually. I get it at the Daily Service, I get it through prayer and reading, and especially at the Holy Communion. I have made it a rule to carry my sins there every Sunday, and have often come away from that holy sacrament feeling as happy and free as a bird."

My friend looked surprised but did not dispute this part of my experience. He contented himself by asking me quietly, "And how long does your peace last?"

This question made me think. I said, "I suppose, not a week, for I have to do the same thing every Sunday."

He replied, "I thought so."

Opening the Bible he found the fourth chapter of St John's Gospel, and read, "Whosoever drinketh of this water shall thirst again."[23] He said. "The woman of Samaria drew water for herself at Jacob's well and quenched her thirst, but she had to come again and again to the same well. She had no idea of getting water except by drawing, any more than you have of getting peace excepting through the means you use. The Lord said to her, 'If thou knewest the gift of God, and who it is that saith to thee, Give me to drink, thou wouldest have asked of Him, and He would have given thee living water,' which should be 'a well of water springing up into everlasting life.'" My friend then pointed out the difference between getting water by drawing from a well, and having a living well within you springing up.

I said, "I never heard of such a thing."

"I suppose not," he answered.

"Have you this living water?" I continued.

"Yes, thank God, I have had it for the last thirty years."

"How did you get it?"

23   John 4:10-14

"Look here," he said, pointing to the tenth verse: "'Thou wouldest have asked of Him, and He would have given thee living water.'"

"Shall we ask Him?" I said.

He answered, "With all my heart."

Pushing back his chair he knelt down at his round table, and I knelt on the opposite side. What he prayed for I do not know. I was completely overcome, and melted to tears. I sat down on the ground sobbing, while he shouted aloud praising God.

As soon as I could get up I made for the door. Taking my hat, coat and umbrella I said I was really afraid to stay any longer.

With this I took my departure, [accidentally] leaving my carpetbag behind. It was seven miles [11km] to Penzance, but in my excitement I walked and ran all the way. I arrived there before the coach which was to have called for me at Mr Aitken's house, but it brought my carpetbag instead. In the meantime, while I was waiting for it, I saw a pamphlet by Mr Aitken in a shop window, which I bought, and got into the train to return to Baldhu. My mind was in such a distracted state that I sought relief in reading.

I had not long been doing so when I came to a paragraph with the words of Jesus in italics: *I never knew you: depart from Me.* The question arrested me: What if He says that to you?[24]

Ah, that is not likely.

But, what if He does?

It cannot be. I have given up the world, I love God, I visit the sick, I have daily service and weekly communion.

But what if He does? What if He does?

I could not bear the thought. It seemed to overwhelm me.

As I read the pamphlet I saw that the words were spoken to persons who were taken by surprise. They were able to say, "We have eaten and drunk in Thy presence, and Thou

24   Matthew 7:23

hast taught in our streets; in Thy name we have cast out devils, and done many wonderful works." Yet, with all this, Jesus replied, "I never knew you: depart from me." I did not see how I could escape if such men as these were to be rejected.

The thought pressed heavily upon me, "What a dreadful thing if I am wrong." Added to this I trembled to think of those I had misled.

Can it be true? Is it so?

I remembered some of my parishioners I had watched over most zealously, lest the Dissenters should come and pray with them. I had sent them out of the world resting upon a false hope, administering the sacrament to them for want of knowing any other way of bringing them into God's favour. I used to grieve over any parishioner who died without the last sacrament, and often wondered how it would fare with Dissenters.

My mind was in a revolution. I do not remember how I got home. I felt as if I were out on the dark boundless ocean without light, oar or rudder. I endured the greatest agony of mind for the souls I had misled, though I had done it ignorantly.

They are gone; lost for ever.

I justly deserved to go also. My distress seemed greater than I could bear. A tremendous storm of wind, rain and thunder which was raging at the time was quite in sympathy with my feelings; I could not rest. Looking at the graves of some of my faithful Churchmen, I wondered, "Is it really true that they are now cursing me for having misled them?"

Thursday, Friday and Saturday passed; each day and night made me feel more dark and despairing than the preceding one. On the Sunday I was so ill that I was quite unfit to take the service. Mr Aitken had said to me, "If I were you, I would shut the church and say to the congregation, 'I will not preach again till I am converted. Pray for me.'"

Should I do this?

The sun was shining brightly. Before I could make up my mind to put off the service, the bells struck out a merry peal and sent their summons far away over the hills. Now the thought came to me that I would go to church and read the morning prayers and then dismiss the people. There was no preparation for the Holy Communion that day, and I had deputed the clerk to select the hymns, for I was far too ill to attend to anything myself.

The psalms and hymns were especially applicable to my case, and seemed to help me. I thought I would go on and read the ante-communion service, and then dismiss the people. While I was reading the Gospel I thought, well, I will just say a few words in explanation of this, and then I will dismiss them.

So I went up into the pulpit and gave out my text. I took it from the Gospel of the day: "What think ye of Christ?"[25]

As I went on to explain the passage, I saw that the Pharisees and scribes did not know that Christ was the Son of God, or that He was come to save them. They were looking for a king, the son of David, to reign over them as they were. Something was telling me all the time, "You are no better than the Pharisees yourself. You do not believe He is the Son of God, and that He is come to save you, any more than they did."

In his tract, *Building From the Top*, Haslam elaborates on the thoughts that led to his conversion during this sermon, but tells it in the third person as though it is happening to another preacher. This is an unedited extract:

These Pharisees and Scribes were not careless and immoral or prayerless men: no, far from it. They were religious to a degree, and yet these awful denunciations! Why? Because they overlooked Christ as the Son of Abraham, now come to be offered, and looked for the Son of David, to restore them to glory! And, in fact, they had overlooked the necessity of a change of heart, and forgiveness of sins through the Blood of the Lamb.

25   Matthew 22:42

In the midst of the discourse it pleased the Lord to show to our friend that Christ was the true and only foundation, and – what the Pharisee did not see – that He was the Lamb of God who beareth away the sin of the world! Now he saw that to work for life was building without a foundation, and promoting sanctification before justification; it was really beginning at the top; building, in imagination, in the air.

I do not remember all I said, but I felt a wonderful light and joy coming into my soul, and I was beginning to see what the Pharisees did not. Whether it was something in my words, or my manner or my look, I know not; but all of a sudden a local preacher who happened to be in the congregation stood up, and putting up his arms shouted out in Cornish manner, "The Parson is converted! The Parson is converted! Hallelujah!"

In another moment his voice was lost in the shouts and praises of three or four hundred of the congregation. Instead of rebuking this extraordinary "brawling" as I should have done in a former time, I joined in the outburst of praise. Then to make it more orderly, I gave out the Doxology, "Praise God from whom all blessings flow."

The people sang it with heart and voice over and over again. My Churchmen were dismayed, and many of them fled precipitately from the place. Still the voice of praise went on, and was swelled by numbers of passers-by who came into the church greatly surprised to hear and see what was going on.

When this subsided I found at least twenty people crying for mercy, whose voices had not been heard in the excitement and noise of thanksgiving. They all professed to find peace and joy in believing. Amongst this number there were three from my own house, and we returned home praising God.

The news spread in all directions that "the Parson is converted," and that by his own sermon in his own

Baldhu church: "The Parson is converted!" Redrawn from an original engraving in *From Death Into Life.*

pulpit! The church would not hold the crowds who came in the evening. I cannot exactly remember what I preached about on that occasion, but one thing I said was, "If I had died last week, I should have been lost for ever."

This was a startling and an alarming word to many of my earnest people, who said, "What then will become of us?"

I replied, "You will be lost for a certainty if you do not give your hearts to God."

At the end of this great and eventful day of my life, my spiritual birthday on which I passed from death to life by being "born from above", I could scarcely sleep for joy. I awoke early the next morning with the impression on my mind that I must get up and go to a village a mile off, to tell James B of my conversion. He was a good and holy man who had often spoken to me about my soul, and had been praying for three years or more on my behalf.

I had scarcely gone halfway before I met him coming towards me. He seemed as much surprised to see me as I was to meet him. He looked at me in a strange way, and then leaning his back against a stone fence, he said, "Are you converted?"

"Why do you ask me?" I replied. "I am just on my way to your house to tell you the good news that I have found peace. My soul is saved."

The dear man said, "Thank God." It came from the very depths of his heart. Shedding tears of joy, he went on to say, "Last night I woke up thinking of you. You were so strongly in my mind that I got up and began to pray for you, but I could not 'get hold'. I wrestled and cried aloud, but it was all of no avail. I begged the Lord not to give you up, but it seemed I could not pray. After trying for more than two hours, it came to my mind that perhaps you were converted."

He continued, "This thought made me so happy that I began to praise the Lord, and then I had liberty and shouted so loud that it roused up the whole house. They came rushing into my room to know whatever was the matter with me. 'I am praising God,' I said. 'Praising God. The Parson is converted, I feel sure he is. Glory be to God! Glory be to God!'

"They said, 'You must be dreaming. You had better lie down again and be quiet.' But it was of no use, I could not sleep. As soon as the light began to break I dressed myself, and have come out to see whether it is true."

"Yes," I said, "it is true. The Lord has saved my soul. I am happy."

I thanked him for all the help he had been, and for the patience he had so long exercised towards me. We spent a happy time together thanking and praising God, and then he returned home to tell his friends and neighbours the news.

After breakfast a visitor arrived who was on an errand of quite another kind. The report had by this time spread far and wide that I was converted. My [clergyman] friend immediately mounted his horse and rode over to see me about it. He at once put the question, "Did you say last night in your pulpit that you were saved, and that if you had died last week you would have been lost for ever?"

I answered, "Yes, indeed I did, and I meant it."

He looked quite bewildered, and stood for a long time arguing with me. Then taking a chair he sat down and began to sympathise and pity me, saying how grieved he was, for he could see madness in my eyes. He tried to divert my thoughts, and begged that I would go out for a ride with him. He called for his horse, but before mounting, he said, "I cannot agree with you, and will oppose you as hard as I can."

"Very well," I replied. "But let us shake hands over it. There is no need that we should be angry with one another."

Then he started off, and had not gone more than a few yards when suddenly pulling up, he turned. Placing his hand on the back of his horse, he called out, "Haslam, God stop the man who is wrong."

I answered, "Amen," and off he trotted.

On the Friday following he broke a blood vessel in his throat or chest, and has never preached since. His life was in danger for several weeks, though in course of time he recovered. I have heard that he has never been able to speak above a whisper. God has most undoubtedly stopped him, while He has permitted me to preach for the last nine-and-twenty years,[26] on average more than six hundred times a year.

From that time I began to preach the Gospel, and was not ashamed to declare everywhere what the Lord had done for my soul. Thus, from personal experience, I have been enabled to proclaim the Word, both as a witness and a minister.

26   Writing this in 1880, at the age of 62.

I, who before that time used to be so weak that I could not preach for more than fifteen or twenty minutes for three consecutive Sundays without breaking down, was now able to do so each day, often more than once, and three times every Sunday.

CHAPTER 7

Revival — 1851

I HAD ONCE MADE a resolution that if I ever had a work of God in my parish it should be according to rule, and that people should not be excited into making a noise – as if God were deaf or afar off. No shouting of praises, no loud praying, no hearty responding, and above all no extravagant crying for mercy such as I had witnessed in Mr Aitken's parish.

On the Monday after my conversion we had our first weekday revival service in the church, which was filled to excess. In the sermon I told them that God had, "Brought me up out of an horrible pit, out of the miry clay, and set my feet upon the Rock, and put a new song in my mouth."[27] I had not spoken long when someone in the congregation gave a shriek, and then began to cry aloud for mercy. This was quickly followed by cries from another, and another, until preaching was altogether hopeless. We then commenced praying for those who were in distress, and some experienced men who were present dealt with the anxious.

I cannot tell how many people cried for mercy, or how many found peace that night, but there was great rejoicing. I, who was still in my grave clothes though out of the grave, was sorely offended at people praying and praising God so heartily and so loudly in the church. I thought that if this was to become a regular thing, it would be akin to brawling and quite out of order. For people to cry out in distress of soul, and to praise God out of the abundance of their hearts, was too much for me. I was sadly perplexed.

27   Psalm 40:2-3

At the close of the service I told the people I would have a short one again the next evening in the church, and after that we would go into the schoolroom for the prayer meeting. Thus ended the second day of my spiritual life.

On Tuesday evening we assembled in the church and went to the schoolroom for the after-meeting. There the people had full liberty to sing, praise and shout too if they desired, to their hearts' content. Many availed themselves of the opportunity. In Cornwall at this time, Cornish folk did not think much of a meeting unless it was an exciting and noisy one.

In this schoolroom, evening by evening, the Lord wrought a great work and showed forth His power in saving many souls. I have seldom read of any remarkable manifestations in revivals, the counterpart of which I did not witness in that room, and I saw some things there which I have never heard of as taking place anywhere else. I was by this time not afraid of noise, so long as the power of the Lord's presence was evident. The shouts of the people did not hinder me, or their loud praying, or their hearty responses.

What tremendous scenes we witnessed whenever Mr Aitken came to preach at Baldhu. The church, which was built to hold six hundred, used to have as many as fifteen hundred packed into it Not only were the wide passages[28] crowded and the chancel filled up to the communion table, but there were two rows of occupants in every pew. The great man was king over their souls, for at times he seemed as if he was endued with power whereby he could make them shout for joy, howl for misery, or cry aloud for mercy. He was by far the most effective preacher I ever heard, or ever expect to hear. Souls were awakened by scores whenever he preached, and sometimes the meetings continued far into the night, and occasionally even to the daylight of the next morning.

28 Here, and elsewhere, when Haslam refers to passages within a church, they are what we would normally call aisles today.

To the cool, dispassionate outside observers and the newspaper reporters, all this vehement stir was very extravagant and incomprehensible, and no doubt they thought that it was done for excitement. Certainly they gave us credit for that, and a great deal more. They did not esteem us better than themselves, and consequently we had the full benefit of their sarcasm and invective.

Cornish revivals were things by themselves. I have read of such stirring movements occurring occasionally elsewhere, but in Cornwall they were frequent. Every year in one part or another a revival would spring up, during which believers were refreshed, and sinners awakened. It is sometimes suggested that there is a great deal of the flesh in these things, more of this than of the Spirit. I am sure this is a mistake. I am quite satisfied that neither Cornish nor any other people could produce revivals without the power of the Spirit, for they would never be without them if they could raise them at pleasure. But it is well known that revivals begin and continue for a time, and that they cease as mysteriously as they began.

Sometimes I have known the children of the school commence crying for no apparent reason when a few words about the love of God in giving His Son, or the love of Christ in laying down His life, would prove enough to kindle a flame. They would begin to cry aloud for mercy forthwith. I have seen a whole school of more than a hundred children like this at the same time. An awakening of such a character was generally a token of the beginning of a work of God which would last in power for four or five weeks, if not more. Then the quiet, ordinary work would go on as before.

Sometimes for no accountable reason we saw the church thronged with a multitude of people from various parts, having no connection with one another. They were all equally surprised to see each other, and the regular congregation more surprised still to see the unexpected rush of strangers. After a time we began to know the cause, and understood that the coming together of the people was by the Spirit of the Lord. So we prepared accordingly, expecting a revival to follow.

On these occasions it was very easy to preach, or pray or sing. We had only to say, "Stay here," or "Go to the schoolroom" or "Stand and sing" or "Kneel and pray" and it was done at once. Such was the power of the Spirit in melting the hearts of the people into entire submission for the time.

CHAPTER 8

The First Christmas — 1851/52

THE FIRST CHRISTMAS DAY during the revival was a wonderful time. The people had never realised before what this festival was, beyond regarding it as a season for domestic rejoicing. It surprised many to see that their past Christmases were a true representation of their past lives. They had tried to make themselves happy without Christ, leaving Him out of their consideration in His own world, as they had on His own birthday.

Now we praised the Lord together for His marvellous goodness to us, and desired that we might henceforth live unto Him, singing in heart and life, "Glory to God in the highest, and on earth peace, goodwill towards men."[29]

When New Year's Eve arrived we had a midnight gathering, and dedicated ourselves afresh to God's service. It was a blessed season, and several hundreds were there, who together with myself were the fruits of the revival during the previous two months.

The New Year opened upon us with fresh manifestations of divine power and larger blessings. I endeavoured to show the people that the Lord was called Jesus, not that He might save us from hell or death, but save us from our sins while we lived on earth.

After the Christmas holidays our schoolmaster and his wife returned. They came back full of disdain and prejudice against the work, and put themselves out of the way to go from house to house in order to set the people against me and my preaching. They said that they could bring a hundred clergymen to prove that I was wrong, but their

29   Luke 2:14

efforts stirred the people to come more frequently to hear, and contend more zealously for what they knew to be right.

The schoolmaster was particularly set against excitement and noise. He said, "It is so very much more reverent to keep still in prayer and orderly in praise. It is not necessary to make such an unseemly uproar."

I had, however, discovered long before this time that the people who most objected to noise had nothing yet to make a noise about. When they had, they generally made as much or more noise than others.

If a house is seen to be on fire, people cannot help making an outcry – but they do not do this when they only read about it. Witnessing a danger stirs the heart, and when people's eyes are open to see souls in eternal danger they cannot help being stirred up and crying out.

Notwithstanding the schoolmaster's opposition, he still came to church and was very attentive to the sermons, taking copious notes. One Sunday when I had been preaching on the text, "Cut it down; why cumbereth it the ground?"[30] he was heard to say, "Thank God I am not cut down yet;" and then he proceeded for the first time to the after-meeting in the school room. When I entered I saw him low down on his knees, and said how happy I was to see him there.

"Oh," he cried, "I fear there is no mercy. The sentence is surely gone forth against me: 'Cut him down. Cut him down.'" Then the poor man howled aloud in his distress.

The people prayed for him with shouts of thanksgiving, while he threw himself about in agony of mind and made a great noise. This only drew still louder acclamations from the people. In the midst of this tremendous din he found peace, and rejoiced with the others in unmistakable accents

30   "Then said he unto the dresser of his vineyard,
        Behold, these three years I come seeking fruit on this
        fig tree, and find none: cut it down; why cumbereth it
        the ground?" Luke 13:7. Cumber: obstruct, get in the
        way.

and as loud as the loudest. Evidently he was not ashamed or afraid of excitement and noise now.

While he was thus engaged, I went round to his house to see his wife and tell her the news. I found her sitting on the stairs in profound dismay as if some dreadful calamity had happened. She was literally dumb with fear and astonishment. When she could speak, she said, "What will happen to him now? Will he die? What will become of us?"

When I assured her that her husband was only just beginning to live, she said, "Must we be Dissenters now? Oh, what will become of us?"

Her sister, who was staying with her, became very angry at hearing of the schoolmaster's conversion. Finding that I could not do much with these two, I left them and returned to the schoolroom where the people were even more uproarious and happy than before. Several others had also found pardon and peace.

The following Sunday the schoolmaster was seen moving out of church as quickly as he could. When he reached the churchyard he was observed to run, then leap over a wall, and next over a hedge into a field. They could not hear him, but he was shouting all the time, as well as running. He afterwards said that the Prayer Book was full of meaning: it was like a new book to him. He said that if he had stayed in church he should have disturbed the whole congregation.

He became a very earnest Christian and took much pains and interest in the religious instruction of the children. There were several revivals in the school while he was there, and many of the children were converted. It was not long before he was able to rejoice over the conversion of his wife and her sister also.

CHAPTER 9

A Young Man in a Tall
Hat — 1851/54

DURING THE REVIVAL the outpouring of the Spirit of God was very manifest and unmistakable, and was seen in various ways. It was astonishing to hear persons, who had been dull and silent before, break out into full and free expression of spiritual truth. Their liberty and power in prayer were no less remarkable. It was as wonderful as the speaking of tongues on the day of Pentecost, with this difference. Those people spoke what they knew, in tongues they had not known. These, in their own speech, declared things which they had never seen or known before.

We had another distinctive sign of Pentecost. While believers rejoiced with overflowing joy – and sinners were pricked to the heart, and cried out, "What must I do to be saved?" – there were those who mocked, saying, "These men are mad, or drunk." But as St Peter testified long ago, these men, women and children were not drunk but under the influence and power of the Holy Ghost.[31]

We had yet another sign. The prophet Joel predicted, "It shall come to pass that I will pour out my Spirit upon all flesh; and your sons and your daughters shall prophesy, your old men shall dream dreams, your young men shall see visions; and also upon the servants and upon the handmaids in those days will I pour out my Spirit."[32]

I think my narrative would be very incomplete, and I should be holding back the truth, if I did not tell of some of

31 See Acts 2
32 Joel 2:28-29

the dreams and visions which continually happened at this time amongst us.

Cornish people at that time, and they may still be the same, lived in a spiritual atmosphere, at least in their own county. I have often heard them complain, when they returned from the shires,[33] of the dryness and deadness they felt there. I can certainly set my seal to this testimony, and declare that those of us who had visions in Cornwall have not had them when out of that district.

I will give a few examples, but only one of a kind, for it would fill the volume if I told all. The reader can judge if there was meaning or import in some of them or not.

At one time there was a depression or check in the congregation, and preaching was hard, praying formal and the singing flat. I invited the people to join with me in prayer, that the Lord would show us what was the hindrance in the way of the work. They prayed with one accord and without consulting one another, almost in the same words, whether in the schoolroom or in their cottages. The substance of their petition was that we might know and put away the obstacle to spiritual blessing, whatever that obstacle might be.

One night I dreamt that I was in the church, feeling very desolate and forsaken. There were very few people there, but soon my eyes lighted on an ugly stranger who tried to evade me. He was a very disagreeable, sullen-looking man. When I spoke to him he gnashed his teeth, and as I approached he drew out a knife and held it out before me. I pursued him notwithstanding, when he backed towards the door and went out. I followed him through the churchyard till he was outside the lych-gate.

As soon as he was gone I saw a troop of happy people, all dressed in white, come in at the same gate leaping and running like so many joyful children, swinging their arms

33 The neighbouring counties (shires) are Devonshire, Dorsetshire and Somersetshire, although nowadays the shire part of each county name is often omitted.

for gladness. They went into the church and began to sing. The dream was as vivid to me as a daylight scene.

I went out the next evening intending to tell it at the schoolroom meeting, but before I began to do so I observed that the people sang more freely than usual. I also noticed that two men who prayed omitted to offer the usual request for hindrances to be removed.

When I told my dream, a man arose and said, "I know all about that. There has been one among us whom we thought was a good man, but instead of this we have discovered that he was most immoral and deceitful, doing a deal of mischief, secretly undermining the faith of some, and misleading others. He has been detected and is gone."

Sure enough our old happy freedom returned and there was liberty in preaching, praying and singing – and souls were saved.

Another time, when I was getting a little impatient with the people, I took a leaf out of my Scripture-reader's book and preached a furious sermon about damnation, representing God as pursuing the sinner to cut him down if he did not repent there and then. I thought I had done it well, and went home rather satisfied with myself, supposing that I now knew how to make the congregation feel.

The next morning a woman called to me as I was passing her cottage, and said, "Master, what d'yer think? I dreamt last night that the devil was a-preaching in your pulpit, and that you were delighted at it."

A sudden fear fell upon me, so much so that I returned to the church. Shutting the door I begged God's forgiveness. Thanking Him for this warning, I asked that I might remember it and never transgress again.

As my Scripture-reader continued to proclaim wrath and vengeance, instead of preaching the Gospel, I parted with him.

My sister[34] came to me one morning, and said, "William, I had a vision last night of a young man in a tall hat, with a green and red carpetbag in his hand. I saw him so plainly that I should know him again anywhere. He was walking up the road when you met him, shook hands, and returned with him to the house. Then you and Frances[35] brought him in at the glass door. On the hall table there stood a basket containing four beautiful and fragrant fruits.

"You took up the basket and offered it to the visitor. Putting his hand upon one, he said, 'Oh, thank you.' Then touching the three others in order, he said, 'That is for mother, and that for sister, and that for...' I could not hear who. You may smile," she continued, "but I heard that, and saw it all as plainly as I see you now."

I was accustomed to hear such things, and consequently thought no more about it, but went on to speak of other subjects. In the course of the afternoon, as I was going out, I met a relative coming along the road and took him back with me to the house. My wife came out to him and we led him in through the glass door.

When he had sat some time, and had some luncheon, my wife said, "I wonder whether this is the young man we heard about this morning?"

"What young man?" asked our visitor hastily. "What young man do you mean?"

"I should not wonder if it is," I replied. "We will see presently."

He seemed very apprehensive, having heard before he came that some mysterious change had taken place in us, and so looked again and again to see if he could detect anything different.

"Come and see my sister," I said, to which he assented.

34   Jane Eliz Sargeant, a visitor age 32 from Stratford, Wiltshire, is listed on the 1851 Census, although Haslam's sister seems to be living nearby.

35   Haslam's wife.

We went across to her house. As soon as we entered her room, she said, "How do you do? I saw you last night."

"What do you mean?" he replied, withdrawing his hand. "Why, I was on board the steamer last night"

"That may be," she said, "but you are the gentleman I saw. Have you not a green and red carpetbag? And did not William meet you on the road?"

Poor young man, he looked dreadfully perplexed.

"Never mind her," I said. "Sit down and tell us about your journey."

After we had talked of this and other subjects, I told him that we were converted, and asked if he had given his heart to God. He said he had. Not being satisfied, I put the question in another form, and yet remained unsatisfied with his answer.

"Do you doubt me?" he asked. "I will prove it to you." He then went up to his room for a little while and returned with a paper in his hand in which was a dedication of himself to God, duly signed and sealed. I had never seen an instrument of this kind before, and asked if he really believed in it.

"Yes, certainly," he replied; "and I mean it, too."

"But," I said, "do you not see that faith does not consist in believing what you write, but in what God has written? You believe you have given, but do you believe God has taken? The Word says He is far more ready to take your heart than you to give it. As surely as you have given, so surely He has taken. Cannot you see that?"

He replied, "I knew that there was something wrong about this, but I did not know what. Thank you. Thank you." Then thoughtfully folding up the paper he went out of the room.

The bell was rung for dinner but he did not appear, and then for tea but he declined taking any. After we had gone to church he found his way down and followed us there. When the service was over he returned again to his room. I was detained at the schoolroom that night until two o'clock in the morning, praying and talking with anxious souls. I returned home very tired.

Going up to bed I saw a light shining under my visitor's door, and hesitating there a few moments I heard him pleading earnestly for mercy. I had a great mind to knock, but was afraid of disturbing him. So I prayed for him and went to bed.

In the morning he came down smiling. "Thank God," he said, "it is all right now. I am saved." In his hand he held three letters: one to his mother, one to his sister and the other to a cousin, in which he invited them earnestly to come to Jesus. Within the week all four were in our house praising God for salvation.

Amongst other people and characters I met with at this time was a good, respectable man who had a remarkable dream. He came to me one day after I had been speaking about Jacob's ladder and said that my sermon reminded him of his dream. I begged him to sit down and tell it to me.

He said, "I dreamt that I and nineteen other young men were living in a beautiful house, in a place where we had everything provided for us, and were free to enjoy ourselves as much as we pleased. We all understood that the premises belonged to Satan, and that we were his guests. As such we were permitted to take our pleasure upon two conditions. One was that we were not to pray, and the other that we were not to go away. We smiled at this and said it was not likely we should do the former, for we were not of the praying kind, and less likely that we should do the latter, for why should we be such fools as to give up our enjoyments?"

He continued, "In the course of time we all became heartily tired of the place and its pleasures, and longed to get away. But we could not. One of us made an attempt to do so, but he was captured and brought back and made more of a slave than ever. At last I and a few others agreed to pray at a stated time in different places, in the hope that if one was caught the rest might escape.

"Upon a set day and time we began praying, each in his appointed place. I had fixed upon a dark corner in a large deserted room where we had stowed away bales of goods we did not care to open. Climbing over the top of these stores I landed on the other side, and went to the spot I had chosen.

"I had not prayed long before I heard our master coming, cracking his whip, and saying, 'I'll teach you to pray!'

"This made me tremble exceedingly and pray all the harder. Hearing that he was very near and coming after me I opened my eyes, and to my surprise there was a beautiful silver ladder before me. As quick as thought I sprang with hands and feet upon it and began to climb for dear life.

"'Ha,' said master, 'I'll teach you to climb!'

"Then I felt the ladder shaking under me and knew he was coming up. I expected every moment to be seized and dragged back, so I climbed all the faster and looked up to see how much farther I had to go. It was such a long way, and there was only a very small hole to get to at last.

"My heart began to fail me so that I almost let go my hold. I felt the master's sulphurous breath on the back of my neck which made me rush forward more vehemently. At last I reached the top and thrust my arm through the hole, then my head and then my other arm. Thus I got through altogether, leaving my old enemy blaspheming and cursing down below. It was a most beautiful place that I was now in, and angels were flying about just as the birds do in this world.

"I saw the Lord Himself, and fell down before Him to give Him thanks. As I remained a long time prostrate, He said to me, 'What is thy petition?'

"I answered, 'Lord, grant that that hole may be made larger, for I have nineteen friends down there in the power of the cruel master.'

"The Lord smiled, and said, 'That hole is quite large enough.' So I awoke."

This dream had the effect of spiritually awakening the man who had it, and of bringing him to the foot of the cross for mercy and salvation.

I noticed that in dreams and visions in Cornwall the Lord Jesus very often appears, and the devil also. These are real persons to the Cornish mind, and their power is respectively acknowledged.

During the summer a young gentleman, whom we invited to our house in the hope of reaching his soul, came to stay with us in spite of his avowed prejudice against us and our proceedings. I took this as a token of encouragement, for I was sure that the devil would have hindered his coming unless the young man had been constrained by a higher power. He spent his time riding about or smoking and made great fun of our meetings and services, though I observed that he was very attentive to hear the sermon whenever he did come.

One weekday evening while we were sitting in the drawing-room and little expecting it, he burst into tears and cried out, "I don't know what to do. I shall be lost for ever."

We immediately sprang to his help, always delighted at such opportunities of working for the Lord. We knelt down to pray, and as we continued to do so he fell into great distress and even agony of soul. He literally writhed as if in excessive pain too great for utterance, and looked as if he was fainting with the struggle. We called all the servants into the room to help in prayer, and while I was praying by the side of my young friend, and pointing him to Christ, one of the maidservants rose up and walked straight across the room.

With a firm hand pushing me aside, she said, "The Lord is here Himself."

I rose instantly and moved out of the way, while she stood with her hands together adoring. She afterwards told us that she saw the Lord stoop down to the chair where my young friend was kneeling, and putting His hand on my friend's head He said something and then stood up. Immediately upon this she saw the veranda crowded with ugly-looking devils, all with their eyes fixed on the young man as he knelt. The Lord then waved His hand and the ugly company vanished.

At that instant the young man lifted up his head, and turning towards the side on which she had discerned the Lord as standing, said, "Lord, I thank Thee," then fainted away.

When the vision was over, she came with tears in her eyes to ask pardon for so rudely pushing me aside, but said that while the Lord was there she could not help herself. "Oh," she said, "He is so beautiful, so grand."

The young man was soon restored to animation, and began to speak in a voice and tone very different to his former utterance. He was altogether a remarkable instance of a change of heart and life.

One more case I will relate, with its solemn end, and then proceed with my narrative.

A careless, worldly man in my parish dreamt one night that he was in the market hall of a certain town. He was surprised to see in a wall a door which he had never noticed before. He went forward to examine it and found that it opened to his touch. He went inside and there he saw an impressive and strange scene. There were a number of men and women walking about, who appeared to be very woeful and in great agony of pain. They were too distressed to speak but he recognised most of them as persons who had been dead some time. They looked mournfully at him as if sorry that he had come there.

He was much alarmed and made his way back to the door to escape, but was stopped by a stern, sullen-looking porter, who said in a sepulchral voice, "You cannot pass."

He said, "I came in this way, and I want to go out."

"You cannot," said the solemn voice. "Look, the door only opens one way. You may come in by it, but you cannot go out."

His heart sank within him as he looked at that mysterious portal. At last the porter relented, and as a special favour let him go forth for eight days. He was so glad at his release that he awoke.

When he told me the dream I begged him to give his heart to God. "You may die," I said, "before the eighth day."

He laughed at the idea, and said he was, "Not going to be frightened by a dream. When I am converted," he continued, "I hope I shall be able to say that I was drawn by love and not driven by fear."

I said, "But what if you have been neglecting and slighting God's love for a long time, and He is now moving you with fear to return to Him?"

Nothing would do. He turned a deaf ear to every entreaty. When the eighth day arrived, being market day, he went to the hall as usual and looked with particular interest at the wall of which he had dreamed. But there was no door there.

He exclaimed, "It's all right. Now I will go and have a good dinner over it, with a bottle of wine."

Whether he stopped at one bottle or not I cannot tell, but late on Saturday night as he was going home he was thrown from his horse and killed. That was at the end of the eighth day.

I do not know whether these dreams and visions were the cause, or the effect, of the people's sensitive state. Certainly they made a deep impression, and even the cold and hardened were ready to hear about the mysteries of the unseen world. I attributed this to the spiritual atmosphere in which they were then living.

CHAPTER 10

Billy Bray — 1852

WHEN ALL THE PEOPLE on the hill where the church was built were converted, there came upon the scene a very remarkable person who had evidently been kept back for a purpose. This was none other than the veritable and well-known Billy Bray. One morning while we were sitting at breakfast I heard someone walking about in the hall with a heavy step, saying, "Praise the Lord! Praise the Lord!"

On opening the door I beheld a happy-looking little man in a black Quaker-cut coat which it was very evident had not been made for him, but for some much larger body.

"Well, my friend," I said, "who are you?"

"I am Billy Bray," he replied, looking steadily at me with his twinkling eyes. "And be you the passon?"

"Yes, I am."

"Thank the Lord. Converted, are ye?"

"Yes, thank God."

"And the missus inside?" He pointed to the dining room. "Be she converted?"

"Yes, she is."

"Thank the dear Lord," he said, moving forward.

I made way for him and he came stepping into the room. Then making a profound bow to the said "missus", he asked, "Be there any maidens?" He meant servants.

"Yes, there are three in the kitchen."

"Be they converted too?"

I was able to answer in the affirmative, and as I pointed towards the kitchen door when I mentioned it, he made off in that direction. Soon we heard them all shouting, and praising God together.

When we went in, there was Billy Bray very joyful, singing, "Canaan is a happy place, I am bound for the land of Canaan!"

We returned to the dining room with our strange guest, when he suddenly caught me up in his arms and carried me round the room. I was so taken by surprise that it was as much as I could do to keep myself in an upright position till he had accomplished the circuit. Then he set me in my chair, and rolling on the ground for joy, said that he was "as happy as he could live."

When this performance was at an end he rose with a face that was beaming all over. I invited him to take some breakfast with us, to which he assented with thanks. He chose bread and milk, for he said, "I am only a child."[36] I asked him to be seated and gave him a chair, but he preferred walking about and went on talking all the time. He told us that twenty years ago as he was walking over this very hill on which my church and house were built – it was a barren old place then – the Lord said to him, "I will give thee all that dwell in this mountain."[37]

Immediately he fell down on his knees and thanked the Lord, and then ran to the nearest cottage. There he talked and prayed with the people, and was enabled to bring them to Christ. Then he went to the next cottage and got the same blessing, and then to a third where he was equally

36   Presumably Haslam understood this puzzling response. Billy is fifty-seven, and may be having trouble with his teeth, or perhaps he is making some obscure spiritual point.

37   This incident would be from 1832, shortly before Billy started building Kerley Downs Chapel a few minutes' walk away. Readers who do not know Cornwall should understand that there are no mountains, although other writers of the period also use this word to describe the Cornish hills. The counties of Devon and Cornwall are for the most part hilly with high moor land, most famously Dartmoor and Bodmin Moor, but Baldhu is in an area of sharp dips and rises of no great magnitude.

successful. Then he told "Father" that there were only three "housen" in this mountain, and prayed that more might be built. That prayer remained with him, and he never ceased to make it for years. The neighbours who heard his prayer from time to time wondered why he should ask for "housen" to be built in such an "ungain" place.

At last, after sixteen years, he received a letter from his brother James to say that they were hacking up the croft to plant trees, and that they were going to build a church on the hill. He was "fine and glad" and praised the Lord. Again he did so when his brother wrote to say there was a Vicarage to be built on the same hill, and a schoolroom also. He was almost beside himself with joy and thankfulness for all this.

In the year 1848, when the church was completed and opened, he came on a visit to Baldhu and was greatly surprised to see what a change had taken place. There was a beautiful church, a Parsonage with a flourishing garden, and a schoolroom, with a large plantation and fields round them.

He was quite "mazed" for he never thought that the old hill could be made so grand as that. However, when he went to the service in the church, his joy was over. He came out "checkfallen" and quite disappointed. He told "Father" that that was nothing but an "old Pusey" He had got there, and that he was no good.[38] While he was praying that afternoon, "Father" gave him to understand that he had no business there yet, and that he had come too soon and without permission. So he went back to his place at once, near Bodmin, and continued to pray for the hill.

After three years his brother James wrote again. This time it was to tell him that the Parson and all his family were

38   Billy is referring to Haslam as "Old Pusey". Haslam had been greatly influenced by Edward Pusey, who was part of the Tractarian or Oxford Movement. This form of High Church service was totally unacceptable to Billy who was a member of the Bible Christians and a preacher in their chapels. More on Pusey on page 105 of this book.

converted, and that there was a great revival at the church. Now poor Billy was most eager to come and see this for himself, but he obtained no permission, though he asked and looked for it every day for more than three months.

At last, one wintry and frosty night in January, about half-past eleven as he was getting into bed, "Father" told him that he might go to Baldhu. He was so overjoyed that he did not wait till the morning, but immediately "put up" his clothes again, "hitched in" the donkey and set out in his slow-going little cart. He came along singing all the way, nearly thirty miles, and arrived early in the morning. Having put up his donkey in my stable he came into the house and presented himself in the hall, praising God, as I have already stated.

We were a long time over breakfast that morning, for the happy man went on from one thing to another, "telling of the Lord" as he called it, assuring us again and again that he was "fine and glad, and very happy." Indeed, he looked so. He said there was one thing more he must tell us. It was this: that he had a preaching-house, what we should now call a mission-room, which he had built years ago. He had often prayed there for "this old mountain" and now he should dearly love to see me in the pulpit of that place, and said that he would let me have it for my work.

Billy went on to say that he had built it by prayer and faith, as "Father" sent him help, and that he and another man had built it with their own hands. One day he was short of money to buy timber to finish the roof. His mate said it would take two pounds' worth. So he asked the Lord for this sum, and wondered why the money did not come, for he felt sure that he was to have it.

A farmer happened to look in the next morning, and Billy thought he had come with the money, but he merely asked them what they were doing, and then took his departure without giving them help. All that day they waited in expectation, and went home in the evening without having done any work.

The next morning the same farmer appeared again, and said, "What do you want two pounds for."

"Oh," said Billy, "you are come, are you? We want that money for the roof yonder."

The farmer then went on to say, "Two days ago it came to my mind to give two pounds for the preaching-house, but as I was coming down the hill yesterday morning, something said to me, 'If you give one pound it will be handsome.' Then I thought I would give only half-a-sovereign; and then that I would give nothing. Why should I? But the Lord laid it on my mind again last night that I must give you two pounds. There it is."

"Thank the Lord." said Billy, and proceeded immediately to get the required timber. In answer to prayer he also obtained reed for thatching the roof, and by the same means timber for the forms and seats.

It was all done in a humble manner, so that he did not dream of buying any pulpit. One day, as he was passing along the road, he saw that they were going to have a sale at the count house of an old mine. He went in, and the first thing which met his eye was a strong oak cupboard with a cornice round the top. It struck him that it would make a grand pulpit, if only it was strong enough. On examination he found it all he could desire in this respect. He thought if he could take off the top and make a "plat" to stand upon, it would do "first-rate."

He "told Father" so, and wondered how he could get it. He asked a stranger who was there, walking about, what he thought that old cupboard would go for. "Oh, for about five or six shillings," was the reply.

While Billy was pondering how to "rise" six shillings, the same man came up and said, "What do you want that cupboard for, Billy?"

He did not care to tell him, for he was thinking and praying about it. The man said, "There are six shillings for you. Buy it if you will."

Billy took the money, thanking the Lord, and impatiently waited for the sale. No sooner was the cupboard put up, than he called out, "Here, maister, here's six shillin's for un," and he put the money down on the table.

"Six shillings bid," said the auctioneer. "Six shillings. Thank you, seven shillings. Any more for that good old cupboard? Seven shillings. Going, going, gone!" And it was knocked down to another man.

Poor Billy was much disappointed and perplexed at this, and could not understand it at all. He looked about for the man who had given him the six shillings, but in vain. He was not there. The auctioneer told Billy to take up his money out of the way. He complied, but did not know what to do with it. He went over a hedge into a field by himself and told "Father" about it, but it was all clear: "Father" was not angry about anything. He remained there an hour and then went homewards.

As he was going along, much troubled in his mind as to this experience – for he still felt so sure he was to have that cupboard for a pulpit – he came upon a cart standing outside a public house, with the very cupboard upon it, and some men were measuring it with a foot rule.

As he came up, he heard them say, "It is too large to go in at the door, or the window either."

The publican who had bought it, said, "I wish I had not bid for the old thing at all. It is too good to scat up for firewood."

At that instant it came to Billy's mind to say, "Here, I'll give you six shillings for un."

"Very well," said the man, taking the money; "you can have him."

Then Billy began to praise the Lord, and went on to say, "'Father' as good as told me that I was to have that cupboard, and He knew I could not carry him home on my back, so He has found a horse and cart for me. Bless the Lord."

Promising to bring it back very soon, he led the horse down the hill and put the old cupboard into the preaching-house. "There it is." he exclaimed, "and a fine pulpit he does make, sure enough. Now," said Billy, "I want to see thee in it. When will you come." I could not fix for that day, or the next, but made arrangements to conduct a series of services the next week, and promised to have them in that place.

There is a problem with the identity of this
"preaching-house" or chapel. Bourne, in *The King's Son*
calls it Kerley Downs, but Haslam says the cupboard was
taken down to the chapel. Kerley Downs is next door to
Baldhu, and at the top of a hill, a fact that would have
been obvious to Haslam. The original Bethel Bible
Christian chapel at Cross Lanes is a more likely location,
as Billy had constructed Bethel, but by this time a larger
chapel had been built in the field opposite, and the old
chapel was used for meetings. Note that Billy seems able
to arrange for Haslam to preach without needing to
consult with anyone. Writing in his *Journal* Billy says the
cupboard was bought by a friend for Bethel, and makes
no mention of an auction. This makes me think that
Haslam was not told the full story by Billy, and into the
facts he was told he inserts a humorous story going
around in later years which had changed in the constant
retelling. He probably believed it to be true. Although
there are several written accounts, not one seems to be
without problems. A detailed investigation into "The Great
Pulpit Mystery" is in my book, *Billy Bray In His Own
Words* published by Highland 2004. Later on, Haslam will
be accused of being a Bryanite (Bible Christian), which
may be a reference to his friendship with Billy.
Cornish-born William O'Bryan (1778-1868) was a
dissident Wesleyan Methodist preacher who felt called to
evangelism in Cornwall, but was unsupported by the
Methodist leaders over the way he wanted to go about it.
The Bible Christian Connexion – the religious body
formed by O'Bryan – functioned in a way that was similar
to the Primitive Methodists.

Before he left us he made a particular inquiry about the two
other houses which had been built, who lived in them, and
especially if all the "dwellers were converted." Then he
declared his intention to go and see the parties and rejoice
with them, and testify how fully the Lord had accomplished

the promise He gave him upon that very hill twenty years before.

According to promise I went to Billy Bray's preaching-house, or mission-hall. It was the first time that I had preached anywhere outside my church and schoolroom since my conversion. There it pleased the Lord to give me much help, and a great work followed such as Billy had never seen in that place before. Several times we were detained there all night through, with penitents crying aloud for mercy, and believers rejoicing.

As a rule the Cornishman would remain at a meeting for hours, and come again the next day, and the day after if needful, till he felt that he could cry for mercy. Then he would begin and continue crying until he felt he could believe.

At the conclusion of these services we returned to the schoolroom where our meetings were continued.

Our friend Billy remained with us at Baldhu and was very useful. He spoke in the schoolroom with much acceptance and power in the simplicity of his faith, and souls were added to the Lord continually.

CHAPTER 11

Perranzabuloe Again — 1852

AS THE SUMMER ADVANCED, it was laid on my heart to go and preach in the parish of Perranzabuloe where I had ministered in my unconverted days. The Vicar, however, would not consent to my having the church, but he told me in writing that he could not prevent my preaching on the common or the beach. I thanked him for his suggestion as to the latter.

As soon as I was able I made arrangements, and giving due notice I went down to the old familiar place. This time I was on a new errand, and it was to me a fresh start in my work. I took my gown for this first open-air service, and on arriving found many hundreds of people already assembled on Perran beach.

After giving out a hymn, which was most heartily sung, I prayed, thanking God for the change He had wrought in my soul. I begged Him to show that He had forgiven the past – by bestowing a clear blessing upon the present service. All this was loudly responded to in Cornish fashion with hearty Amens and various other cries to which I was well accustomed. Then I read the beginning of the fifth chapter of St Luke, taking for my text the words of Jesus to Peter, "Launch out into the deep, and let down your nets for a draught."

Having reminded the people how hard I had worked amongst them for four years without seeing any conversions, I went on to show them that Simon Peter had toiled all night and taken nothing. But when he went forth at the Lord's command, he enclosed a great multitude of fishes.

At the close we found at least fifty people in that great throng on their knees crying for mercy. It was a most triumphant and joyful time, and the people were loath to separate.

The open-air preaching at Perran led to many similar services there, and at other places. On one occasion I was invited to a neighbouring parish, which formerly used to be united with Perran at the time when I had sole charge of it. Here on the appointed Saturday afternoon I found not fewer than three thousand people assembled on the common. They had erected a kind of platform, with a canvas awning to shelter me from the wind which always blows with more or less violence in Cornwall, even when it is not raining.

There I stood and beheld this concourse of people, evidently full of large expectation. I gave out the hymn, "Oh for a thousand tongues, to sing my great Redeemer's praise."

This was heartily sung. After prayer for a blessing I announced my text, and spoke from the fact that Christ Jesus came into the world to save sinners. Upon enforcing this as worthy of all acceptation, I pressed the thought that the Lord Jesus came more than eighteen hundred years ago, and that He is present still and able to work greater miracles than He wrought then. Indeed, He only began then to do and to teach what He is doing and teaching continuously now.

A mighty power of the Spirit of the Lord came on the people. Several hundreds fell upon their knees simultaneously, and many began to cry aloud for mercy. The strange part was that the power of the Lord appeared to pass diagonally through the crowd, so that there was a lane of people on their knees six or eight feet deep, banked up on either side by others standing. It extended from the left-hand corner near me, to the right-hand corner in the distance.

It was quite impossible to go on preaching. So I gave out another hymn, and then went in among "the slain of the Lord".[39] After about an hour someone suggested that we should go to the schoolroom, as it was getting dark. The clergyman of the parish was on horseback in the lane close

39 Biblical reference probably Ezekiel 37:8-10

by, watching proceedings. I asked him if we could have the use of the schoolroom.

"Oh yes," he said. "Yes, certainly. Certainly. Anything." He seemed very frightened.

The men and women in distress of soul were led to the room, crying and praying as they went. When I reached the place I found it impossible to get in, for it was already full, with a throng standing at the door. I was taken to a window at last, and getting in through that I stood on the schoolmaster's table which was near.

Against the wall the men had in miners' fashion set up in clay some candles, which were beginning to bend over with the heat of the room. The place was densely packed, and the noise of the people praying for mercy was excessive. I could do no more than speak to those who were near me round the table. As they found peace one by one, and were able to praise God, we asked them to go out and let others come. In this way the meeting went on till ten o'clock, when I left, and it continued to go on all night and all the next day without cessation.

It will scarcely be credited, but that same meeting was prolonged by successive persons without any intermission, day or night, till the evening of Sunday, the eighth day after it began. This kind of thing was not unusual in Cornwall, for we had the same in our schoolroom at Baldhu for three days and nights. But eight days is the longest period of which I have any personal knowledge.

I went again and again to see how they were going on, but the people were too absorbed to heed my presence. Those who were then seeking mercy were strangers to me, and had not been present at the service on the previous Saturday.

CHAPTER 12

No Law Against It! — 1852/53

AT THIS TIME I did not confine myself to my own church at Baldhu, but frequently went out to preach in other places as opportunities occurred. These were, for the most part, brought about by remarkable and unsought-for incidents.

One Sunday a lady and gentleman came to my church from one of the neighbouring towns. They were professors of religion[40] and members of some Dissenting body. My sermon that evening was upon wheat and chaff: the former was to be gathered into the garner, the latter to be burned with fire unquenchable. I said that we were all either one or the other – to be gathered or burned.

They went away very angry, and complained one to another of my want of charity. They also remarked that I took good care to let the people know that I was not amongst the chaff which was to be burned! The arrows of the Lord had evidently found them, and had pierced the joints in their harness.

They could not sleep all night for anger and distress. In the morning the gentleman rose early, and before breakfast had his horse out and galloped over eight miles [13 km] to see me. He came with the intention of finding fault, but instead of this he burst into tears and told me that he was the greates of sinners.

He was in sore distress, which increased all the more as he gave vent to his feelings. I could not help rejoicing. I told

---

40 Not academic professors, but people who professed
    to be Christians. Billy Bray uses this term frequently
    in his writing, applying it to nominal Christians with
    either no real faith, or a lapsed one.

him that God had wounded him, but that He only wounds to heal, and kills to make alive.

"Ah," he said, "that is the first thought of comfort I have had. It is like balm to my soul."

We knelt down and prayed. Then I had the privilege of leading him to Christ, and we praised God together.

I gave him some breakfast and rode back with him to see his wife whom he had left in the morning in great trouble of mind. We found her up and rejoicing. It was most touching to witness the mutual surprise and joy of these two loving ones when they discovered that they were now united in the Lord.

She told us that after her husband's departure she was in such terrible trouble that she got up to pray, and that while she was on her knees she saw a vision on the bedcover. Before her was printed, in large visible letters, "Thy sins be forgiven thee."[41] She could scarcely believe her eyes, but with her own finger she traced the letters and was sure they were there. Taking them as a message from Christ she rose and thanked Him, and now felt quite sure she was saved. I could not help telling her not to believe in her eyes or her visions, but in Jesus, and the fact that He had died for her.

Having thanked God together they next began to think of their servants. So we sent for them, and both master and mistress told them what the Lord had done for their souls. While we were praying, they all three cried aloud for mercy and found peace.

This was the commencement of a good work in that town by drawing-room meetings, and many were gathered to the Lord. Amongst the number was the mayor of the town, who in his turn wished to have a meeting at his house. As soon as I was able to fix the day he invited his friends, but on finding that so many more desired to come than he could accommodate, he announced that the meeting would be held at the Town Hall. Great interest was excited, and it was soon

41   Words from Matthew 9:2

evident that even this building would not be large enough, so it ended in the Temperance Hall being selected.

The Vicar, hearing about it, wrote to protest and asked me to call on him before I went to the place of meeting. He said it was bad enough for me to come to his parish to private houses, but to come to a public room, and that a large one, was quite out of the question.

I endeavoured to show him that the lecture or address I had come to give was not an official or ministerial act. But he would not see that. I also suggested that there was no law against it. He, begging my pardon, insisted that the Conventicle Act had not been repealed yet, and therefore no one could lawfully hold a meeting of more than twenty persons.

"But surely," I replied, "that is virtually repealed by the Toleration Act[42]. A clergyman ought not to be in greater bondage in England than a layman, or more restricted. Anybody else can come and preach the Gospel in your parish, and you cannot hinder it. Do not hinder me. It will do you no harm."

He said, "I cannot conscientiously allow it. It is against the Canons."

"Which Canon is it against?" I asked.

He took down a book and showed it me, but casting my eyes on the one before, and another which followed, I found that we neither of us observed the one or the other. Why then be so zealous about this?

"Besides," I said, "you are not responsible. You have not asked me, nor have I asked your consent. Your conscience need not be troubled about the matter."

"But," he said, impatiently, "I am determined that you shall not preach in this parish. I will inform the Bishop."[43]

42   The Toleration Act, 1689: "Exempting their Majesties' Protestant Subjects, Dissenting from the Church of England, from the penalties of certain laws."

43   Bishop Phillpotts of Exeter.

I replied, "The Bishop has not any jurisdiction in this case. There is no law on the subject. The Conventicle Act only refers to worship, not to service or preaching."

He said he could see no difference whatever between worship and service.

I said, "I am sure the Bishop knows, and will acknowledge the great difference between these two."

Changing his tone, he said, "Now, come, there's a good fellow. Don't preach at the Town Hall."

"My dear man," I answered, "I am not a 'good fellow' at all. I cannot give it up."

"Then," he said, "at least please to defer your address for a week, till we can get the Bishop's decision."

He asked so kindly and earnestly, and made such a point of it, that I consented to wait for the Bishop's answer and defer the preaching for the week. He was very pleased, and said that I was indeed a 'good fellow'; but the praise I got from him barely satisfied my conscience, and I was ashamed to meet my friends.

I had not gone far before my courage failed, so going back, I said, "I must withdraw my consent to defer the meeting. I will take the consequences and responsibilities, and go on."

"No, no," said the Vicar. "I will arrange for the postponement of your meeting. Look here, I have written out a notice for the crier. He shall go round the town at once and tell the people that the meeting is unavoidably deferred for a week."

I was very reluctantly persuaded to yield, and then went to my friend and told him what I had done.

He was very much vexed with me, and said, "Then we must go at once and tell the mayor, before he hears the crier."

We did so, and found that this personage was disappointed too, and advised me to go away out of sight of the people. Accordingly, my friend and I went to a house which commanded a good view of the town and principal streets, from whence we could see the people assembling, and then dispersing. A large throng of them stood opposite my friend's house and asked if I would not preach to them in the open air. When they ascertained that the Vicar had hindered the preaching, they were much exasperated.

In the evening I went back to my own parish, and had the usual service which I found very refreshing after so much bickering about technicalities.

The Bishop's letter arrived in due time. In it his lordship said that "he always had entertained a great esteem for me and my obedience to authority, and highly commended me for postponing or giving up my service at the above town."

As he did not say a single word of prohibition, I immediately wrote to the mayor to expect me on the following Tuesday, saying, "The Bishop has not forbidden me." I also wrote to the Vicar to the same effect. Large bills, with large letters on them, announced that, "The Rev William Haslam will positively preach in the Temperance Hall at three o'clock on Tuesday next."

On behalf of the Vicar, the churchwardens of the parish were requested to attend the meeting and protest, and also to present the Archdeacon's monition.[44] They stood beside me all the time, and after the service they showed me the archidiaconal instrument with a great seal appended to it. They said that they, "Dared not stop that preaching," and so they took their monition back.

This gave rise to a long correspondence in the newspapers, some taking part on my side, and some against me. Thus the question was ventilated, and finally concluded by a letter from someone, who said, "The Bishop of Exeter is one of the greatest ecclesiastical lawyers we have, and if he cannot stop Mr Haslam the question is settled; for be sure his lordship has all the will to stop this preaching, and would do so if he had the power."

From that time I never hesitated to preach the Gospel in any parish or diocese where I was invited. However, so few

44 A formal ecclesiastical notice warning a person not to commit an offence.

of the clergy asked me that I was obliged to go out in spite of them, or at any rate without asking their consent.

A general disposition has arisen amongst the clergy since then, from one end of the land to the other to have "missions". Now, there is no need to work independently of clergymen but with them, and very cheering it is to be thus employed. It was not pleasant at this period to witness the scowl and the frown, nor to get the cold shoulder. Thank God times are changed now.

CHAPTER 13

Billy Bray Again — 1853

MANY OF THE PROCEEDINGS in our parish were, I confess, more tumultuous than I could justify, and more noisy and exciting than I thought needful. If the people had been brought up to ideas of propriety and self-control, the impulse of Divine power which filled them might have found expression in a more quiet and orderly manner. But to hinder their rejoicings would have been to withstand the Spirit of God.

One day, by way of change, I had a meeting for the Bible Society and invited some of the clergy who sympathised with its object. They attended, and others came out of curiosity "to see these revival people."

We had a large gathering and everything began smoothly. My Scripture-reader, who was a most excitable and noisy man, tried to do his best before the clergy. He spoke of the sweet words which they had heard from the reverend speakers. It was charming, he said, to hear of a good cause supported in such "mellifluous accents" and so forth.

He got a little wild towards the end, but on the whole he was to be praised for his efforts to give a quiet tone to the meeting. By this time our friend Billy Bray had appeared on the scene, and gave us chapter and verse from one end of the Bible to the other on the subject of "dancing for joy". He propounded his theory that if a man did not praise God he would not rise in the resurrection. If he only praised God with his mouth he would rise like those things carved on the tombstones, with swelling cheeks and wings. If he clapped his hands – suiting his actions to the words – he would have a pair of hands as well at the resurrection; and if he danced with his feet he would rise complete. He hoped to rise like that, to sing, to clap his hands, dance and jump too.

The worst of jumping in this world, Billy said, was that he had to come down again. But in heaven he supposed the higher he danced and jumped, the higher he would be. Walking in heaven, to his mind, was praising God. One foot said, "Glory," and the other, "Hallelujah!"

The people were warming up and becoming a little responsive, and Billy himself was getting excited. In reference to some remarks which had been made by a previous speaker about Samson, Billy said he felt as happy and strong as Samson.[45]

Then suddenly he put his arms round me as I was making signs to the people to be still. Taking me up as he had done once before, he carried me down the schoolroom, crying out, "Here go the posts! Glory! Hallelujah!"

It was useless to resist, for he held me with an iron grasp. So I remained still, hoping at every step that he would put me down. I suppose he imagined himself to be Samson carrying off the gates of Gaza. The people got what they called "happy", and shouted and praised God most vociferously. I gave out a hymn, but the joy of the Cornish people could not be restrained within the bounds of a tune or form of words. Some of them became very excited and unmanageable.

Only those who have witnessed such scenes can understand what I mean. The power of God was great, though the demonstrations were very human. My visitors trembled with fear and made their escape as precipitately as they possibly could. To those who are not in the power of the Spirit, such rejoicings are unintelligible. Lookers-on are offended because they only see and feel the human manifestation, and not the Divine power. They are like people who get all the smoke and none of the warmth of the fire.

I made up my mind for the worst, for we had a reporter there, and some others who were only too ready to make the most of such a scene. Nevertheless, I would rather have the same thing over and over again than have the most stately

45   See Judges 16

and orderly ceremonials conjoined with spiritual death. Such ceremonials, with all their proprieties, are very chilling to living souls, and all the more hurtful because dead souls are satisfied by them instead of being disturbed.

Dear Mr Aitken was very angry with us when he heard the things which were reported. Like a good spiritual father he came over to teach us better. He preached one of his own strong sermons on the difference between emotion and principle, and after beating us down very hard his dear heart relented, and he tried to cheer and lift us up. This last is always an easy thing to do in Cornwall.

The people soon responded to his efforts, and began to praise God. Then he took fire and praised too. Being excited, his powerful voice could be heard above the din of hundreds of shouting voices. The dear man was happy in his soul, and so was I, and we did not care a halfpenny for the outside world, newspapers or anything else.

Even to my personal friends I could not give satisfactory explanations of these things. One suggested that I should read a paper at the next Clerical Meeting and give a statement in exposition of my views and practices. This I consented to do, and Mr Aitken kindly helped me to write it. On the appointed day I undertook to read it, on condition that no one interrupted me till I had finished. It was a hard task for them to sit still, but they did manage to do so, and at the end burst out upon me in a volley of censure and disapprobation. Finally I was obliged to tell them that they were not converted, and therefore could not understand these things.

CHAPTER 14

A Visit to Veryan — 1853

I WILL TELL of a clergyman to whom I was much attached, although we were diametrically opposed to one another, especially in my Puseyite days. He was Evangelical and I was then High Church. Consequently we fell out more or less at every meeting, though we never really quarrelled.

After my conversion I felt sure this friend would sympathise with me, but I found to my disappointment he was in reality more opposed now than before – because I had become, as he called it, a Dissenter. He would scarcely speak to me and said he was not so sure of my conversion. He would give me seven years to prove it, and then pronounce.

I said, "You are an old bachelor and know nothing about the treatment of babies. We do not put our babies out on the lawn for seven days before we decide whether they are born or not!"

He could not resist joining in the laugh against his inexperience in this respect, although he was not over-pleased. With all his head-knowledge of Gospel truth he had not seen anything of the work of the Spirit. Because I had announced some sacramental views after my conversion, he fancied that I must be dead still. But these were only the grave-clothes in which I used to be wrapped.

One day he came to me, and said, "I have been thinking for some time that I should like to come to your church one Sunday and see your work."

I agreed to this with thanks, as the first sign of sympathy I had found in him, and said, "Shall I go and take your services in exchange?"

"Oh no, certainly not. I wish you to be present in your own church. I will preach in the morning, and be there to see and hear you in the evening."

We soon fixed upon the day.

He came to dinner with us on the Saturday, but before he would sit down he wanted to go into the Church and adjust the height of the pulpit, and see that all other things were to his taste. He asked me if I would remove the candlesticks from the communion table and let him preach in a black gown. These were all matters of indifference to me now, so I readily acceded to his wishes.

Having completed his arrangements we spent a very pleasant evening together, talking over the work in the place. Then we went to the weekly prayer meeting, but he took no part. On Sunday morning the service was conducted at his request in the usual manner, excepting that he stood away in the eastern corner of the north side of the table, "scrootching" away like a Papist, as the people described it. They had been accustomed to see me stand at the western or outside corner of the north side. He was much amused at this criticism.

Then he went into the vestry, having asked for an interlude on the organ before the last verse of the Psalms which we always sang in the metrical version. While this was being played, he came sailing out again and swept up the steps into the pulpit. He gave us an excellent sermon, preached as the Cornish say "to a form" – that is, with a manuscript before him, though he did not look at it much.

He showed it to me afterwards. It certainly was a curious thing, done in ciphers and hieroglyphics of his own. Again and again there appeared a figure with two horns and a tail. This, he told me, stood for Satan. There were also many other striking signs. He preached with far more animation than he was wont, and towards the end of his sermon seemed to forget his manuscript altogether, leaning over the front of the pulpit, gesticulating with his hands and looking at the people.

They got very excited and followed every sentence with some response, till he became excited also. When he came down from the pulpit, he said that he had never preached with such help before. He had quite enjoyed his own sermon, and now he thought he understood the secret of what I called being "converted".

He came in the afternoon to the catechising of the children, and expressed himself very pleased with their behaviour and their readiness in answering questions.

In the evening he sat in a part of the church where he could see both the congregation and me as the preacher, and so make his desired observations. The service was perhaps a little more animated than usual, and the sermon may have been so too. After this was over he went with me into the schoolroom where he heard the people pray and thank God for the morning sermon. Several souls were brought in that evening.

About ten o'clock that night we returned home, when my friend declared he had never known a day like this in all his ministry, and never heard of such things as he had seen. "Your congregation," he said, "is like the waves of the sea, and mine like a glassy millpond. Now I must have you come and preach in my church. I wonder what the effect will be."

I agreed, and we fixed upon the second Sunday as he wanted a week to announce my coming.

I was quite eager for the time. When Saturday arrived I set off, intending to stay for several days. On Sunday morning the church was filled from end to end, the people being on the tiptoe of expectation. Many anxious ones remained after the sermon, to be spoken with about their souls. The church was scarcely cleared before the men came to ring the bells for the afternoon service. This time the passages, chancel, pulpit-stairs and every available corner were crowded, and the congregation certainly did not look like a "millpond", but more like "the waves of the sea".

At the close of this service the people begged for another in the evening.

The Vicar said, "Oh, that is impossible, for I dine at six o'clock."

"But," I involuntarily added, "I do not mind missing dinner. I can come if you like."

He gave me such a look.

I continued, "I have had dinner enough for today. I can take the service alone if you are agreeable."

"But we have no lamps for the church. It cannot be."

I was silenced now, and gave up the point. Then the churchwarden came forward and said he would be responsible for lighting the church.

The Vicar at last consented, on condition that he was allowed to have his dinner in peace. As the time approached, however, he put off that important meal and joined me in a cup of tea, after which we went together to the third service.

This time it was as much as we could do to get in, and when we did succeed a most striking sight presented itself. The whole church was lighted from the pews. Some of the wealthier people had lamps, but the others had candles: one, two, or more in their respective compartments. From the pulpit it looked more like a market scene than a church congregation.

I had liberty in preaching, and the people were greatly moved. Some were greatly agitated – indeed, so much so that the Vicar thought he would not have another service in the church, and accordingly announced that the Monday evening meeting would be held in a building which he named in a village about two miles off. This was a large barn-like structure where they cured fish in the season, but at other times it was unoccupied.

The next day happened to be very wet, and in the evening it began to blow as well. Despite this inclemency, when we arrived at the "fish-cellar" as it was called, we found it crammed with people. The women and children were occupying the ground, sitting there on straw which had been provided for the occasion. The men and boys were sitting on the crossbeams of the roof.

The heat in the place was stifling beyond all description, for besides being densely crowded below and above, the wooden shutters were closed because of the wind and rain. The people's wet clothes were steaming, and there was a strong smell of stale fish. At first we felt as if it would be impossible to bear it, but after a little time we had other things to think about.

I gave out a hymn, and after a short prayer commenced the address, speaking as loud as I could so that all the congregation might hear me. During the sermon the responses were most vociferous and hearty, and the attention very encouraging. After speaking for about thirty minutes I observed a tall, fine-looking fisherman in large high boots, who had come in late. He was standing in the little space before the table on which were placed two candles and a glass of water.

I saw as the address went on that though he was very quiet, his breast was heaving with emotion as if something was passing in his mind. All at once, without a moment's notice, he fell on the ground and bellowed out a loud prayer for, "God's mercy! I want God's mercy!"

Besides upsetting the table – candles, water, and all – which went down with a great crash, he fell on one or two women who screamed in their fright and consternation, as only women can.

If this had been a preconcerted signal it could not have been more effectual, for there was instantly a simultaneous as well as a universal outcry. The whole place was filled with a confused din of voices: some were praying, some singing, some shouting and others exhorting, all at the top of their voices in order to be heard. In the midst of this I began to sing a hymn, hoping to restore order, and many joined me. But it only added more sound to the uproar.

The good Vicar was overwhelmed with fear and dismay, as well he might be at this tumultuous scene. He made for the door and beckoned me to him.

When I came, he suddenly opened it and drew me out, saying, "There will be no peace till you are out of this place."

The extreme change from the hot cellar, into the cold and pitiless wind and rain, was so great that we fled precipitately to the cottage which stood opposite. Happily the door was on the latch and we went in. I felt about in the dark for a chair, but not finding one I sat on the table, listening to the noise and din of the meeting.

The Vicar vainly thought that the tumult would subside as soon as I was gone, for he said that I, "Made as much noise, if not more, than any of them."

He went back into the storm to get my hat and coat, and the inevitable umbrella without which no one can get on in Cornwall. He was a long time absent, during which a man with heavy boots came into the dark cottage where I was sitting. Tumbling down on a seat somewhere, he heaved a heavy sigh. He evidently did not suspect that anyone was there.

After sighing and groaning several times, he said to himself, "What shall I do? What shall I do? The man is right, sure enough. He is right, I'm sure on it that he is."

I disguised my voice, and asked, "What man?"

"Oh," he said, "are you there, neighbour? Couldn't yer get in? Why, I mean the man what's been speaking inside."

"What did he say?"

"He said, 'the devil's no fool'. And of course he ain't. He has hooks in all his baits, and I have swallowed lots o' them. Oh, what shall I do? What shall I do?"

Then I heard him shuffling to his knees, groaning and praying. I sat unmoving on the table, saying, "Amen, Amen," every now and then to his prayer, till he became terribly in earnest, and at last got into a state which the Cornish call "wrastling in prayer". In this condition he was quite past heeding anyone's presence.

I helped and guided him to the Crucified One, and then he found peace and began to praise God. On coming to himself, he recognised my voice.

"Why, you are the very man," he cried, and putting his great heavy arms round my neck he nearly strangled me. The Vicar, who I did not know was back in the room, here interposed and got my release.

"Here you are," he said, "at it again. They are getting worse and worse in the barn. Whatever is to be done? We cannot go home through this rain, and the carriage will not be here for at least an hour. What am I to do?"

I said, "Let us go then to the barn for a short time, just to see how they are getting on."

After some hesitation he went in with me, and found the people praying and rejoicing; but, as I expected, far too much absorbed to observe our presence.

Later some lads noticed me, and cried out, "The Parson is here! The Parson is here!"

In a moment we were surrounded by a number of happy people who were so demonstrative that they made the poor Vicar tremble, as he told me afterwards, with a strange fear.

They said, "You will come again tomorrow?"

"Certainly," I replied.

"Oh, no," rejoined the Vicar. "On no account! One night of this work is quite enough – more than enough."

I was very loath to give up, but a man said, "Never mind, we will carry it on. This revival will not stop for a week or fortnight, for certain."

This was terrifying news for the Vicar, who turned, and looking at me with astonishment, said reproachfully, "How did you do it?"

I replied, "This is not my work. I did not begin it, neither can I stop it. Nor would I, even if I could. I dare not. I have known persons brought under heavy judgments for hindering a revival. Take my advice and let these men go on. They know what they are about."

Soon the carriage came and we returned to the Vicarage, but the dear man was much put out and evidently very sorry that he had asked me to come and disturb his millpond. Indeed, he said as much. So I concluded my visit the next morning.

Going through the village I heard that the meeting on the previous evening was continued till two o'clock in the morning, and that it was announced there would be one in the chapel that evening. As the Church refused the blessing, there were others happy to receive it.

At Golant [north of Fowey on the south coast] I preached with great effect in the church, and when the work abated I proffered a visit to the High Church Rector who had asked me to come over and tell him the secret of my success.

He readily fixed upon a day, so I went over to luncheon, after which we began to talk. The Curate who was present, and who had heard some ranters shouting and screaming in the "shires", kept on every now and then putting in a word of caution to restrain the Rector from admitting too much, for little by little he was yielding to me.

I spoke of letting down the nets for a draught and catching men, not to smother and kill them in some Church system, or by some erroneous teaching, but to keep them alive. "This," I said, "is the meaning of the word in the original." We looked it out in the Greek. It was very interesting. We then talked over the difference between the Church system and that of the Bible. The one, I said, makes apostolic succession and the sacraments the channel of salvation; the other the Word of God, as applied by the Holy Ghost.

We had a great battle on this point, two against one, but having the Word of God on my side I stood by my experience. I had myself been on the other side, and was then ten times more zealous and earnest than these two were. I said, "I used to preach salvation by Church and sacraments once, but I was not saved that way. I used also to teach that the new birth was by Baptism, but I was not born again when I was baptized. Were you? Are you quite sure that, with all your faith in Baptismal Regeneration, you are born again of the Spirit? Are you satisfied that you are now saved because you are in the Church?"

They were dumb. I went on to say, "I have no party or sectarian object in my work. My only desire is to bring souls to Christ Himself for salvation. I used as a priest to think I was mediator between Christ and the sinner, and that I had received by delegation some power for this purpose. But now that I have been over the ground from experience, I would as soon blaspheme God in your presence as dare to absolve a sinner, or come between Christ and him. My orders are to bring them from the power of Satan to God, and to Christ crucified for forgiveness of sins."

At this point the Rector brought out a printed sermon by Dr Pusey on Justification by Faith, which he had been carefully reading. I asked him to read it to me. The first few pages contained statements of the doctrine in New Testament words, with a fair exposition of them, but when the author came to his own thoughts about the subject he said that Baptism was the cause of justification.

Here I challenged the statement, and said, "Have you any references there?"

"Yes," he answered, "references to the Fathers."[46]

I replied, "The Fathers were not inspired. There is no such thing as Justification by Baptism in the Scriptures. It is by faith only, as you will see in the fifth chapter of the Epistle to the Romans."[47]

My two High Church friends were not convinced, though they could not answer me. It was a question in their minds who was right, Dr Pusey or this "Fanatical Revivalist."

"Come," I said, "there is your man-servant [Sam] outside in the garden. He was converted two weeks ago, and though he cannot read I feel sure he knows more about this experience than the author of that learned sermon. Let us call him in and read a few pages."

We did, and told him to sit down while we read a little while.

The Rector began, and as he went on Sam's face lit up with joy until the Rector came to the sacramental passages. Then anyone could see Sam's interest was gone. He became very restless, and at last interrupting, said respectfully, "If you please, sir, is there much more of that?"

"Why, Sam," said his master, "don't you like it?"

"No, sir," he said; "that man ain't converted at all!"

"Well, that is strange," said the Rector. "I saw his interest went off just at the very point where you took exception to the sermon. You and Sam understand something that I do not know."

I had stayed already two hours longer than I intended, and was tired of talking. The Rector asked me to remain and

46 The Church Fathers – the early Christian theologians, particularly those of the first five centuries of Christian history, not the writers of the New Testament.

47 For example, verse 1: Therefore being justified by faith, we have peace with God through our Lord Jesus Christ.

dine with him, and promised that he would send me to church in the evening in time for the service. I agreed to this, so he kindly took me upstairs to wash and rest.

Coming into the room with me he shut the door, and said in confidence, "I know you are right. My mother taught me all this when I was young."

"Then," I said, "we had better kneel down and pray about it."

We did so. In his prayer he entreated very earnestly that the scales might fall from his eyes, and that these truths which he loved when he was young might be brought to him again.

He was only praying for truth and not for pardon and salvation, so I pointed this out to him.

"Yes, yes," he said. "Lord, save me! Lord, save me! Pardon me!"

I believe he found peace before he came down to dinner, and it was not long before he roused the anger and contempt of his wife and Curate, by saying, "I am converted."

They tried hard to laugh him out of it, and asked him which of the chapels he would join? They suggested he had better be a Bryanite; Mr Haslam is king of the Bryanites; and so on.

When I was leaving for my service, the Rector in bidding me goodbye said that he "was sorry he could not go with me, but would I come and preach in his pulpit on Sunday?"

I promised that I would. Thus the revival which began on one side of the river passed over to the other and brought out people from another town and also villages beyond. There was a great wakening in that part of the country. The Curate found peace on the Sunday, and many more with him; but not the Rector's wife. She continued her opposition most vigorously.

CHAPTER 15

Trouble in Dorset — 1854

MY FIRST JOURNEY to "foreign parts", as the Cornish call it, was to a town in Devonshire where I stopped three or four days. The day I arrived I preached in the church because it was the regular evening service. Special services were not then known, unless it was for some Missionary Society or other such advocacy. The idea of preaching to awaken souls was considered very strange and fanatical.

The church I preached in had high pews which prevented my seeing the occupants. I was told that it was full, and certainly there were faces visible here and there, but the whole congregation was so still that the dropping of the proverbial pin might have been heard. It was all very chilling and dead. No Amens! or Glory! as in Cornwall. Indeed, the stillness had such an effect upon me that I found it difficult to get on. After making two or three hard appeals, and meeting with nothing but silence for a response, I came away much disappointed and disheartened.

Walking through the town the next day, a tall mason with a large whitewash brush in his hand came running after me. "Are you the man that preached last night?"

I said, "Yes, I am."

"Oh," he replied, "will you preach tonight?"

I answered him somewhat doubtfully, "I suppose not," for the Vicar did not know what excuse there could be for my preaching a second time.

He continued, "Will you come to my house and preach this evening? I have a large room at your service, and can promise you a congregation."

I assented, so we fixed the time and made all other necessary arrangements. On coming down in the evening I found my mason friend had invited his neighbours, and finding more had promised to come than his room would hold, he had opened the folding doors between two rooms upstairs. By taking down three large bedsteads, and having borrowed forms and chairs, he was able to accommodate seventy people. As many as this came, and more, for men and women stood on the stairs and landing besides.

We sang heartily, and after prayer I felt a little more at home than I had done on the previous evening. But it was not up to Cornwall yet. In my address I had liberty and power to hold the people, and we had some conversions that evening and the following one also. My mason friend was greatly cheered and revived, and from this time began preaching himself, carrying on meetings in various cottages and farm places.

From there I went on into Dorset and arrived at the Vicarage to which I was going, rather late on Saturday night, very tired, and was glad to go to bed as soon as possible. On Sunday morning I went to church and preached to a large congregation the words which God gave me.

On coming out, the Vicar's wife said, "If I had sat up all night telling you about the people, you could not have preached more appropriately. Indeed, I am sure that some of them will think that I told you what to say!"

It was so, for this same lady was later accused of telling me to put before some of the congregation things which her husband dared not. In the evening the church was crammed to excess, and the people were most attentive and eager. Some of them could scarcely restrain their feelings, so powerfully did the Word come home to them. At the conclusion of the service I announced that I had come there to preach every night for the week, and would visit them during the day. Accordingly, in the morning I called at several cottages, in one of which King George III used to attend a prayer meeting with the country people.

We had a very good time that evening in the church, and there was much power and blessing. At the close of the service I gave out that I would preach again the following evening, and having no opportunity for an after-meeting, the word preached was left with prayer for a blessing on it.

The next morning there came an unexpected, as well as a most abrupt, opposition to the work; and no wonder, for it was not likely that Satan would permit it to go on smoothly. A Vicar from the neighbourhood who had formerly been a military man, and had still the commanding manner of such, presented himself and tried to terrify my good and kind friend the Vicar. He told him that he was deputed by other clergymen to come and ask that my preaching might be stopped. Then he went on to say that I was nothing less than a Jesuit in disguise.[48]

Turning to me, he said, "Sir, you know you are!"

I replied, begging his pardon, "I can assure you I am not. You must be altogether misinformed."

But he said, again turning round and sternly looking at me, "You know I am not mistaken or misinformed. Your countenance betrays you!"

I smiled at this, not knowing how my countenance looked. He was quite satisfied with himself, and rather more so because he thought he had succeeded in extracting a promise from the Vicar that the services in question should be stopped.

This officer-clergyman then went away, saying that he was quite convinced in his mind that I was a Jesuit, and nothing should ever dissuade him. This interview had confirmed his thoughts on the subject. My dear good friend was so afraid of that loud, overbearing man that he consented to give up the services after that night.

Presently another clergyman, evidently in concert with the former, called on the same errand. His more gentle manner and plausible words had greater effect, so that the Vicar more than half decided to have no service, even on that evening.

Before he had fully made up his mind, it so happened that there came on a tremendous thunder-storm accompanied with hail and vivid flashes of lightning. This was

48   A member of the Society of Jesus, an order of the
Roman Catholic Church, founded by Ignatius Loyola
in 1534. A strange accusation!

considered by him quite providential, and an indication that God wished the services stopped.

When the sexton came over to the Vicarage a little before the service time, the Vicar said, "Don't ring the bell for church tonight. It is of no use. No one can possibly come out this weather."

"Why, sir," said the sexton, "the church have been crammed full this half-hour. It's no use ringing the bell, sure, for we ain't got no room for no more people."

"Now, that is remarkable," said the Vicar. "I do think, after all, the Lord would have us go on. What do you think?" he said, turning to me.

I replied, "Without doubt I think so. I cannot suppose that the Lord would send such men, in such a tone, to stop His work."

"Well, then," said the Vicar, "we will go on till the end of the week."

But this could not be. I had already written to a cousin of mine in the neighbourhood asking him to get me to the parish church for the next evening – and the letter had gone.

I spoke that evening, and announced that I would do so again on Thursday. On the following day I went on this promised visit to another part of the county, and was not long in the company of my cousin before I found out that she had been brought up in Evangelical doctrines and hated Puseyism, but had never been converted.

In the evening we went to the Minster Church, the use of which she had obtained for me. There I preached from the words, "Behold, I stand at the door and knock." I did not know then, as I do now, that this is a text for believers.[49] Accommodating it for my purpose, I explained that many people assented to evangelical doctrines without yielding to

49 Revelation 3:20. In spite of Haslam's changed point of view, many Bible scholars see this verse as applying especially to the unconverted, and Christians use it to great effect in drawing people to Christ, as Haslam does here.

them: that is, they heard the knocking but did not open the door and receive the Saviour. Therefore they remained unsaved, and if they died like that they would be lost for ever.

When I first ascended the pulpit, which stood outside a high chancel screen, I looked towards the nave and saw it filled with high pews which, as I thought, were for the most part empty. I could see that the choir and chancel which was brightly lighted was full of choir-men and boys, besides many people. So instead of turning my back upon the many in the lighted chancel, and addressing myself to the unseen few in the large dark nave, I turned round in the pulpit, and looking through the screen preached to those I could see.

The people in the nave, however, were most attentive to hear. After the sermon they came up and asked me why I had turned my back on them, for they could not hear all I said. Evidently they had heard something which had interested them. Seeing so many were anxious, we invited those who wished for further help or instruction to come home with us. Many did so, and we held a kind of after-meeting in which my cousin and several others found peace.

I could not promise to stay there any longer, having settled to return on Thursday to resume services in the church previously referred to. Accordingly I went back to the neighbouring town where my good Vicar had appointed to meet me. He did so, and without delay commenced telling me that he had had a long talk with some of his brother clergymen, and had given his word that the services were positively to be discontinued after that night.

He also told me he had booked my place on the coach, and I was to start for Exeter the next morning. Then he went on to say that he found it would be dangerous to keep me any longer, for he should have the whole neighbourhood up about it. In his timidity he would rather let the work stop, than be embroiled with the neighbourhood.

The evening service was crowded, and the people were very disappointed that I was not allowed to remain. However, I told them it could not be, and so took leave of them.

The next morning we rose early and breakfasted at six o'clock, then drove out to the turnpike road to meet the coach at an appointed corner at seven. It arrived in due time, piled up high into the air with passengers and luggage. Having an inside place secured for me we were not dismayed at the outside appearance. The coachman got off the box, and instead of opening the coach door as we expected, put some money into my hand and with a grinning countenance, said, "There's your money, sir. Sorry to say can't take you today. Hain't got a crevice of room anywhere. Good morning, sir."

In a moment more he was up on his box, with reins in hand. "Take you tomorrow, sir, same time. Good morning." And off he went.

Imagine our surprise at being left on the roadside in this unceremonious way. My good little Vicar was most indignant at being thus treated. "I'll make him pay for that," he said. "I'll punish him. It's against the law." And then, as if a new thought had suddenly come to him, he said, "Ah, I know what we will do. Jump into the carriage again."

Putting my luggage in, he got up and drove me to the next town. He said, "We will take a post-chaise and make the coach people pay for it. That's it. That's what we will do."

I suggested that I did not think we could do that, having received the money back.

"Ah, that's nothing," he said. "That's nothing. We will take a post-chaise."

This scheme was prevented, for on arriving at the hotel there was not a carriage of any kind to be had. "Are you sure of that?" said the Vicar, as if all the world was in league with the coach proprietor. "Are you quite sure?"

"You had better come and see for yourself," said the ostler in a surly tone.

We went into the yard and found the coach-houses quite empty,

"That's very remarkable," said the Vicar. "But these people are connected with that coach. It changes horses here. We will go to the next inn."

There they did not let out carriages at all.

"Well now," said the Vicar, "this is very remarkable," and was silent.

"Perhaps the Lord does not mean me to go today," I said meekly.

"It seems so, certainly. I must say it is very remarkable."

I suggested that I would stay at the inn till the next morning, as there was no means of getting on. "Shall I do so?"

"Oh, no, certainly not. Certainly not," said the kind man. "Not at all, not at all. We will go back again."

In due course we arrived again in sight of the Vicarage gate, and there we saw the Vicar's wife with her hand up in astonishment. She exclaimed, "What, are you come back?"

"Yes, we are indeed," said the Vicar, and he was going to tell her how it was – but she was too impatient to listen, having something more important to communicate. She said, "After you went away this morning, the weather being so fine, I thought that I would go into the village and see some of the people who were at church last evening. In passing by widow S's cottage, on my way to another, I saw her door and window open, and heard her praying very earnestly, 'Lord, bring him back, bring him back!'

"I thought she was praying about her husband who had recently died, and that I would go in and try to comfort her. So I knelt down by her side and repeated the words, 'I shall go to him, but he shall not return to me,' when she turned round and said, 'Oh, I don't mean that!' And then, as if she grudged every breath which was spent in other words, she went on repeating, 'Lord, bring him back! Lord, bring him back!'

"'Who do you mean?' I said. 'What can you mean?'

"She went on, 'O Lord, I saw him go away. I saw them take him away. Lord, bring him back! Bring him back!'

"I again said, 'Who do you mean?'

"She took no heed, but went on, 'O Lord, when I opened the window I saw him coming out of the Vicarage gate. Lord, bring him back! Do bring him back!'

"At last I understood that she was praying for you to be brought back. Then I said to her, 'Dear woman, do get up from your knees and let me talk to you.'

"No, she would not get up. 'No, I can't get up. Lord, bring him back! Bring him back!'

"I said, 'He is on the coach by this time. A long way off.'

"The woman became frantic at the thought. 'Oh, what shall I do? What shall I do? Lord, bring him back!'

"Seeing that I could do nothing in the matter, I went to call on some other people, and coming back found the widow still on her knees, urging the same petition without stopping."

"Well, that is remarkable," interposed the Vicar.

Without a moment's pause I set off to show myself to the widow.

"Now, there you are," she said. "The Lord has sent you back. I lay awake best part of the night thinking of some questions I wished to ask you, and when I saw you go away like that so early in the morning it gave me quite a turn. I thought I should be lost for ever."

Her questions concerned her soul's condition. On my putting Christ and His salvation before her for her acceptance she found peace, and afterwards became a good helper in the parish. There were some other anxious ones she urged me to visit, which I did. On referring to my letters, written at the time, I find a record of five persons who professed to find peace that morning.

In the evening we had a kind of service in the schoolroom with as many as we could get together, and spent a very happy time in prayer and praise.

The next morning I started for home, which I reached late on Saturday night, or rather early on Sunday morning, and appeared quite unexpectedly among my people again. I gave them an account of the state of things in the "shires". This, my first experience of "foreign missions", was not encouraging.

CHAPTER 16

A Trip to the Midlands — 1854

THE WORK AT BALDHU, which had been going on almost incessantly for three years, was now beginning to flag. That is to say there was not that ardent and eager attendance at the services and meetings to which we had been accustomed in the revival time. Occasional lulls like this before did not last more than a few weeks, but this dullness was continuing longer than usual.

The crowded congregations were falling off, strangers did not come from a distance and people at home were not so lively. However, the classes were continued, also the services at the church, and the number of communicants did not decrease. Still, anyone could see that the revival was over. It was rather discouraging to me – and a cause of triumph to some outsiders – but we were occasionally cheered by work amongst visitors and sick-bed cases.

While ruminating on these things and praying over them, I was surprised by receiving a letter pressing me to come at once and preach in a parish in Staffordshire, near Birmingham. Mr Aitken had stopped a night at this place and preached one of his alarming and awakening sermons. The effect was so great that the people, together with their Curate in sole charge, were in much trouble and anxiety about their souls. There was a gloom hanging over them, as if they had been sentenced to some dreadful doom and did not know what to do or how to avert it.

In his perplexity the Curate went to see Bishop Lonsdale of Lichfield. When his lordship had ascertained the cause of the trouble, he took up a pamphlet of which I was the author, and said, "If you cannot get Mr Aitken back, send for this gentleman and pay his expenses."

The letter urged me to come at once. I started off that night, and reaching the place on Saturday afternoon I opened a mission the same evening without further notice. On Sunday I preached three times, and went to the schoolroom for the after-meeting. There we had a scene which, for noise and confusion, was quite Cornish. Men and women cried aloud for mercy, while some believers shouted for joy.

The Curate in charge was completely bewildered but felt he could do nothing. Seeing, as he remarked, that I appeared to understand it all and know what I was about, he thought he had better remain quiet till the noisy meeting was over. That same night before he retired he gave his heart to God.

The work went on in this place with the force as of an explosion, just as if hungry desires had been pent up a long time, and now they had vent and opportunity to be satisfied. The church was crowded every day, even in the week, and we were kept in the schoolroom night after night till twelve and one o'clock.

The town was a dark, smoky place, and the air filled with exhalations from the various works. Everything was black and dirty, and the red fires from the furnaces around glared all night long. To come from the pure air and beautiful scenery of Cornwall into such a place as this was most trying and uncomfortable, but the reward was great. The work was deeply interesting and scores of men and women of all classes, besides five clergymen, professed to be converted that week.

The devil did not leave us alone. He was very angry and raised up a great opposition. The Rector of the old church who used to be most benevolent and smiling, suddenly changed and made it his business to call on the Curate in charge of the church, to tell him that he was quite sure that his friend the Vicar – who was away at the time due to ill health – would never have sanctioned this excitement. The Curate said that the Bishop had bid him invite Mr Haslam, and that he had done so, not knowing anything further about me or my work.

The Rector went off to write to the Bishop forthwith, and in the meantime ordered bills to be posted all over the town warning people against "the Cornish fanaticism at St

James's." This, of course, had the effect of drawing out a greater assembly of people.

What with excessive work and bad air, by Friday evening I was quite exhausted. I came out of the pulpit to the vestry remembering that Cornish miners, in order to recover themselves after climbing ladders, often found it necessary to lie down flat on the ground. I thought I would try the same plan for a few moments while the people were going out to the schoolroom. I did so, and while I was in this position a clergyman came in and asked me if I was ill.

"No," I said, "I am only resting for a short time."

"Very well," he said, "rest on, but listen to me. The Bishop has sent me here to see and hear you, and this is my report to his lordship."

Opening out a paper he held in his hand, he read: "St James's crammed to excess with a most orderly and devotional congregation; their attention to the sermon marked and riveted; sermon from St Luke 15:2, 'This Man receiveth sinners, and eateth with them.' The exposition of chapter most vivid and instructive; never heard better, or so good; the application fervent and pointed; altogether, most edifying service.

"There," he said, "that is my report, so you need not be afraid of anything you hear. I will tell the Bishop all about it. Thank you very much for what I have heard. God bless you. Goodnight!"

"Oh," I said, springing up from the ground, "do not go yet. The best part is to come. You have only seen me let down the nets. Come now to the schoolroom and see them pulled up."

He seemed a little afraid and asked many questions. When we reached the place we could scarcely get in, and the noise certainly was tremendous.

"What is all this confusion about?" he asked. "I think I had better not go in tonight."

"Oh, come in, come in," I said. "Do not fear."

But somehow he slipped off in the dark, and I did not see him again. When I entered, I noticed the two Curates of the parish church taking notes. However, I did not heed them or ask to see what they had written, for I would always rather have real work, even with a noise, than orderly, respectable stillness and spiritual death.

On Saturday I rested, but was very unwell all day and did not know how I should be able to work on Sunday. When the morning arrived, my strength and voice were gone, and it was impossible to preach. The people met together and had a prayer meeting before the service, asking the Lord to restore me.

[A converted doctor helps Haslam recover, and he preaches twice more that Sunday before returning to Cornwall.]

I never heard any more of the Rector of the parish, or of the Bishop, but was frequently cheered by letters saying that the work thus begun was going on week after week in the same place. Some years after, when I was passing, I stopped there for a few days and gave them "a lift" as they called it. I saw with half a glance that they had become practised workers – that both clergymen and people were fitted to missionise the whole countryside.

One's great purpose in this mission work is not only to save souls, but to encourage believers to do their part so that the effect of a mission may be continued and extended. God has a twofold blessing for us. He says "I will bless thee, and make thee a blessing." It is well to remember that the benefits we receive are not so much to be kept for ourselves, as to be imparted and transmitted to others, even as they were transmitted to us.

CHAPTER 17

Water Clear as Crystal — 1854

WHEN I RETURNED from the far-off mission in Staffordshire, whether from over-fatigue or other causes, I was much depressed in mind as well as body, and quite out of heart with the Church of England. I observed that some people over whom I rejoiced as converted went back to their former worldliness. This perplexed and troubled me more than I can describe. I knew from my own experience that conversion was necessary to salvation and a new life, but when people professed to be saved and did not live a new life, I was sure there was something wrong.

My dear friend Mr Aitken said, "My brother, this work is the Lord's. You must go to Him and ask what is wrong. Lie on your face before Him, till He shows you His will about the matter."

Shutting myself up in the church I cried to the Lord, till I felt that an answer would come in due time.

Soon after, I was led to preach from the text, "Through this Man is preached unto you the forgiveness of sins: and by Him all that believe are justified from all things."[50] This opened my eyes to see that through Christ Jesus pardon was offered to any and every sinner. Moreover, by the same Christ Jesus, every believer – that is, everyone who had received the forgiveness of his sins – was justified from all things.

I urged the people to consider that we were not created and redeemed to be saved, but saved to glorify God in our lives. I grieve to say that this teaching did not meet with the

50   Acts 13:38-39

acceptance I hoped for. I wondered at their slowness of heart to believe in the risen Christ.

This brought me into the deepest distress and perplexity of soul, to think that after my experience of conversion, and all I had done for the conversion of others, I was still such a self-condemned sinner. I even began to think that I had never been converted. It appeared to me that my whole life was nothing but intense selfishness: that I availed myself of the blood of Christ for my salvation and happiness, and led others to do the same, rejoicing with them in thus making use of God for the purpose of getting quit of hell and gaining heaven. It was a clear case of making God serve me instead of my serving Him.

On Sunday morning as I was going to the early Communion my soul was set at liberty. I felt as if a great cloud was lifted up. The light shone into my soul and I had deliverance. I was exceedingly happy in the knowledge that the risen Christ Himself was my help; that He, who had hidden His presence in a pillar of cloud and fire, now was Himself present in Person, my omnipotent Friend and Leader.

This was quite a new experience and one I had not known before. I thought that I had not even heard or read of it, and therefore began to suspect whether it was a temptation. I determined to be wise and not commit myself too soon, so I made up my mind that I would not refer to it in the pulpit. But at the close of the service a stranger came into the vestry to thank me for my sermon, and when we were alone he put the question to me: "How long have you known Sanctification?"

I replied, "Do I know it now?"

"Yes," he said, "you preached it from experience this morning, and I shall be very much surprised if you have not some inquiries on the subject before the day is out."

I felt reproved before this stranger's steady gaze, and confessed that I had received the blessing that very morning; but thinking that it might be a temptation I had determined to say nothing about it.

He said, "That was a temptation from the devil, sure enough, to hinder you; for the Lord spoke on this subject through your sermon as clearly as ever I have heard. Do not be afraid but go on and tell others."

So in the evening I preached on Sanctification and we had an after-meeting in the schoolroom. Many believers stayed behind to ask questions upon the subject of my sermon. I do not remember how I replied to them, but imperfect as my statements must have been it nevertheless led others to desire to enter into the experience of this same blessing.

Soon after this I was holding an afternoon Bible-class in another part of the parish and we discussed Sanctification. One woman called Hannah, who was more advanced in general knowledge and experience than most of the others, declared that she did not believe in Sanctification for she had known so many who professed to have it and had lost it.

"Lost what?" I said. "You cannot lose an experience. The joy of it may depart, and certainly does where people rest on their feelings instead of the fact." I told her to go home and pray about it and ask the Lord that, if He had anything more to give, to let her have it.

She was sullen and hard to persuade, but after a little more conversation and prayer she consented to lay aside her prejudice and do as I had told her. She did so, and came again the next morning to see me. I was not in my house but shut up as my custom was in the church for meditation and prayer. She followed me thither, but being engaged with my Master I answered no knocks or taps whether at the doors or windows. When I came out I heard that Hannah had called and wished very much to see me.

She wanted, "To hug the dear head of him, if she could catch him." She was happy beyond expression for she had had a dream, and what is more she said that she had entered into the "second blessing".

In her dream she saw a well of water as clear as crystal. It was beautiful, and the clean pebbles at the bottom glistened with brightness so that she could count them. "There, there," she said, "what does anyone want clearer and cleaner than that?"

As she looked into this clear well, my voice said to her, "Throw a pebble into it." When she did so, in an instant the water became thick and dirty.

"Ah," said the voice again, "the water of grace is always clear as crystal, but the well in which it is – that is your heart – is most unclean. The Lord can give you a clean heart and renew a right spirit within you."[51]

She woke up from her sleep and immediately began to pray, asking the Lord for a clean heart, until she obtained it.

Some may say, "But what did she obtain?"

This question is seldom if ever asked by persons who know the experience of this blessing, but to those who do not it is very difficult to convey an idea of what it is by definitions. Let it be enough to understand that there is something desirable to be had, which may be obtained by doing as this woman did.

After this, Hannah became a restful, peaceful soul; and many others, with her, found that quiet confidence which can only belong to those who can and do trust a risen and living Christ.

It was quite a new era in the work and called out fresh energies, but like every new thing it absorbed too much attention, to the exclusion of the simple Gospel for the unsaved. "Christ died for our sins," is only part of the Gospel, though a very important part. "Christ rose again the third day according to the Scriptures,"[52] is also a part which should not be omitted in its due time and place. These two important truths, I am sure, are needful for scriptural work, and they should both be systematically preached.

I was soon to discover it was a great mistake to replace the preaching of the truth, as it is in Jesus for the forgiveness of sins, with the higher subject of the risen Christ. In the freshness of this new-found truth, and thinking that the want of it was the secret of our depression, I was urged on to press it upon the people.

One day a Christian friend came on a visit. He begged me to be patient with the people, as God had been with me, and exhorted me not to scold or discourage them. He told me to

51   Psalm 51:10
52   1 Corinthians 15:3-4

lead them out of the low standard of truth in which they lived, to a higher and deeper one. His visit was a great comfort and encouraged me very much, but before leaving he plunged me into another gulf of difficulty. At the railway station as he was going away, he said to me, "Brother, do you believe the Lord is coming again?"

"Certainly," I replied.

"What will He come for, do you think?"

"Why, to judge the quick and the dead, of course." Seeing he was not satisfied, I added, "What else would you have me say?"

He replied quietly, "I thought you would say that, but there is not time to speak about it now. Goodbye." And so saying he stepped into the train and was soon out of sight. I was left behind wondering what he could mean.

One morning the postman brought me a packet of tracts on the Second Coming, but somehow I did not connect this with my friend's question and I put them aside. Then a stranger came to church, and in conversation after the service he asked me if I would read a little book and give him my opinion of it. It was called "Jesus Comes Quickly."

Even this did not enlighten me, and I told him that I thought the writer considered the end of the world very near, but that I did not care to dwell on such gloomy subjects while we had the brightness of a present Saviour before us.

One morning I awoke with a strong impression on my mind that I ought to read those tracts which had been sent me. I therefore rose earlier than usual, and taking up the packet went into the church to consider them. The first one I read was on prophecies concerning the Lord Jesus. The prophecies concerning the Lord's humiliation were fully accomplished: they did literally pierce His hands and feet stood staring and looking at Him, parted His garments among them and cast lots for His vesture. He actually had His death with the wicked and His grave with the rich.

If these prophecies [of the crucifixion] were so completely fulfilled, we may expect other distinct prophecies to be so, at least as fully and clearly. He who came in "weakness" shall come in "power." He who came "lowly, and riding upon an ass," shall come "in the clouds of heaven;" and "His feet shall stand upon the Mount of Olives."[53] These are the words of Scripture.

Altogether I had come into a new region of thought, and wondered where I had been all my life that I had never seen these things. How could I have misunderstood or overlooked such clear and plain Scripture words? I gave up all engagements that day and applied myself to investigating texts, and read over again the tracts which had been sent me. They were well selected, and referred all statements to the Bible itself for verification.

I felt now that I had possession of a secret which very few would believe, and I could not help seeing the startled or suspicious look with which people regarded me when I ventured to utter it. The Christian hope – that Christ was coming in person, to take us to Himself to live with Him for ever – was a most cheering prospect. It brought the Saviour Himself more vividly before the mind.

Instead of death and hell, heaven and judgment, it was Christ in His coming glory which filled my mind. I began to lose faith and interest in hymns which referred to Christ as the Judge of all. As a Christian I was now looking for a Bridegroom and not a Judge. Nor could I follow the prayers of people who spoke of a judgment to come, for I believed that Christ had been judged and punished for us that we might not come into the Judgment.[54]

53 Zechariah 14:4
54 John 5:24

CHAPTER 18

A Bishop Full of Tricks — 1855

ABOUT THIS TIME I was invited to go to a parish in Plymouth [in Devon], to a church where sacramental teaching was the rule. The incumbent was evidently as much dissatisfied with the state of his congregation as I was with mine. He wanted something new, and I thought that I did likewise. Accordingly I went and preached in his pulpit, and the word spoken produced a marked sensation.

My sermon brought to the Vicar's mind many truths he had heard and loved in early days, and for this reason he urged me to stay and preach again. Then to my surprise he invited me to leave Cornwall and come to Plymouth to take a district in his parish, so that I might help him occasionally in his church.

This was altogether such an unsought-for thing, and so unexpected that I took time to consider. The next day I told him that I could not entertain his proposition. I said, "I am sure that Bishop Phillpotts would not consent. Besides, I have a debt laid on me by my patron for nearly three thousand pounds which I spent in building the church for him. Finally, I am responsible for a debt of three hundred pounds as security."

He still urged it, and said he would go and see Bishop Phillpotts and speak with him on the subject. In his zeal he set off that very morning.

The Bishop at first said flatly, "No." Then upon further inquiry he recalled the request, and said, "You may try it if you will."

The Vicar returned in the evening with this information, which surprised me greatly. But what made me wonder still more was the receipt of two letters the next morning by the same post: one from London and the other from Paris, releasing me from the responsibility of the two debts – and this without any request on my part. The three difficulties, which were like mountains before me only three days before, were now removed. I did not know what to say, and therefore determined in all haste to go home and consider the step.

When I had related these astonishing circumstances to my wife we agreed to go together to consult with Mr Aitken. On arriving, I said to him, "You must please to sit still and hear all before you speak." Then I told him of the invitation to go to Plymouth, the result of the preaching, the unexpected proposal to remove hither, the Bishop's answer, and the remission of the three thousand three hundred pounds.

"Now," I continued, "what do you say?"

"You must go, my brother," he replied. "You will never make Catholics[55] of the Cornish people. The Methodist mind is far too deeply rooted in them."

Our friend's decision was firm, so there remained nothing for us to do but to follow it. When the decision was given and accepted, then Baldhu seemed to lift up its voice and urge its claims. Certainly it was a strong tie which bound us to this place, but on our return home I wrote to the Bishop and proposed to resign my present incumbency in order that I might take a district in Plymouth.

He replied in due course that he would accept my resignation.

After I was thus pledged, my wife's mind veered from her consent to go. Mr Aitken changed his tone also and said that the text had come to him, "Cast thyself down,"[56] and that I was tempting God. Yet all the steps I had taken had been in prayer, and had been taken reluctantly, for I was much attached to Baldhu.

---

55 Not Roman Catholics, but presumably members of the worldwide Anglican Church, even though here and later Haslam uses a capital C.

56 Matthew 4:6 and Luke 4:9

For nearly three months I was torn with distractions. I did not know what to do. The work at home had come to a stand, but my successor was not yet appointed. Nor had I signed my resignation. Therefore every now and then the thought came over me that I would stay.

Then a letter came from Plymouth urging me to come away at once, "for the iron was hot for striking."

Sometimes people came in and said, "You had better go."

Then others would come and say, "You will do no good if you do go."

It was desolating, as well as disturbing beyond description. I had a family of six children[57] and three servants, and it was a great expense to move there. Yet if God was calling, it was quite as easy for Him to move eleven people as to move one. At last suspense was over, for my successor was appointed and the day fixed for our going. I signed my resignation having to pay four pounds ten shillings for it, and then suspense was changed into unmitigated sorrow.

I had designed and built that church and house, and had seen them rise; had made the garden, and had many happy and wonderful days in this place. But it was done now, and the friends who had advised me not to resign seemed to have their triumph, and those who advised to go were discouraged and grieved at my sorrowful state. My dear wife cheered up when she saw me down, and rose to the occasion. She began to pack up as if delighted at going, and went about everything most cheerfully.

I told the people that I could not bear a leave-taking, but there would be a service in the church with Holy Communion at seven o'clock on the morning we were to leave. Many came, but the majority could not sum up the courage to do so. I put my resignation on the offertory plate and gave it to God with many tears.

A kind neighbour came to officiate for me, so that I did not take any part in the service, being exceedingly dejected and overwhelmed with sorrow. It was chiefly for fear lest I

57   See Appendix 3 for family details.

was doing that which God would not have me do, and taking my family out from a comfortable home, I knew not whither or to what discomforts.

One thing I certainly saw plainly enough: that my affections were too deeply rooted in earthly things. I had no idea till then that the place of my own creation had taken such a hold upon me. It was well to be loose from that and free for my Master's service.

After breakfast we left the old place. Many people stood weeping by the roadsides. Some ventured to speak, and others only thrust their hands into the carriage windows for a hearty grasp without saying a word. It was indeed a sorrowful day, the remembrance of which even now makes my heart sink, though it is more than twenty-five years since.

In the evening we arrived at the house of some friends who had kindly invited us to break our journey and remain the night with them. In the morning we proceeded on our way to Plymouth. When we reached the house we found our furniture unpacked and distributed in the various rooms, and the table spread ready for us to take some refreshment. The word "welcome" was done in flowers over the door, besides many other demonstrations of kindness; but I am afraid we were all too sorrowful at the time to show our appreciation or to enjoy them.

We never settled in that house, and did not care to unpack anything more than necessary, or hang up the pictures and texts. My work did not prosper here for I found I was unequally yoked with strangers, and accordingly felt dry and wretched.

I had sent my resignation of Baldhu to Bishop Phillpotts, and with it my nomination and other necessary papers, saying that I would wait on his lordship for institution on a certain day.

At the appointed time I went to him, when to my great surprise he very calmly said he could not appoint me to that district. I could not understand this, for as I told him I had only resigned conditionally. I reminded him that I had asked his permission to resign specifically for the purpose of taking this district.

"How can I consciously appoint or license you to anything in my diocese?" he said, looking me full in the face. Then in his courteous way he laid his commands on me to stay to luncheon, saying he would be obliged "if I would do him this honour." He then bade me walk in the garden as he was busy and would be occupied till luncheon.

I felt that I needed a little quiet and fresh air to get over this climax of my troubles. Out of one living and not into another – and that with a wife, six children and three servants, with very little to live on. Here was a state of things. I had plenty to occupy my thoughts and prayers. I feared and mourned, above everything, lest God should be angry with me. "Oh, if I could only know this is the will of God, then I should not care a fig for all the Bishops on the bench, and would not ask one of them for anything."

I was soon roused from my reverie by the presence of Miss C, the Bishop's daughter[58] who had come out at her father's request to show me the garden and the view. I had known this lady slightly for several years. She talked so cheerfully and pleasantly that it came to my mind, "Perhaps, after all, the Bishop is only trying me. He will not appoint me to this bare district because he has something better with which he means to surprise me."

This thought cheered me up greatly. At luncheon the Bishop was as friendly to me as he used to be in other days. After the repast he summoned me to his study again.

"Now," I thought, "I shall hear where I am to go."

Instead of this he said that he was "much engaged, and must take leave of me."

I was more than astonished, and said, "I can scarcely believe that you refuse to appoint me."

"I do then, most positively."

"But I have a copy of my letter to your lordship, and your answer."

"Then you may urge your claim by law, if you please."

58   Bishop Henry Phillpotts had 18 children.

"No indeed, my lord, I do not think I will do that." And then after a short pause, I said, "You have done for me what I could not dare do for myself, though I have often been tempted to do it."

"And pray what is that?" he inquired.

"To give up parochial ministration, that I may be free to preach wherever I am led."

"Could you do that?"

"I could not do it conscientiously myself, but now that you have stripped me of one harness I will put on no more."

The Bishop made his bow and I made mine, and that was the end of our interview.

In my unconverted days I used to be an ardent and enthusiastic admirer of this man: his charges, his speeches and especially his withering, sarcastic letters to Lord John Russell and others who came under his tremendous lash. This to my mind made him a great hero. His straightforward manner also commanded my respect, for generally speaking I had found Bishops very smooth and two-sided, or rather both-sided; but in his case there was no mistake.

It used to be a proud time for me when this Bishop came into Cornwall, and I was permitted to accompany him and to act as his chaplain at the consecration of a church or burial ground, or to attend him when he went to a Confirmation. Sometimes I had the happy privilege of rowing him in a boat on the sea. He seemed to take such an affectionate and intelligent interest in my parish and my church work. He asked various questions about my neighbours, just as if he lived among them and knew all their circumstances. He struck me as a wonderful man, and I was his champion upon all occasions in my unconverted days. Notwithstanding this, he was too honest to his own views to favour me after my conversion.

On my return home without a licence I had but a poor account to give, and the future prospect looked very gloomy.

CHAPTER 19

The Whitewashed Apostles — 1855

I OCCASIONALLY PREACHED in the parish church,[59] and went to the daily Communion and the daily service. My spare time I occupied in painting the church. I laboured for hours and hours to try and make this great chalk-pit of a place look somewhat ecclesiastical. Among other paintings, on the bare wall at the end I painted a life-sized figure of our Lord, as a Shepherd leading His sheep. This together with a few other pictures of Christ warmed up the building very well. Then for the chancel I had a most elaborate design. First, there was a beautiful gilded pattern over the very lofty chancel arch, which I managed to reach by means of a ladder. Professional people need scaffolding and platforms, which I dispensed with. Inside the chancel I had twelve niches, with tabernacle work above them, for the twelve apostles. These were all duly represented after a true mediaeval pattern, but the local newspaper made great fun of these paintings.

The reporter would have it, that "these lively saints looked very conscious of being put up there, and that they were constantly 'craning' their necks to look at one another, as if they would inquire, 'I say, how do you like being there?'"

My favourite figure, St John, upon which I bestowed extra pains, the provoking man would have it was "St Mary Magdalene, leering at the apostle next to her," or at the one opposite – it did not seem quite clear to him which, but her head was down on one side in a bewitching attitude.

59   Presumably still in the Plymouth district, as the start
     of this chapter in the original, as here, follows
     straight on from the episode with Bishop Phillpotts.

In the middle of the great undertaking I was called away for a few weeks. During this time the reporter came again and again, but saw no progress. He therefore put an advertisement into his paper to this effect:

"Stolen or strayed, a monkish priest who paints apostles. He is not to be found. Any person or persons who can give information concerning this absent personage, will greatly oblige."

My preaching was not acceptable in this church, neither was my connection with it. My apostles were no better appreciated, for they were soon whitewashed over and disappeared like a dream. Sometimes in damp weather they were still to be seen, much to the amusement of the chorister boys, though with a kind of veil upon them. Doubtless in a future generation, when the plaster begins to blister, some antiquarian will discover this "wonderful mediaeval fresco" and call the attention of the public to it!

This church to which I had come was one in high credit for much private and public devotion, but alas I found what I might easily have expected: that without spiritual vitality everything must be dry and dead. A lady presided at the organ, and had the teaching and training of the choir. Much of her own personal and religious character were imparted to the performances, which in tone and manner were admirable and precise. She made the boys understand the sense of the words they sang, till I have seen them even in tears during the singing.

The verger who headed the procession at least four times a day, up and down the church, was a very important and successful part of the machinery, and from him up to the highest official everything was carried out with exact precision. But oh, how unsatisfying and disappointing it was. How could I be so foolish to give up a living, where there was vitality, for such a superficial religion?

One day when I was feeling more desponding and wretched than before, a lady called and said she wanted to speak to me. Would I come to her house for this purpose? I went, and she was not long before she opened the conversation by charging me with being very uncharitable. "You say we are all unconverted."

I replied, "Of course, as children of Adam we are, till conversion takes place. There can be no mistake about that. But when did I say that you were unconverted? Is it not your own conscience that tells you that? When we preach to people as unconverted, those who are changed and brought from death into life know that we do not mean them. They pray for a blessing on the Word, that it may reach others as it once reached them. They do not sit there and resent the charge, for they know what has passed between God and their souls, and are anxious for others to share the same blessing."

She was silent, so I continued, "May I ask you the question? Are you converted?"

She replied, "I do not know what you mean."

"Well then, why do you suppose that I mean something uncharitable or bad?"

"Because I know very well it is not a good thing to be unconverted. But," she added, "it seems such an unkind thing to put us all down for 'lost' while you suppose yourself to be saved."

"Will you allow me to ask you one thing: Do you believe in the Lord Jesus Christ?"

She replied indignantly, "Of course I do. Now, this is the very want of charity I complain of – the idea of asking me such a question!"

She was one of her confessor's favourite devotees and had been absolved by him for several years. The very idea of asking her if she believed in the Lord Jesus Christ made her quite impatient, as well as indignant.

I said, "Do not be angry with me, but what do you believe about Him?"

"Believe everything, of course! I believe the creed."

"Yes, I do not doubt that, for a moment. But do you believe that Jesus died for you?"

"Why, yes, certainly. How could I do otherwise. He died for us all."

"That is not the point. I mean, do you believe that He died, and that you have a personal interest in His death?"

She hesitated, and then looking at me said, "Do you mean objectively or subjectively?"

"May I ask what I am to understand by these words?"

"The Reverend Doctor taught me that 'Christ died' is objective, and that 'Christ died for me' is subjective."

"Very good indeed," I answered. "I like that very much. It is quite true. But it is one thing to know about subjective faith, and quite another thing to have it. Now I will come back to my question. Do you believe that Christ died for you?"

"You evidently mean something that I do not understand," she said in a perplexed manner.

Then looking at the crucifix on her table, I said, "What does that remind you of?"

"Oh, I pray before that every day, and ask the Lord to take my sins away."

"Then you do not think your sins are forgiven yet. How can you ask for forgiveness, and have it at the same time?"

"Do you mean to say then," she replied, with surprise, "that you have no sins?"

"Yes, I mean to say that my sins were atoned for once for all on the cross; and that, believing this, I have peace and remission of sins. My past sins are cast like a stone into the deep. As to my daily sins of omission and commission, I do not take them to the cross like a Romanist, but to the throne of grace where the risen and living Christ is now making intercession for me."

She was silent; and so was I, inwardly praying for her.

Presently she looked up, and said, "I do thank Him for dying for me. Is that what you want me to say?"

"Thanksgiving is an indication of living faith. How can I believe that Jesus died for me, and not thank Him?"

"But I do thank Him, and it is very uncharitable of you to say we do not thank Him. We all thank Him!"

"You remind me," I said, "of three ladies of good position whom I met last year. They all professed to thank God for

Christ's death, but they had no peace and were not satisfied. Seeing they were in real earnest, I proposed to go over the General Thanksgiving in the Prayer Book with them.[60] They did so, and thanked God for creation, preservation, and all the blessings of this life; but above all – then as I emphasized this 'above all', they said, almost together, 'That is where we are wrong. We have not put the redeeming love of God as shown in Christ's death, above all.' These three ladies found peace and pardon that same evening."

"That has been my mistake too," said the lady, interrupting me. "I have never put Jesus above all. But I do desire to do so, and that with all my heart."

"Then do so," I said; "and thank Him for His love in dying in your stead, and shedding His blood to wash your sins away."

"He shall have all my heart!" she exclaimed.

So saying, she knelt before the crucifix, and bowing gracefully and most reverently she reproached herself for not putting Jesus first, and said, "Thou art worthy. Glory be to Thee, for Thy great love to me."

Then she rose from her knees, and once more turning to me, said, "Thank you so much. God bless you for your kindness and patience with me. I cannot tell you how much I thank you."

I knew that she could sing and play, so pointing to the piano I asked her if she would sing a hymn. "Find 'When I survey the wondrous cross,'" I said.

She did not need to find the music, for she knew it without. So sitting down she began to sing till the tears came into her eyes, and her voice broke down. "I never knew the meaning of these words before," she said. "'Sorrow and love flow mingled down.' How could I be so blind and ignorant?

---

60 We bless Thee for our creation, preservation, and all
    the blessings of this life; but above all for Thy
    inestimable love in the redemption of the world by
    our Lord Jesus Christ.
                        (Book of Common Prayer 1662.)

'Love so amazing, so divine,' does 'demand my life, my soul, my all!' O Lord, take it!"

After this I had a few parting words with her, and pointing to the crucifix, I said, "Remember, Christ is not on the cross now. He died: that is past. He is risen and has ascended up on high. The throne of grace is not the crucifix or the confessional, but where Christ sits – at the right hand of God. We as believers may in heart and mind thither ascend, and with Him continually dwell. Have done, then, with this dead Popery.[61] You know better now. Testify for the glory of God."

This lady's conversion vexed her husband greatly, and brought down the frowns and disapprobation of the Reverend Doctor. Altogether it did a deal of mischief. The lady was not allowed to speak to me any more, but I hope she continued to go to the true throne of grace, and not to the crucifix – to a living, not a dead Christ.

61   This is Haslam's condemnation of the Roman
     Catholic and High Church doctrine as he saw it at the
     time. There are, of course, many members of these
     churches today who share Haslam's certainty, and go
     straight to the "throne of grace" to meet the risen
     Christ who has died for our sins.

CHAPTER 20

St James in Hayle — 1857/59

I WAS AT THIS TIME invited to preach in a church in Devonport [just west of Plymouth, but still in Devonshire], where it pleased the Lord to give blessing to His word. But despite some encouragement I felt as if God had cast me off. I can now see that this trying and perplexing dispensation through which I was passing was not altogether such a barren desert as I felt it to be at the time. It was fraught with many lessons which have stood by me ever since, though I must confess I never think back to this period without many unhappy memories.

I felt as if my life, with its work, was cut off in the very beginning of its usefulness, and that there was no more for me to do. As the weather became hot with the advancing summer, I was more and more dejected in mind and body. I lived now among strangers and had no settled occupation, nor could I apply myself to study.

About this time my dear wife became exhausted in health and spirits, so much so that we felt anxious about her. I went to a famous physician who was in the neighbourhood and asked him to come and see her. He did so, and after careful examination, he said, "She will be perfectly well if you take her away into the country. You must do this at once, for the longer she remains here the weaker she will be."

He refused to take any fee, and said he would send a carriage at two o'clock and we must be ready to start by that time. This was more easily said than done; for where could I take the children, or how could I leave them at home? However, as the doctor was adamant, we prayed about it and considered how we were to accomplish the task.

At this critical moment a friend arrived in his carriage and said he had driven in from the country to bring some relatives of his to the train, and did not care to go back alone.

"Would one of us, or both, take pity on him and give him our company?"

As soon as he heard of our position he greatly rejoiced, and said, "Come, all of you. I have plenty of room!"

He took the invalid with some of the children. I shut up the house and followed with the others and the nurse in the fly, which duly arrived at two o'clock. By five o'clock we were all out in the green fresh country, and my wife was already revived and walking about the garden.

There happened to be a farmhouse vacant, which we took. Removing some of the furniture we made it comfortable for the present.[62]

When my family were all settled and surrounded by kind friends, I went off to the north of England on a visit to a clergyman who had invited me. He had already suffered for inviting me on a previous occasion, in the diocese of Oxford. There the Bishop took away his licence because he had me to preach for him. The real cause of offence was that there was a revival in the parish, and complaint was made to the Bishop that people were kept up till "all hours of the night, howling and praying."

His lordship had sent forthwith for my friend's licence, and I had advised him to send it, saying, "He will be sure to return it to you, but perhaps with a reprimand."

62 Although Haslam makes no mention of it, he was
     appointed Perpetual Curate at Carnmenellis in 1856.
     Carnmenellis is halfway between Camborne and
     Falmouth in Cornwall, 60 miles (nearly 100 kms) and
     too far to be reached in a three-hour carrige ride - if
     the Plymouth area is where the family was living at
     the time. Haslam later mentions being at Tregoney
     (sic) and implies that his family were lodging there.
     Tregony is about 30 miles (50 kms) west of Plymouth
     and therefore a possible destination for the family
     now. Haslam's first entry in the Carnmenellis baptism
     book is for December 1855, where he gives his title as
     Officiating Minister. His first entry as Perpetual
     Curate is May 1856, and his last entry August 1857.

Instead of this the Bishop kept it, and said that he would countersign his testimonials to go to another diocese. My friend was at first disgusted, and disposed to rebel, but he bore the treatment patiently and went to another position in the north of England.

Thither, nothing afraid, he invited me to come. Here I soon regained my spirits and got to work in earnest. A revival began at once, and every day we had people crying for mercy very much in the way they did in Cornwall.

When it was time to be returning southward and homeward, I did this by several stages, stopping to preach in various places on the way. At length I reached the village in Cornwall where my family were lodging in the farmhouse I have already mentioned.

Early in the [following] spring I went on a mission to Worcestershire, and there the Lord vouchsafed a great blessing, which has more or less continued to this day; though I grieve to say the present Vicar has no sympathy with it. The work is still carried on, out of church hours, by people who continue to go to church.

While meditating upon my present position and wondering what I was to do next, I received an invitation to take charge of a district in another part of the country, near the sea, which suited my health.[63] There was a large population which gave scope for energetic action. Moreover, the people were careless and Godless, and as such were not preoccupied with other systems. So I thought it was the very place in which I could begin to preach, and go on to prove the power of the Gospel.

There were two large iron factories here, besides shipping. Many of the workers were drawn from other parts of England, and were what the Cornish call "foreigners". They had no love for chapel services or revivals, and no

63 The parish of St James, Hayle. Hayle is on the north
coast of Cornwall, east of St Ives. Now a popular
holiday resort, it was then involved in heavy industry
for the tin mines, shipbuilding and fishing.

sympathy with Cornish views and customs. Not having a church to go to, they were left pretty much to themselves.

With this attractive sphere before me I gave up my living and work in the country, and accepted the curacy at 120 pounds a year with a house rent free. My Rector was a dry Churchman who had no sympathy with me, but he seemed glad to get anyone to come and work amongst such a rough, and in some respects unmanageable set. He had bought a chapel from the Primitive Methodists for Divine service, and had erected schools for upwards of three hundred children. These he offered me as my ground of operation, promising with a written guarantee that if I succeeded he would build me a church.

Here was a field of labour which required much prayer and tact, as well as energetic action. In accordance with Scriptural teaching, I determined to know nothing but Jesus Christ and Him crucified.[64] I made up my mind that I would not begin by having temperance addresses for drunkards, nor lectures on "The Evidences of Christianity for the Unbeliever", but simply with preaching the Gospel.

In this undertaking I knew and understood that without prayer and dependence upon God, to work in me and by me, my mission would be altogether unavailing. I therefore looked about, and found some Christians who consented to unite in pleading for an outpouring of the Holy Spirit. We agreed to pray in private, and also met together frequently during the week for united prayer. Finding that many of the petitions offered were vague and diffuse, I endeavoured to set before those assembled a definite object of prayer. I told them that the work was not ours but the Lord's, and that He was willing and ready to accomplish it, but that He must be inquired of concerning the work of His hands. Also, in order that our prayers should be intelligent and united, I put before them the fact that the people we had to work amongst

---

64   1 Corinthians 2:2

were lost – not that they would be lost by-and-by if they died in their sins, but were actually lost now.

At first there were very few people in my congregation, but by degrees more came and listened attentively to the Word. After preaching for four or five Sundays I asked the people during my sermon what in the world they were made of, for I was surprised at them! They came and listened to God's truth, and yet did not yield themselves to Him.

That next morning it came to my mind that I must go round to the people and ask them what they were thinking about. I had done so from the pulpit; now I would go from house to house and do the same. That Monday I rejoiced over five people brought to the Lord, and then the work began in real earnest. Every week remarkable conversions took place, besides many ordinary ones. Some of these are described at length in tracts published in a volume entitled *Building from the Top, and Other Stories*.

A married woman heard people talking of the work which was going on. It seemed to her to be such a strange thing in connection with a Church minister that she came to a cottage meeting to judge for herself, without the remotest idea of being converted. God's ways are not as ours: while she was listening, the word reached her with power so that she was convicted and converted, and came out of that cottage a rejoicing believer lost in wonder, love and praise. She was indeed strikingly and manifestly changed, and did not hide it. It was such a joy 'and surprise to her that she could not help telling everyone. Out of the abundance of her heart her lips spoke to tell of the loving kindness of the Lord.

The church [formed from the Methodist chapel] in which I now ministered had been intended to accommodate the largest number of people for the smallest amount of money. It was scantily built and almost square, with galleries on three sides. On the remaining one there used to be a pulpit, conspicuously placed in the middle of the wall. This was now removed to one side to make room for a Communion table, and the seats in front we arranged chancel-wise, facing one another for the choir. This place was quite a damper to my ecclesiastical tastes, besides being ugly in the extreme.

However, once the Lord began to bless the Word and souls were awakened, despite all anti-ecclesiastical appearances, my heart was drawn towards the ugly building and I loved it greatly. I could never have believed that my former tastes and tendencies could have been so completely changed as they were.

In those days it was unusual to hold an after-meeting in a church. Therefore I took the anxious ones and others to my own house for the inquiry meeting after the evening service. Having taken up the carpet in the drawing-room, we fitted it up with chairs and forms to accommodate ninety people, while half as many more occupied the hall, and often numbers stood outside the windows. In this house it pleased God to give us very many souls who were brought in week by week for several months. I believe every room in that house, like the rooms at Baldhu Parsonage, was consecrated as the birthplace of one or more of God's children.

The number of those who attended the after-meeting became so great that we found it necessary to go to the large schoolroom. This place will also be remembered in eternity, and many a soul will say of it, "I was born there!"

A glorious work of salvation was going on without the extravagant noise and excitement we used to have in former years. I was exceedingly thankful for this, and began next to consider what was to be done with these new converts. Besides inviting them to the church services, for which they needed no pressing, I urged them to read their Bibles at home, bidding them to mark any passages where they wished for explanation, that I might have something good and profitable to speak about when I visited them. Then I invited them to Bible-classes instead of to experience meetings which Cornish people rely upon so much. On these occasions I endeavoured to instruct the people from God's Word, and put Christ before them as the object of faith, hope and love. After prayer I encouraged them to ask questions, which made these gatherings interesting and instructive.

It is an awful thing to see and know that people come for bread, and get a stone; for fish, and they get a serpent; and for an egg, they are offered a scorpion.[65] Exceedingly trying it is to be frowned upon by clerical brethren in the presence of Dissenters who, to say the least, do know the difference between life and death. In one church we have the service elaborately rendered, and the sermon is nothing. In another the sermon is everything, and the service most slovenly; and, too often, souls remain asleep and perishing on all sides.

It so happened, that as we approached the term of three years, that my dear friend Mr Aitken came to pay us a visit. He preached with more amazing power than ever. His appeals were altogether overwhelming, and I do not wonder that the people fell on their knees and cried aloud for mercy.

As soon as Mr Aitken had gone, the Rector came to see me. He appeared to be somewhat embarrassed at first, but after a little time said, looking on the ground, "You know I am no revivalist. I do not like all this uproar. I cannot have it."

He then went on to say that he wished me to leave, for though he had given a guarantee that if I succeeded he would build me a church and endow it, he could not do anything of the kind now for he did not consider my work any success whatever. Quite the contrary. "These converted people, as you call them, are no churchmen!"

I replied that I had taken his voice as from God in inviting me, and I supposed that I must take the same for my dismissal if he really intended it. But I urged him to consider the matter well before he broke up the work which was going on there, for whatever he thought about it, it was undoubtedly a work of God, though one certainly not very common in churches.

Without saying another word he took up his hat and went away. His departure was so abrupt that I could not

65   Luke 11:10-12

believe he intended me to receive this as six months' notice. Consequently I went on with my work as usual, finding plenty to do, more especially after Mr Aitken's energetic visit. There were many new converts to add to our classes, anxious ones to be guided and led to Christ, and broken hearted and despairing ones to be comforted and built up. The work under such a preacher is by no means finished with his visit, however long or short it may be. On the contrary, it may rather be said to begin there.

After some months the Rector came again to remind me that he had given me notice more than five months before. He wished me to leave at the beginning of the year, as he had secured the services of a clergyman whose views were in accordance with his own. I was much grieved at this, and could only lay it before the Lord and beg of Him to order all according to His will.

The following morning without any seeking on my part I received an invitation from Bath, asking me to come and take charge of the district of St Paul's in the parish of Holy Trinity. Thus was the door shut behind me, and another opened in front. This was so unmistakable that I could not but be satisfied and acquiesce in the manifest will of God.

Naturally I felt great sorrow at having to leave the people and the work I loved so well. I said nothing about my dismissal, but went on with my various engagements as usual, though I had only a little more than three weeks left me.

By some means it appeared in the newspapers that I was appointed to a district in Bath, and another clergyman was named as my successor at St John's, Hayle. This fell as a great blow upon my people who were both grieved and angry, but I could not comfort them any more than I could help myself.

The last Christmas Day came and went, a sad and sorrowful day it was; then the last day of the year and the last night. We held our watch-night service as usual, thanking God for the mercies of the past, and entered upon the New Year with thanksgiving and prayer.

Thus ended my work and eventful sojourn at Hayle, a little more than three years after it began. A very sorrowful trial it was, and one of bitter disappointment. But the Lord's leading was clear, and I have since proved that it was right, though at the time it was most mysterious and very dark.

I felt very sad to leave my Cornish congregation – all the more because I knew that they would mourn for me. Even before I had any idea of leaving, some of my people had expressed misgivings, and said: "What will become of us when you go away?"

Notwithstanding this the call was so clear that I determined, in simple dependence upon God, to step into the unknown future.

Yet Not I

Contents of Yet Not I

Chapter 21

Bath — 1860

IF I HAD KNOWN nothing of Bath I might have rejoiced in the prospect of labouring in such a great and influential city, but this was not the case. I had visited that place on two former occasions. Each time I had left it discomfited and glad to get away, saying, "I will never settle in Bath."

As at Hayle, I determined again to know nothing "save Jesus Christ and Him crucified" as the foundation of my work. The brazen serpent was the only remedy for the dying Israelites,[66] so now Christ crucified must be the only door of salvation for perishing sinners in Bath. I could see that I must hold up Christ, so that the Holy Ghost might take of the things of Christ and show them to the people. I must begin with conversion – out-and-out salvation by God – and nothing else.

On reaching Bath I went to the place appointed for my temporary abode. I found that the lady of the house was a Christian person, and with her I was at home at once. I have said she was a Christian, but she was certainly not one after the Cornish type. She knew and believed many beautiful things about Christ and His Church, but the salvation of souls did not occupy the prominent place which I thought, and still think, it should do in the heart of a true lover of the Lord. She supposed that salvation would come or follow in due time somehow, while people were learning about the doctrines of Christianity.

After a night's rest I set out to make the acquaintance of my Rector who was a hearty and generous man.

66   Numbers 21:9

Avon Street, Bath, redrawn from an original engraving in *She Spake of Him* by Mrs Grattan Guinness. The old Wesley chapel, used by Haslam for his church, is the building on the right with the two high windows and circular ornament.

"Now," he said, "let me tell you about your parish. It is very rough, but you shall preach in my church sometimes." This he said out of kindness, and I accepted it as such.

When he saw that I was willingly going to the work in that "rough place", he said in his candid way, "I could not go there myself for the world, but I will set you perfectly free to work as you will. Don't come to me for anything but money. You will want that, I think."

We had a quiet talk about Cornwall and Bath, and then it was time for him to go to his daily parish meeting in the vestry. Punctually as the clock was striking twelve he took his place to listen to the various cases of distress or deception which were brought before him, the latter of which he was very quick to discover. The adroitness wherewith he discharged his work proved that sharp, short and decisive was his motto.

By one o'clock his business was done, and he took me into the district of St Paul's. He showed me Avon Street with its many courts, and said the policemen always went down there in couples as it was not safe for them to go alone. Avon Street consisted of fine houses of three and four storeys which had once been inhabited by fashionable people.

In the middle of the street was a chapel built by the Wesleys. It had been deserted by their followers, who had gone into a more respectable part of the city and built themselves a finer edifice. They had let this one to an undertaker to keep mourning coaches and hearses in, but the Rector having offered a higher price obtained possession.

Finding the Wesley pulpit in a corner, he put it up and furnished the place for divine service. This was to be my church. A public house, which had failed, was secured for a penny bank and as a residence for the Bible-woman and others. I was introduced to the Scripture-reader belonging to this part, and made an appointment with him to go round the district the next day.[67]

In the evening I took a quiet peep at my district by myself and fell in with the Scripture-reader. My talk with him was anything but encouraging. He had been many years in the place and had settled down into a routine, delivering so many tracts, paying so many visits, in so many hours. As to seeking the salvation of souls he never seemed to dream of such a thing.

"I am convinced," he said, "you will never do anything of that kind in this street."

"What do you do," I inquired, "when you visit them?"

"Why, I read a chapter or tract, and sometimes have a little talk."

"Shall we go and see someone now?"

"No," he replied. "It is after five, and I must go home."

"Then tell me as we walk along what you say to them."

67 See page 18 for more information on these two job titles.

"Oh, I tell them that the way of transgressors is hard, you know, and that they had better give up drinking, fighting and sinning. Sometimes I persuade them to follow my advice, and they do it for a time but it seldom lasts. The women are worse than the men, and the children more impudent than all."

"That is a pleasant prospect!" I replied.

I left him to return home feeling heavy-hearted and discouraged, yet strong in the conviction that there is nothing too hard for the Lord. Surely, I thought, if there is one set of people more than another on whom the Lord has compassion it must be these degraded people steeped in sin and vice. Surely He cannot bear to see these immortal souls perishing – poor sheep without a shepherd.

I never could understand Christians who do not care about the salvation of souls. Teaching and building-up are very important, but what is the use of building up dead souls? Even the work of edifying believers is not so urgent as that of rescuing the perishing.

CHAPTER 22

No Water, but Plenty of Beer — 1861[68]

THE NEXT MORNING, having provided myself with some sandwiches for luncheon, I set out for a day's work with the Scripture-reader. In the course of conversation I found out that whatever he had known of conversion in his own experience had completely slipped out of its place, and that the even tenor of his daily routine consisted in relieving temporal distress with very little, if any, spiritual teaching.

There were about one hundred houses in Avon Street alone, and more than eighteen hundred people. Whole families lived in one room. The filth and bad atmosphere were beyond all description. How human beings can live in such places, or be content to have them so, I cannot imagine.

We visited one old man who mended shoes. He lived in a cellar that was cold, and green with damp. Yet he was cheerful, and content to call it his home.

I asked him if the water ever came in.

"Oh yes, when the tide be high it do come up here for a hour or two."[69]

---

68 The date in all editions of the original *Yet Not I* for this and the next chapter is shown as 1863. From the context and later events it seems that 1861 would be correct. Chapter 4 in the original, 23 in this book, appears to have been correctly headed 1861.

69 Bath is above the tidal reach of the Avon, but at that time defences erected nearer Bristol to keep high tides out also slowed the downstream flow. During heavy rain the river could back up as far as the Avon Street district of Bath "for an hour or two".

"Why," he said, suiting his action to the words, "I puts my legs up on the stool and goes on with my shoe mending. I keeps my tools up there," he continued, placing his hand on a shelf, "where they be safe from the wet"

In his person he was a dirty and grimy man who apparently never washed himself from one month's end to another.

Bad and vile as these dwellings were, from attic to cellar, their occupants with a few exceptions were far worse. It was easy to see that drink had a great effect in stupefying and drowning their senses. Twenty, thirty and sometimes forty people might be found living in one house without any adequate supply of water. The company turned the water on once or twice a day, but there were no cisterns in the houses to hold or keep it.

The little vessel each tenant brought out to be filled with this most useful commodity would not hold anything like sufficient for their need. Neither could they, in such a poisonous atmosphere, keep the small quantity they had sweet and wholesome. These poor people had no chance of making tea or coffee for themselves, and little or no opportunity to drink water. So there was nothing for them but the beer sold in the public houses. These, I need scarcely add, abounded in this street and neighbourhood.

In a similar cellar I later found a family of five all huddled together in a most miserable condition. Their story moved the compassion of a kind lady who commissioned me to take better and more healthy lodgings for them at her expense, and remove them out of that wretched, damp place. She said she could get no sleep for thinking of these poor creatures.

I soon obtained a two-roomed lodging for them with a good fire, but this failed to please them as well as their old abode. The following day, on calling, I saw that they had darkened the windows with paper.

"The light," they said, "made them feel so cold."

In a day or two I found to my surprise that they had gone back to what they called their "own sweet cellar." There's no place like home! I could not help thinking, "What is the use of the Gospel if it cannot touch such people? What place is there in all Bath that would excite the attention and sympathy of the Lord Himself more than this?"

As we went on in our round, passing from house to house and room to room, I took notice of the sick, making a list and promising to visit them on the following days. Now and then we found some poor but comparatively respectable people.

Two tidy-looking women who lived in adjoining rooms told me that they went out at five o'clock in the morning for three hours to sweep shops, from which they were allowed to bring away the sweepings. Every two or three days it took them several hours to sort the rags, pieces of paper, pins, needles and a number of other articles. Sometimes they found coins. They sold the rags, paper, pins and needles, and were paid so much a week for sweeping.

After a long night of troubled sleep I awoke in the morning rather disheartened, tempted to give up the work altogether. Better men, and more persevering ones, had tried it and failed. Why should I hope to succeed, and what would be the end of my success if I had it? Happily, with my morning prayer and reading, these dark clouds dispersed.

At family worship I was led by the subject we were considering to say that introspection was very discouraging to the Christian. We ought to look away from self to Christ who is our Life. For our work we ought to look not to our talents, gifts and resources, but to Him who alone can use them aright. The work is His, not ours. We may be sure that whatever He means us to do, He will open up the way and provide the necessary help and strength – if we continue to trust Him.

After breakfast I set off to visit the sick people whom I had promised to see. At first I rather shrank from going into these dens of dirt and stench alone, but I braced myself with the recollection that I was not alone. I then went forward, praying the Lord to give me the right word.

I had made a special mark against the name of a dying shoemaker in the street. I can give no description of the state of the atmosphere on entering the house before any windows or doors had been opened. It gave me quite a turn, but I went in to see the poor sick man. He looked pale and very ill, and was so afraid of the cold that he would not have the window opened.

He was too poor to secure the services of any medical man except the parish doctor, and that gentleman had already given him up and told him he would die. This, however, did not harass or alarm him. In his ignorance he thought he was sure to go to heaven, because he had "suffered a sight in this 'ere world."

I suggested that people did not go to heaven because of their sufferings here, but for what Christ had suffered on their behalf. He was very unwilling to give up his hope, though it was so groundless, for he had been cheering himself with the fancied prospect. It was hard to take away the little comfort he had, but I could not help trying my best to do so. I spoke to him about salvation and the forgiveness of sins through the blood of Jesus Christ, and told him that he was a lost sinner.

"Oh no," he replied, "I'm not lost at all. Not I. Poor people don't go to hell as far as I knows. It's only the rich. I'm sure on it, for I've read it somewhere in the Scripture."

I offered to pray with him. How to kneel down in that dreadful place I did not know, and to bring my face nearer to that bed was very distressing. However, down I went and told the Lord as plainly as I could about the poor man, his darkness of soul and serious illness. Not that the Lord did not know these things, but I did it for the sake of the poor sufferer, that he might hear it. I besought God to open his eyes by the power of the Holy Spirit, and show him his dangerous condition and the great salvation there was for him in Christ Jesus.

When I first commenced to speak in prayer the poor fellow was very restless, and resented the things I was saying about him. He muttered to himself something to this effect: "It's no good praying like that. I ain't as bad as all that." And so on.

When I rose from my knees, he and his wife looked at me as if they thought I must know all about them. She thanked me, and he asked me to come again.

"Come," he said, "this afternoon."

In the afternoon I returned to the poor shoemaker who was now in a very different state of mind from that in which he had been in the morning. Then he wished to die; now he was afraid lest he should die before he was saved. He wept much when I told him of God's love for sinners, and His willingness to forgive them for Jesus' sake. I prayed with him again, thanking God for opening his eyes thus far. I felt much encouraged by the change I perceived in him, for I was sure that the Lord had really taken him in hand.

After a little further conversation, and bidding him trust in God, I went away, promising to return in an hour or two. I did so, and encouraged this dear man to thank God for saving his soul, and for prolonging his life till the good news of salvation had reached him.

"Oh, wife," he exclaimed, "only think, if I had died before, I should have been lost for ever. Now, thank the Lord, I'm saved. I'm so happy!"

I went for the Scripture-reader to come and rejoice with us, but he was not to be found. Perhaps it was as well, for afterwards when I told him what had passed he said that he had no faith in such conversions.

Once again I went to see my converted shoemaker and found him very happy. He had spent a joyful night in praising God, and intended sending for his neighbours that day to tell them what great things the Lord had done for his soul.

The next morning, my first Sunday, I passed along the street while the church bell was ringing, and invited the loiterers to come with me. Some of them laughed aloud at the idea. Others, mocking, said, "Oh yes, we'll come. We're all on us coming!" Another man suggested that he would come if I paid him. "That is the way to get us along to church." This remark caused much merriment. I stopped and said that I thought they ought to pay me for coming to do them good!

On arriving at the church I was grieved to find but a few people there. They were respectably dressed and not like those I had seen in the street. After the service I took a chair, and standing on it at the church door I spoke to the crowd outside. They were very quiet and gave me a patient hearing.

In the evening we had a larger congregation and I felt more encouraged. I had much liberty in preaching the Word, and declared that my expectation was not from my preaching, but from the Lord through His Word which was sharper than any two-edged sword, and must cut.[70] It will either cut sin from the soul – or the soul, sins and all, from God.

70   Hebrews 4:12

CHAPTER 23

The Nasty Little Man from the Tramps' Church — 1861

THE SECOND WEEK of my work in Bath happened to be the Week of Prayer, a time set apart for united supplication all over the Christian world for the outpouring of the Holy Spirit. Unhappily, the Church people and the Dissenters had their united meetings in separate places, if not at different times. This was not a good omen for successful prayer, but it was well that the Week should be kept at all.

On the Monday evening I went to the Church of England meeting and was introduced to several of my clerical brethren. One of them told me that the meeting was for special prayer for the outpouring of the Divine Spirit upon Bath. This had a refreshing sound, and delighted me.

I went on to ask whether they had already received any droppings of a shower. I suppose I was unfortunate in the person I addressed, for he said he "did not quite take in my meaning."

I asked him more plainly, "Have you had any conversions?"

"Oh yes. I suppose God does that."

I said, "In Cornwall, when we met together to pray for the outpouring of the Spirit we expected it – and what is more we received it. The believers praised God, and sinners cried aloud for mercy."

"We never have such a thing as that here," he said.

I said, "Suppose, while we are praying, the Lord answers prayer and sends down His Spirit. Then the people are moved to cry out, 'What must I do to be saved?' How would you act then?"

"Oh," said one who had been quietly listening to our conversation, "we do not allow such things. We should at once send for the police and have them put out."

I told him, "A little girl who once heard the prayer for rain in church in the morning, came out on a fine Sunday evening with a big umbrella. When the Vicar met her, he said, 'Well, my little girl, what is the umbrella for?' 'Please, sir,' she said, dropping a curtsy, 'did you not pray for rain this morning?'"

"We have no Cornish girls here," he replied, laughing. Then looking at his watch, he said, "It is time to go in."

On entering the hall we found a large company assembled. The chairman took his seat, and we clergymen arranged ourselves on the platform near him. After a few introductory remarks about the whole world being girded with prayer, he gave out a hymn. Then followed a long prayer about a great many good things, but with scarcely an allusion to the special object for which we had met. After this a portion of Scripture was read, with an exposition. We then had another long and beautiful prayer, and the chairman gave out a second hymn.

This chilly meeting was concluded with the benediction, exactly as the minute hand reached the hour. I must confess it seemed to me that nothing had been done or said that would or could "move the Hand that moves the world" to send down a blessing upon the city.

In another part of Bath the Nonconformists were holding their gatherings. Unknown and unintroduced, I went into one of these to see how they were conducted. Here I was disappointed even more than before, for my idea of Dissenters was very different to what I now beheld. I had, it is true, only seen Wesleyans in Cornwall, but I had a supposition that all who separated from the Church did so because they had an exuberance of life. Here I heard nothing but platitudes and eloquent utterances.

There was much display of oratory, and one speaker vied with another in using difficult words and long sentences. I noticed that each of them concluded with the verse of a hymn or poem before he sat down exhausted, while the people applauded. Their prayers were as oratorical as their speeches.

The previous year we had held a Week of Prayer at Hayle. There we commenced at five o'clock in the morning, by desire of those who were obliged to go to work at six. We had a meeting again at midday, and another in the evening. The thought that Christians were praying all over the world at the same time, for the same thing, had stirred the hearts of our men. Men who could not make a speech upon any subject whatever, were able on their knees to shake the whole place when they prayed. Their souls soared away on strong wings to regions altogether beyond this world. Theirs were prayers that came from the heart, and brought out spontaneous responses from hearts lifted by the same Spirit.

In spite of numerous discouragements and difficulties, I went on working in my little church and district with unceasing energy. I found that the Scripture-reader's depression of mind was by no means without cause. The people had deceived him so often and so long that he despaired of them altogether.

One day a lady who had good intentions and much knowledge, who had heard the best of sermons from the most eloquent of preachers, and had made volumes of notes, was drawn by curiosity, having heard of strange things which were said to be done in my church. When she came she saw it was but a small place and not full, and as she afterwards told me the sermon was "neither eloquent nor particular."

At the close of the service the people were asked to remain to an after-meeting. This she could not understand, and asked the doorkeeper what it meant. He bade her stop and see. She did so.

On observing a stranger at the end of the church, I made my way down to her and asked whether she had given her heart to God.

She replied that she "did not know what I meant."

I said, "Do you know any people who have given their hearts to the world? Have you seen how the world lays hold of them and carries them off?"

"Yes, indeed I have," she replied, for she had sisters and brothers at home who lived for nothing else.

"In the same way," I said, "if you give your heart to God, who is really entitled to it, He can take it and employ you for Himself and His work. Would you like to give yourself to Him?"

"I was never asked the question before."

"Well, it is time you were. You had better think about it, and I will come to you again presently."

As I was going away she put her hand on my sleeve to detain me, and said, "What shall I do?"

"Kneel down and give your heart to God at once. Say, 'Lord, take my heart and give me Thy Holy Spirit, for Jesus Christ's sake.'"

Deliberately and quietly she knelt down, and I prayed with her. As I was leaving, she said, "Thank you," and soon after went away. I did not know who she was, or where she came from.

The third day after this she called at my house with a note to tell me she had obtained peace with God and was very happy. I bade her come in, and we thanked God together. I then asked her if she did not wish to thank God in her life as well as with her lips, and whether she would help us in the work in Avon Street.

She was willing, but shrank from the task, saying, "I am so ignorant. I used to think I knew a great deal, but now I feel I know nothing as I should. I have no experience."

I showed her the text in Acts 26:16, "I have appeared unto thee for this purpose, to make thee a minister and a witness, both of these things which thou hast seen, and of those things in the which I will appear unto thee."

"There, you see, God wishes you to be a witness only of what you have seen, and then He will show you more."

She promised to come and make a beginning, but before leaving asked whether I would consent to hold a Bible-class if she could prevail upon a few others to attend. I readily and thankfully agreed to do this, and arranged to open a weekly Bible-reading. This began with ten persons, but speedily increased till it was necessary to have two a week, and afterwards more than that.

The winter this year was a most inclement one. The frost continued for many weeks, and while those who had time and health for skating amused themselves to their hearts' content, the poor suffered. Coals and blankets were in great request in my district, and were generously and abundantly supplied.

At that time I had not equal acceptance anywhere else in Bath. I remember on one occasion when I preached in the Abbey upon the Full Assurance of Faith, I was regarded with great suspicion and distrust. When preaching in another part of the city, a lady resented what I had been saying, and remarked; "The very idea of that nasty little man from the tramps' church coming to teach us!"

But here in the "tramps' church" I had free scope. I could speak out all that was in my heart, and work till I dropped.

One day, while the frost continued, my helpers came to me and said, "There's a woman and two children up in a garret, starving. They have had no food for days, and the neighbours say they have not seen them go up or down stairs. They must be ill."

I went to the place, knocked at the door and was told to come in. On entering, I found a woman in bed, with a boy and girl on each side of her. There was nothing in this desolate chamber in the way of furniture but a broken chair with an earthen pitcher of water on it, and the pallet bed on which they were lying. I asked if they were ill.

"No," answered the woman.

"Then why do you not get up?"

"Oh, we are keeping ourselves warm here, for we cannot do anything in this frost. So we lie in bed and drink cold water."

"How long have you done that?"

"This is the third day."

"We are very hungry, sir," said the boy.

"Get out of bed then, and I will send you for something to eat."

With this he sprang up from under the covering in his ragged clothes, and I took out my silver pencil-case to write an order for two shillings' worth of groceries. The boy was gone in a trice, and we heard him clattering downstairs in his old shoes which he had put on while I was writing. When he had gone I asked the woman as to her way of livelihood.

She told me that she sang in the streets with the children, and that on the whole she made a good thing of it. "But lately," she added, "the frost has been so stinging, we cannot sing."

From the tone of her voice and manner of speaking I suspected that she must have been an educated person. This I afterwards found to be true, for she informed me that she, "had been brought up for a drawing-room."

While sitting on the one chair by her bedside, I took up a book from the mantelshelf with a name, under which was written, "From my affectionate mother." I said, "Is this your writing?"

"Yes," she replied.

After a little more conversation she acknowledged that she was a surgeon's daughter, and a surgeon's widow. She added that her father had died from drink, and her husband too. After this she took to drinking so that her mother, who had married again, would have nothing more to do with her.

Her story touched me, and I said, "Do you like this kind of begging life?"

"No, not overmuch," she answered. "But I have followed it now for several years, and it seems to agree very well with the children."

"But what a dreadful way to live and to bring up your children. Are you disposed to try a different life?"

"Yes, if you please, sir," she said meekly.

"What can you do?"

"Do?" she repeated. "Why, do anything, everything. I can teach, and children are obliged to obey me. Let me teach the children in the streets. There are hundreds of them running about wild. I will bring them up for you."

By this time the boy had returned with the various articles from the shop. There were tea, sugar, bread, butter and bacon; a little coal, sticks and matches. He had borrowed a kettle, a tea-pot and a frying-pan on his way upstairs. In a few minutes there was a fire burning cheerfully in the little grate. While the kettle was singing there was the sound of bacon frying, the fragrance of which spread over the room. The woman and her daughter threw off the bed covering and were quite ready for their breakfast. Though it was late in the afternoon, it was to them a break of three days' fast – literally a break-fast.

I said I would leave them to their meal and come back later on, to have a little further talk. Before leaving I happened to put my hand into my pocket, when to my dismay I missed my pencil-case.

The woman, seeing my look of astonishment, said gravely, "What's the matter, sir? Have you lost anything?"

"Why, yes," I said, "my pencil-case has gone."

"Perhaps you did not bring it, sir."

"Oh yes, I did. I wrote that order for you with it just now."

"I ain't got it," interposed the boy, who was very busy with his cooking.

"Perhaps you dropped it," said the mother, looking about the room.

At last, on moving the pillow, I saw the missing article. I was only too delighted to have it back again, for I valued it.

"How did it ever get there, I wonder?"' exclaimed the woman.

I said as little about it as possible, for I had no doubt whatever but this creature picked my pocket while I was talking to her, or perhaps when I was watching the clever operations of the boy at the fireplace. It was evident to my mind that this woman wanted changing very much.

After an hour or so I returned, and with the same pencil wrote an order for clothing to a good man whom the Lord had sent to my help. He was a pawnbroker, and took a great interest in my work. Of his own free will he offered to let me have garments for poor people, at the price at which they had been deposited with him. He had a room full of unredeemed clothes which were far more suitable for my protégés than new ones. Having rigged up this family, and made them look respectable for a comparative trifle, I began to think seriously of the woman's proposal to teach the children.

At last I concluded that I could not do better than let her commence a school for some of the hundreds of neglected street children. I did this, hoping that no one would recognise my beggar woman when she was dressed up as a schoolmistress. She said she did not want any salary, but only a place where she could assemble her scholars.

Thinking that there would only be a few of the quietest of the children to begin with, I told [the woman whom I now knew as] Mrs C that she might have the use of the lower part of the church till I could provide a suitable room. She agreed to this and undertook to begin at once.

Walking up and down the street, she invited the ragged and dirty children who were running about to come with her, at the same time promising to teach them.

She soon got a small crowd round her, which increased as she moved along. In less than half an hour there was a large gathering. I admitted them into the church, but instead of occupying the lower part only, they filled the whole place.

I must say that they entered in a most orderly and quiet manner, and took their seats as they were directed, or rather silently pointed to do. There they sat as mute as if they could not make a noise anywhere. Mrs C was like a monarch who knew her power, and exercised it with serene confidence.

In an hour's time I looked in and there I saw my incorrigible ragamuffins in most obedient and beautiful order. They were spell-bound, and learning a verse of a hymn. The children were told that when they knew the words they would be taught the tune; and then, that they would walk up and down the streets and sing it. By twelve o'clock the hymn was learned and duly rehearsed. Then out came these unmanageables, walking two and two, more than a hundred of them singing, while the others followed trying to keep step.

They were all eager to come again in the afternoon, but the schoolmistress said, "No, bring a halfpenny tomorrow morning at nine o'clock and we will have school every day, morning and afternoon till Saturday."

The next day at the appointed time the doors were besieged. There were more children than we could well accommodate, so we took in the foremost of the crowd and their halfpence till we could take no more, and then we shut the door. Their names were written down and they were duly installed as scholars. Thus my school was begun.

Boys and girls came the next week with a penny each, rather than not get in, and our trouble was enhanced. While other workers had the anxiety of getting their schools up, we had the novel one of keeping it down. We wanted no salary and no books, for the children were taught orally and simultaneously. Certainly a very manifest and good effect was produced upon them.

Mrs C had a little assistance from her son and daughter, but otherwise the whole affair was governed by her eye, or the mesmeric or other marvellous power which she possessed and exercised. I was happy to see these dirty, ragged children being thus civilised and brought into something like training. Mrs C was also listening to the Gospel, and everything appeared fair and promising.

Unfortunately this state of things did not last long, for some officious person put a letter in the newspaper, saying, "The new clergyman of Avon Street is employing a beggar woman – a common tramp – to teach the children."

This caused a dreadful upset and great consternation, but I did not care to reply to it. I thought if such children were taught, it would do good; that I had better take no notice and go on quietly. But the hubbub increased, and the opposition was led on by people who did not know the circumstances of the case. They certainly had a good handle against me, and they plied it rigorously.

I was at first disposed to resent this unwarrantable interference, but as I could not be altogether sure of my school-mistress and could not defend the position, I was persuaded to yield. My friend the Rector promised to look out for a more suitable schoolmistress.

Mrs C, seeing the trouble I was in, took a house in another part of Bath and thus spared me the painful task of dismissing her. There no one ever suspected who or what she had been. The school she opened rapidly increased and was a great success. I have also every reason to believe that the Gospel was blessed to her soul, and that she was changed in heart as well as in outward life.

Several years after this, when I was preaching in London, three respectable-looking people presented themselves to me. These were none other than Mrs C, her son and daughter, living in prosperity as good members of society and Christian people.

My flourishing school came to an end, and the children were turned adrift to run about the streets as heretofore. This was a great disappointment to me, but hoping for better days and a better school, I went on with my work.

CHAPTER 24

To Freshford and Back — 1861/62

AMONG MY POOR degraded people I had some of all kinds, and of every denomination, who were more or less steeped in this fatal vice of drunkenness – Roman Catholics, Gipsies, Dissenters and Church people, to say nothing of the members who were regardless of creeds and names. In our temperance meetings, however, I classed them all under one category – that of drunkards.

I gave the people to understand that temperance was not religion. I merely wanted to remove the hindrance in the way of so many men and women, so that with clear heads they might hear and receive the Gospel, and that converted men might not be overpowered by strong drink.

"Suppose," I said, "one of you came to hear a sermon and had a bad habit of knocking your head against the wainscot, making a noise, disturbing other people and hurting yourself. I would certainly move you away from it. So, I want to move you away from this terrible habit of drinking."

My Temperance Society greatly prospered, and proved to be an immense help to the Gospel preaching. We had also a Band of Hope, for even children were frequently seen reeling about the streets in a drunken state, the cause of sport and merriment to their elders. It was high time that some effort should be made to overcome this evil.

When I preached the Gospel I addressed them still as of one kind, namely children of Adam "dead in trespasses and sins." My course was definite and plain enough, to ignore all differences and press the points, "You must abstain from intoxicating drinks to be free – and you must be born again to be saved."

At our temperance meetings, during the free conversation after the address, I had opportunities of bringing out the truth as it is in Jesus. I pointed out to one who was trusting in his Church for salvation, that the Church of Christ was not intended to take the place of the Saviour, but rather to be a shelter for the saved. I took some pains to explain the difference between the shepherd who found the sheep, and the fold in which he kept it. This man saw his mistake, and all the more clearly when I told him from my own experience that I myself was once under that delusion, and thought I was safe – but the Shepherd had not found me then.

This man gave up the shadow for the substance, and surrendered himself as a sinner to be saved; and thank God, he was saved.

I asked another man, "What was finished on the cross?"

Not receiving any answer, I went on to say, "Our salvation was finished there. That being so, there is no need for you to be 'doing' in order to obtain salvation. The religion of four letters is better than that of two. That is to say, the religion which rests on what Christ has done is better than that which depends on what you can do."

This man also was persuaded to give up his error, and in the light of truth to seek for pardon and peace from Jesus Himself.

In the summer I was advised to go away into the country with my family for five or six weeks. For this purpose a lady generously gave me an ample cheque, and when I accepted it, she said, "Now, you are bound in honour to go, you know – and stay away. None of your going out and being here too, remember. You must go and remain away, all of you. If you want more money, write and say so."

Having acceded to her wishes, I asked, "Where shall we go?"

She said, "To Freshford."[71]

The necessary arrangements being completed, we took a carriage and drove out into the country. On our way we passed one or two enticing-looking villages but they were

71   Just over 6 miles (10km) south of Bath, in the picturesque Limpley Stoke Valley.

not Freshford. So we proceeded onwards and in due time arrived at the place of that name.

Not meeting with any suitable lodgings, we were on the point of returning to Bath when we heard of Mrs M's house, which we were told had been vacated that very morning. On arriving there I inquired of a nice-looking young person who opened the door whether they had any apartments to let.

She said that she would go in and ask her mother, who forgetting perhaps that everyone was not as deaf as herself, said aloud, "Are there any children?"

"Yes," answered her daughter.

"Then say No."

Something more was said, which I did not wait to hear, thinking I had heard quite enough. I went back to the carriage, saying, "They will not take children here, so we had better go back again."

Just then Mrs M herself came out, and after a few minutes' conversation said, "Come all of you in. I'll make you as comfortable as I can."

She afterwards told us that when she bid her daughter refuse, the Lord rebuked her for her selfishness; and although the girl urged her not to receive us, saying, "There's such a lot of children,[72] and they look like sickly, troublesome people," she was yet obliged to come out and accept us. She had found we were neither sickly nor troublesome, but Christian people whom the Lord had sent to bring a great blessing to her house and to the neighbourhood.

In the evening we invited her and her household to our family worship. This she "enjoyed very much," as she said, and begged to be allowed to come again in the morning.

To our surprise there were eight people, besides her family, assembled for morning prayers. These all professed

72   There were ten children at this time. See Appendix 3.

to be "much pleased," and said that they would like to come again in the evening; but "could we be so good as to hold our meeting at eight o'clock?"

"Certainly," I said.

At that hour the room was full, also the passage outside, so we opened the window for the benefit of those who were standing in the garden. Mrs M's two daughters were awakened that night, and one of them found peace. The other did so four days afterwards, then their brother, and lastly their father. Thus all the family were brought to know and rejoice in the Lord.

In the meantime the village was roused, and I was asked to hold my meeting in a vacant schoolroom which was placed at my disposal. There it pleased God to commence a good work at once. It seemed as if the train had been laid and everything was ready, needing only the match to be applied for the fire to burn. Burn it did, and the lamps of many were kindled at it, who lived to be bright and shining lights in the neighbourhood. It was most interesting to see the readiness with which people came to the meetings, and to witness the prepared state of their minds. It was great joy to show them the simple way of salvation. Young and old, rich and poor together, were under the melting influence of the Holy Spirit.

Of course all this did not take place without opposition. Not a few of the neighbours, instead of rejoicing in the Lord's work, became exceedingly angry. Some of them called after us in the street, and when we were assembled in the meeting they gratified themselves by throwing heavy stones upon the roof. I begged the people to be still and not to notice this wilful disturbance.

"It is all right," I said. "I would far rather have this opposition than smooth indifference, though I am sorry for the persons who thus employ themselves."

Another day stones were thrown at the windows with disastrous effect, so that the people put up their umbrellas toward the side which was being assailed. Well it was they did so, for the broken glass came against the outspread calico or silk, and cut through more than one of these shields.

Again I bid the people be still, adding, "I am delighted to see and hear this disturbance, for it is a sign the Lord is working and that the devil is angry at the Gospel being brought to this quiet place. I think we shall have much blessing here. It is not at all unlikely that some of these very men and boys who have broken the windows will be converted. I will have the windows mended tomorrow, and perhaps before the month is out those who broke the glass, or instigated others to do so, will pay for the damage."

And so, indeed, it came to pass. In these and other meetings souls were converted every day, and the work continued without interruption all the time we were there; and was carried on by others after we left, and spread to several villages beyond.

The Vicar of the parish who lived half a mile off heard of these things, but he did not come near us, nor did I care to make him in any way responsible for myself or my doings. Therefore I did not compromise him by asking his consent. I heard that the "lady bountiful" of the parish was very angry with us, and did what she could to urge him to stop our proceedings. For all that, he did not appear on the scene, or utter any prohibition.

On the contrary, one morning as I was riding up to a gate he kindly opened it for me, and taking off his hat politely, said, "You have been opening the door of salvation to my people: I am happy to open this gate for you. Good morning."

He then went off, as if not caring to say too much. Soon after this he sent a note inviting me to preach in his church on a particular Sunday, as "I was popular amongst the people, and he wished to go away." This I was happy to do. So far we had his concurrence, which was pleasant.

The Sunday that I officiated for him we had the church filled from end to end three times. The great lady was not there. How she settled the matter with the Vicar for going away at such a time, and worse still, for leaving a wolf like me in charge of the flock, I do not know!

There was great power, and God's presence was very manifest in the church. I believe the word of God was not spoken in vain that day.

Our sojourn at Freshford was a truly happy time, and one of much blessing, with many converted. We had a change of air together with plenty of work for God, and we returned to Bath with renewed health and zeal.

I had abundantly proved that God was not unmindful of my domestic circumstances, for my stipend was only one hundred and twenty pounds a year. Though this amount had sufficed in Cornwall with a house rent free, it was manifestly not enough to live upon in Bath, with rent and taxes to pay. I had a wife, ten children, and two servants dependent on me, but I was dependent upon the Lord and He did not fail me.

Unsought for, a friend wrote to ask me to put two of my sons on the foundation of his grammar school. Another, a lady, the daughter of a Lord Chancellor, bade me send my daughter to a school at her expense. A gentleman who had a nomination to Christ's Hospital gave me that for another of my sons.

My house rent was regularly paid by some unknown benefactor. A butcher's boy came twice a week to the door with a joint of meat. A tailor called in occasionally to measure me for a greatcoat or other clothes. Indeed, we never wanted.

In addition to all this, a Christian physician attended us for nothing, and said he was "our debtor." It was like carrying an empty purse, but always finding money convenient according to the need. In some way or other the Lord did provide.

One day a clergyman whom I had often heard of as slandering and opposing us, called on me at a time of some defection from our ranks – at which I knew he was delighted – and said he had heard so much about the work that was going on under my teaching that he wanted to know further particulars. He asked whether I was satisfied and happy. "Do you find that any of your converts go back, my brother?"

"Go back?" I repeated. "Of course they do. Do not your converts go back?"

He did not answer.

"Did you ever know or hear of a work of God anywhere, in the Bible or out of it, when some did not go back? I do not for a moment assert that all are saved among my so-called converts, but merely that they profess to be so. Time shows whether or not the work is real. I have observed that some who at first make a loud profession go back, while others who make none come forward and abide. Truly, 'the wind bloweth where it listeth.'[73] I cannot undertake to tell whence it cometh and whither it goeth. I only act up to the best judgment I have."

He said he had paid me quite a long visitation, and was very glad he had called; for, after all, he found that he agreed with me a great deal more than I supposed, and so on. With this he took his departure.

I fully expected greater opposition than ever, and am convinced that I should have had it if he had not received "preferment" as he called it, and been removed from the city.

The services in the little church [in Avon Street] were continually blessed in a very manifest way. The number of persons who attended regularly increased to such an extent that it became necessary to enlarge the building. I made this the subject of prayer, but did not otherwise mention it. Soon the Lord put it into the heart of a lady to say, "You ought to enlarge your church. I will give you one hundred pounds towards it, or if you build a new one I will give you a thousand; and I know someone else who will add five hundred or more."

My soul was now all astir for building, and I felt as if some of my old architectural fervour was coming back. It was clear to my mind that the new church ought to be in Avon Street, near the poor people for whom it was intended. Some thought otherwise, and suggested that I should build a good one in a more respectable position, with the idea that

73   John 3:8

it would take these people out of the dreadful scenes of degradation to which they were accustomed, and in this way elevate them.

I could not agree to this proposition, for I saw that they did not care to go to such churches, though they had them within easy reach. I felt sure that to build a handsome church in a better situation would be but to add another fashionable one to the city, which had already a great many.

No, I preferred a site in the street, and found a most suitable one near the river on a plot of ground covered with dilapidated cottages. This belonged to the Corporation, and what is more, was offered for sale at the easy sum of three hundred pounds. Making sure of obtaining it, I at once designed a plain, homely though architectural church for the poor, and set on foot inquiries about purchasing the ground.

In course of time I received a most encouraging letter from an influential member of the Corporation, who said, "If I would apply on a particular day he would propose that the site should be granted me for nothing, because I had saved the town much expense in prosecutions."

I remembered that there used to be a long column in the daily papers headed *Avon Street* which contained a list of various crimes and offences. But now I saw that the charges for a whole week were not so many as they used to be in a single day in former time. This was encouragement for me to go on with my work, and press for the church to be built among the people.

However, the opposition was greater than I cared to contend against, so I gave up the idea and fell back upon the original plan of enlarging my little church. Thus it was left to another to build the "handsome church" of St Paul's in a more respectable part of the city, which was done a few years after I left.

Strange to say, I happened to be passing through Bath the very day the first stone of St Paul's Church was laid, without previously knowing that it was to be. I was present again, though only accidentally, when it was opened at its completion. I hear that it is now a crowded and fashionable place of worship, and one to which the ragged people do not venture.

I set to work to enlarge my little church by building behind the end wall. When the new addition was roofed and closed in, we took down the wall between so that the services were not hindered. This enlargement being accomplished, the building was in the shape of a T, and held double the number of people it did before. We put up an organ, and an organist was provided for us, also a lady who was responsible for the choir and singing.

The old part of the edifice next to the street was made available for our present purposes. I used to call it "The Factory". There we had the Sunday school, the Mothers' meeting, and afterwards the day school. The first, the Sunday school, was an overwhelming perplexity because of the unruly character of the lads and lasses who attended. Happily our superintendent, on his own responsibility, obviated the difficulty by transposing the classes, giving the girls to the men teachers, and the boys to the ladies. Then the school prospered. I record this as a hint, which I hope may prove as useful to others under similar circumstances as it did to me.

The Mothers' meeting was much needed for civilising the women, and teaching them to make proper garments in place of the rags in which their offspring were usually arrayed.

I had desired a day school ever since the break-up of that promising one already mentioned. The great need of a school had been so pressed upon me that I went to a lady who held a Bible-class for young women, to ask whether she could recommend anyone suitable for a schoolmistress. She said that she thought the locality would be a difficulty, but promised to give me a definite answer on Monday afternoon.

Strange to say, on that very Monday morning, altogether unsolicited, there came a cheque from a lady of title who had received good at the church in Avon Street. It was "for the benefit of the place, and towards a school if possible." For this I thanked God and felt sure of success.

That same afternoon I called upon the lady who had promised to inquire about a governess. She told me that one of her class had offered to take the situation, and had said, "It is an honour I could scarcely have aspired to, to work for the Lord in Avon Street. I will undertake it with pleasure, and a friend of mine will assist me. Now," added the lady, "what about the money?"

"Here," I said. "is a cheque the Lord has sent today."

Looking at it, she exclaimed, "It is the Lord's school, and is sure to be a blessing. Will you let me have the management?"

I need scarcely say that I accepted her offer, and we thanked God together. The school was opened the next day and did become a blessing to many. It was worked most efficiently in connection with the Mothers' meeting.

One of my lady helpers at this time had a brother, a colonel from India. He was very irate that his sister, "such a beautiful and accomplished young lady, should be working in a dreadful place like Avon Street. She sleeps at home, to be sure, but she lives down there all day. She must be mad!"

To my great surprise one night I saw this same colonel on his knees among the beggars at the after-meeting. I could scarcely believe my eyes. I found him thoroughly broken down and in deep distress of soul. His sister's prayers were heard, and the Word had at last penetrated his armour and brought him in penitence to the Lord.

He became an out-and-out Christian, and worked diligently for the Master in this as well as other parts of the city. Before his conversion his idea of Christians was that we were a very selfish and indulgent set. He said he had "observed in India, and in this country also, that if there was one chair or sofa in a luxurious drawing-room more comfortable than another, there was sure to be a Christian in it!"

One day after his conversion, when he was paying me a visit, I sent the servants upstairs to fetch down a large and particularly comfortable chair from one of the bedrooms. They brought the unwieldy thing down as well as they could, laughing as they came into the room where we were sitting.

"There, Colonel," I said. "Look, there is the Christian's chair, and now you are entitled to sit in it."

"Ah, yes, yes," he said thoughtfully, "I remember all that, and a deal more. I am ashamed to think how strong my prejudice was. I used to feel quite a hatred against some of the Lord's people, though they tried to be kind to me."

He went about his work for God in a most methodical and businesslike way, finding out anxious souls and sick people, also some cases of real temporal distress. Among other things, he arranged Bible-readings and drawing-room addresses for me. By this means I had sometimes as many as three or four gatherings a day, besides all my work in the district.

CHAPTER 25

Is Mr Haslam on Board? — 1862

IN THE FOREGOING CHAPTERS I have given a brief account of one year's work. Obviously space would not allow me to dwell with the same fullness of detail on the work of successive years. Suffice it to say that it went on with increasing interest and energy, though not without difficulties and opposition. The work was not mine, and if I laboured abundantly it was as the Apostle Paul says, "Yet not I, but the grace of God which was with me."[74]

In the beginning of the summer of 1862 I received a letter from a Vicar in the far west of Cornwall, asking if I could arrange to come with my family for six weeks and take charge of his church and parish during his absence. This was exactly what I desired. So thanking God, I accepted the invitation and arranged to go. The weather being calm and fair we decided to take the steamer from Bristol to Hayle, and accordingly wrote to our friends to expect us the next morning.

Along the Bristol river and past the Holmes the water was very smooth. As we went farther west, however, the vessel commenced to roll and pitch, causing us all to blanch and feel uncomfortable. There was a strong headwind, and the waves of the great Atlantic were sullenly rolling in long hills and valleys after some storm by which they had been stirred. Our vessel was sadly tossed, and the passengers were very ill.

To our dismay, when the time arrived at which we expected to get into harbour and smooth water, we were told that we had missed the tide and must stay out in the bay

74   1 Corinthians 15:10

for eight or nine hours longer. Here the waves were larger and the ground-swell much heavier than ever. It was a dreadful morning, and we were helplessly and hopelessly sick, and had to remain like that all day till nightfall.

At last to our joy we saw the harbour signal denoting that there was water enough to carry the vessel over the bar. We crossed it in safety and entered the little tidal harbour at Hayle about ten o'clock at night, after a voyage of twenty-five hours instead of fourteen or fifteen. We were very ill, starved, dejected and feeling as if no one cared for us – the natural consequences I suppose of our condition.

As we advanced we could see a great crowd of people on the shore, and soon I distinguished a loud, familiar voice shouting to the captain, "Is Mr Haslam on board?"

"All right," the captain replied; "they are all aboard."

Immediately there went up a loud and long cheer from the people. When the steamer reached the quay, friends came jumping on deck to greet us. One immediately claimed us for his guests. I thanked him and assented. While I was engaged in looking after our luggage, another friend took possession of my dear wife and carried her off with two or three of the children. A third, who found that he could neither get her nor myself, made off with the nurse and the remaining children.

Thus we were all scattered here and there at eleven o'clock at night. I did not know where to find my wife, and she did not know where to look for me or the rest of the children. There was no doubt whatever that they were all most affectionately housed and cared for, long before I was. So being far from well I retired, determining to carry out a search the next morning or, if necessary, to send round the crier.

The next day we spent among our warm-hearted friends, and we heard with tears many stories of their unhappy and spiritually starved condition. They went for bread and got a stone, and sometimes it was "cruel hard." Yet many of them were "sticking on," as they called it, to the Church.

In the evening we proceeded to Paul-beyond-Penzance,[75] and there found a happy people ready to receive us. We had a meeting of course, and the next day also, which made a good preparation for Sunday.

On Sunday the church was filled to excess three times. We held the after-meeting in the evening at the schoolroom, which was also filled. Souls were given that night, and many nights after. We had believers rejoicing aloud and sinners crying for mercy at the same time. This was the best cure for sea sickness and every other ailment.

I cannot describe what a joy it was to live and breathe again in a land of spiritual liberty. It was so good of the Lord to send us out for this refreshment. To those outside it might have looked like a very laborious holiday to be employed talking, praying and singing all day long – and a good part of the night too! But it was real rest of soul – rest in comparison with the hard work in Bath. Taking Christ's yoke, we find rest to our souls.

We had many remarkable conversions in that church, and some wonderful scenes. One I will endeavour to describe.

At an afternoon service on a certain Sunday there was a very large congregation, and the choir was in full force almost filling the capacious gallery at the west end of the church. They had prepared a grand anthem for the occasion, which was taken from the Prayer Book version of the twenty-sixth Psalm. The striking parts were repeated over and over again: "I will wash, I will wash my hands in innocency, O Lord; and so will I go to Thine altar."[76]

While this was in lively execution, the portly clerk stood still and firm as a rock in the front of the gallery, presenting a striking contrast to the band of numerous musicians behind him who were in energetic action, arms and heads all going. There were upwards of a dozen violins, a bass fiddle,

75   Paul is a village between Newlyn and Mousehole,
      south of Penzance.
76   Psalm 26:6

trombone, ophicleide, brass bassoon and other instruments of music, besides a host of singers. This vigorous demonstration was quite exciting.

I could not help wishing that their feet did indeed stand aright, and that they had really washed their hands in innocency and could praise God from their hearts. In the sermon, referring to this, I said that so many people lived and rejoiced as if they were safe. They came to the house of God and praised Him in voice, as if no heart were required. I added a great deal more to the same effect.

At the end of the sermon the choir scarcely joined in singing the psalm that I gave out, and while I was praying some of them began to cry to the Lord for mercy. I went up to the gallery as soon as I could, and oh, what a scene presented itself. The violins were lying about in all directions, and the various other instruments of music were laid aside. The players were on their knees praying for mercy, the clerk himself being among the number.

It was a glorious afternoon. There were people praying and rejoicing in the body of the church, and the gallery was resounding with cries, first of distress, and then of praise. Many began from that day to praise the Lord in the congregation, with their feet standing on the Rock. The churchwarden, with others, was helping to lead the anxious ones to Jesus.

One day I went to Mousehole, a fishing village about two miles from the church, to give an address to the sick and aged who could not come to the services. The room was all too small, and I had to stand in the open street opposite, and speak to those within the room and those without. Amongst others there came to the meeting a stout, heavy woman upon crutches. As the address went on she was so excited in praising God that she tossed her crutches into the air, and shrieked out, "I'm haled! I'm haled! I can walk and leap too!"

Leap she did, with a power that astonished me and everyone else present. She rose from the ground at least as high as the table which was placed out in the road for me to stand upon.

She exclaimed, "My soul is full! Hallelujah!"

And so, it would appear, were the souls of many others – if noise and outward demonstration were any proof.

Another time, preaching at Newlyn in the open air, there was so great a crowd assembled that I was obliged to climb up into a high fishing-smack which was stranded on the beach. There, standing on the deck, I let down the nets and truly the Lord gave us a miraculous draught of fishes. It was indeed a day of joy and gladness.

In this far-off West we had some Philistines also, who wrote to Bishop Phillpotts to inform his lordship that I was preaching at Paul-beyond-Penzance. Then came a letter to the Vicar in the well-known handwriting, with H Exeter in the corner. I need not say I did not forward the Bishop's document. The following week came another in the same handwriting, with the same veritable signature, and I put it with the first on the mantelpiece. In a few days another, and yet another, each of them more angry than the one before. At least, I had no doubt it was so – and so it was. At last there were five letters all in a row waiting the Vicar's perusal by the time I left to return to Bath.

I had taken my departure several days before the Vicar returned. He saw his letters and opened them one by one. Upon inquiry he found that my sojourn in the parish had been blessed to many souls. The people were full of my visit; the choir almost without exception were converted; the schoolmaster changed; the churchwarden rejoicing, and the clerk also.

The Vicar wrote to the Bishop at once to tell him all this, and said that even if his lordship's letters had been forwarded he could not have dared to stop the work. He went on to say that "the people were begging him to ask me to come again;" and he added, "unless, my lord, I have a good legal reason for not doing so, I feel it my duty to write and fix the time for another visit from Mr Haslam.

After the lapse of a few months he did this, and invited me to come for a week for missionary and other meetings.[77]

77   This is the only reference in the original to a return visit.

CHAPTER 26

Off to Scotland — 1862

DURING MY VISIT to Cornwall I received an invitation to go to Aberdeenshire – from the extreme West to the extreme North. It came from the Earl of Kintore, whom I had met in Bath in the previous spring under the following circumstances.

On that day, as the congregation was dispersing from my church in Avon Street, I observed a couple on the pavement before me whose appearance presented a great contrast to that of the people about. On nearing them I overheard the gentleman say to the lady, "It is hurrah for sinners here. There is nothing for us."

"So it appears," was the lady's quiet reply.

When I came up with them I looked round, intending to make some remark.

Before I could speak, the gentleman handed me his card, and said, "I understand you do not go out to dinner, so come and lunch with me tomorrow."

Accepting the card and the invitation with thanks, I went on to speak about the dreadful place and the discouraging nature of the work, till we reached the end of the street. Then we parted, as our paths lay in opposite directions.

On looking at the card I was surprised to see who my unknown companions were. Nothing terrified, however, I went the next day to their residence for luncheon, and had a most interesting time in prayer and thanksgiving with the Earl and Countess. The Lord there and then gave me these two to be my friends. Through many years their friendship proved helpful and encouraging, as it has ever been steadfast and unwavering.

Subsequently I had the joy of seeing his lordship grow in grace, and expanding year by year in Christian happiness and usefulness. In the midst of his joyful career it pleased the

Lord to take him home suddenly one Sunday evening. He is now for ever with the Lord, but his departure has made a terrible blank in his family and among a large circle of friends.

These kind people invited me to their family seat in Scotland, and at the same time asked if I had any objection to preach in a Free Church.[78] I answered that I was willing to preach anywhere – in a church, school, hall, drawing-room, barn or in the open air. Having accepted this call I hastened back from Cornwall to Bath for a Sunday or two, and then set out early one Monday morning for the far North.

It may be asked, what became of my congregation during my absence? I made full provision for them as to the Sunday services, and beyond this there was little need. The majority of the poor people in the street followed the fashion and left town. The beggars like their betters went to the seaside and to watering-places. Others went out fruit and hop picking into Kent and Sussex until the middle or end of September. Therefore there was little to do in my district.

Travelling night and day I reached my destination at Keith Hall on Tuesday afternoon. Having promised that I would preach the same day if required, the drummer was sent round on my arrival to announce that a clergyman from England would speak in the open space in front of the Town Hall at five o'clock.

On coming to the place appointed, we were surprised to see a large concourse of people; and more so to find two Free Church Evangelists already addressing them. It appeared that these gentlemen happened to be passing through the town in the afternoon, and thinking that the announcement

78   In the national Church of Scotland, landowners could
      nominate ministers, whether these ministers were
      Bible-believing Christians or not. The leaders of the
      evangelical movement in the Church of Scotland
      viewed this as an intrusion by the State in the affairs
      of the Church. The result was that in 1843 some
      evangelicals in the Church of Scotland formed the
      Free Church of Scotland.

given was for them, they went down even before the time and began their "exercises".

I was pleased to witness the scene, and thankful to hear what was being so well and faithfully said. I was also not a little curious to see for myself how the Scotsmen conducted such services, for they were not common in those days. I remained quiet and unknown till they had finished. Then my friend went forward and stated the case, to the dismay of the two Evangelists, saying that the English clergyman for whom this meeting was convened was present and would now address the meeting.

I did not detain the audience long, but merely gathered up the points of doctrine which had been well and firmly stated, and applied them from experience. I saw clearly that these ministers were much better versed in Christian doctrines, and in ability to state them, than the great majority of our English clergy. They talked well, and evidently knew what they were speaking about. After I had finished, the Free Church minister of the place invited the people to his church at half-past seven the same evening, and announced that the three ministers who had been addressing them would do so again.

At this service I asked the two Scotsmen to speak first, and leave time for me to follow. I tried to impress the people with a sense of the eternal realities to which we had been listening. My friend having fixed upon the next day for a gathering of his tenants, I announced with due permission that I would speak again on Thursday and Friday evenings in that church.

The tenants' feast was held in a capacious barn, which was prepared and decorated for the occasion. When we had assembled, the tea and hot cakes and other good things ready, the minister of the parish was called upon to say grace. He rose to do so. On and on he went, slowly and per-severingly till ten minutes had passed by, and five more added to that, and yet there seemed to be no sign of termina-tion or the slightest indication of it. The people stood and bore the grace patiently as if they were accustomed to it.

My friend whispered to me, "He will not stop till he gets to the angels and archangels." The "exercise" passed slowly on till it came, at last, to the welcome angels. Then my friend looked at me, and true to his prediction, the long grace was over and we sat down to cold cakes and colder tea.

The repast being finished, I rose and gave my address to the farmers and labourers. It was on the subject of the Gospel feast to which all are invited. It was a banquet, I said, worthy of the Great King, and most joyous to the guests. I was led to dwell upon two facts – the freeness of the invitation and the happiness of the invited.

"You were on very tender ground," said my friend. "You know many of the Scottish people do not believe in that 'free invitation', neither are they the joyous people you would have them to be. Their mirth is very solemn."

However, in my innocence of these facts, such was the message. After this I went round, making the acquaintance of some of the tenants and conversing with others. They seemed interested in hearing truths put, as they said, in "quite another way."

The Thursday and Friday evening services in the Free Church were well attended. An English clergyman was certainly a novelty, and they were not disappointed to hear that he was to preach twice on the Sabbath.

It seemed a gigantic labour to conduct these two services in the Presbyterian mode. I had never done such a thing in my life before, though I could not say I was unaccustomed to public speaking; but this was a great undertaking. I prayed to be sustained and guided through those services, and believe I was. During the exposition of Scripture the people listened very attentively.

While I was preaching, the quiet attention was very perplexing to one who had just come from Cornwall. I felt as if I could not move them; they were altogether imperturbable. I was dismayed to find that my appeals fell flat and dead, again and again. The people looked as if their faces were of stone. They never moved a muscle, though their eyes were fixed upon the preacher.

When the service ended I was heartily thankful, for it appeared to be needlessly heavy throughout – to say nothing of the singing. As to the tunes, they were most mournful and complicated. When I expected the notes to go up they went down, and when I thought they would go down they went higher. Altogether it was to me anything but a joyous service.

On coming out, my friend who was waiting at the door took my arm, and said, "Well, you gave it to them very faithfully."

"Did I not give it to you also?" I asked.

"Well, yes, there was a good word for us all."

Evidently, however, it had not hit him, nor did I feel I had reached anyone. I was sorely discouraged by the apparent coolness of the congregation and could not help speaking of it.

"Oh," said my friend, "I have seldom seen the people so interested. You may be sure they took it in. We will talk to some of them as we go along."

In the afternoon the Free Church was fuller than in the morning. I preached, feeling that the people were all attention, notwithstanding that they looked like so many stones set up in rows before me. In the evening I spoke at the schoolroom, and had an after-meeting when souls were gathered. Every night during the week I preached somewhere.

I may say that coming from the South I was surprised to find so much Bible knowledge, especially among the working classes. Their intelligent acquaintance with Christian doctrines also surprised me, though not so much when I saw in the little shop windows the children's lesson book, with the ABC on one page, and a short Catechism on the opposite side. I believe that this early planting or teaching of God's truth, coupled with the daily reading of the Bible, is the secret of Scottish stability and influence.

In some country parishes in England I have found it hopeless to allude to Scripture characters. I remember one day speaking of Joseph at a small meeting, taking it for granted that everyone knew who I meant. A woman came forward afterwards with tears in her eyes, to ask whether I could tell her Joseph's other name, and what prison he was in, for "her poor boy Joseph was in prison!"

In the course of one of my sermons in the Free Church I happened to make a Scripture reference, naming chapter and verse. In an instant hundreds of hands were stretched out to take up their Bibles. The rustling of leaves was so great that I had to wait till the text was found. This made a break in my speaking which I did not care for, so I gave no more Bible references. In exposition and teaching it may be better to prove the statements as you go on, by referring to chapter and verse, but when speaking from heart to heart these interruptions are a hindrance. At least I found it to be so.

I strongly commend familiar knowledge of the Bible and accurate acquaintance with Scripture truth, even though it be only mental. I find that when people are converted who have no such acquaintance with the Word, they are compelled to fall back on their own feelings. Consequently, they are too frequently tossed hither and thither by feelings, whereas those who know the Word are confirmed and established in the work of the Spirit which they have experienced, and are able to set to their seal that God is true.

This visit to Scotland was a blessing to many, besides being a great benefit and enlargement to my own soul. After three weeks I returned home, refreshed and strengthened for my future work.

CHAPTER 27

Leaving Bath — 1863

AMONG MY LADY HELPERS in Avon Street was Miss Geraldine Hooper, of whom I shall have more to tell hereafter.[79] She was indeed eminently useful to me. The cheerful readiness with which she acceded to my wishes, and the wonderful ability and success with which she accomplished what she undertook, were truly astonishing. If she conducted the Temperance meeting – though at that time she had not commenced giving addresses – by her winning way she obtained more pledges than anyone else. If she took a Bible-class it was crowded. If she held a prayer meeting, even in the early morning, it was sure to be full.

She was a great favourite in the street, universally and deservedly esteemed. In short, her will was law; and a very pleasant law it seemed to be, for the people rejoiced to do her bidding, and she exercised her authority in a cheerful and cheering manner.

When there was to be a service in the church, it was amusing to see her coming down the street beckoning and summoning people to attend, and then waving on with her hands the little crowd before her, adding to them as she passed along till they arrived at the church door. Here she took her stand and bade the people go in and sit down. Then she went to the lower end of the street to bring others in the same way. In the church she would play the organ if required, lead the singing, keep children in order, or what

79   In 1863 Geraldine Hooper was twenty-two, a year
     younger than Haslam was when this book starts.
     (Haslam is 45 now.)

was more difficult still, at least to most people, constrain a drunken man or woman to be quiet and orderly if any such had strayed into the congregation.

In our street-preaching her help was most valuable, for she not only swept up the people from all sides to the appointed place, but moved about among them to ensure order, or to encourage them to sing.

These open-air services I made as attractive as I could, by reference to familiar objects. One day I referred to the fountain at the head of the street, and spoke of the ever-flowing water without which people were obliged to drink beer and spirits, as those who neglect the fountain still continue to do. So, in like manner, I said, till the people hear God's Word they are obliged to do the best they can with men's falsehoods, and consequently wander farther and farther from the truth till they perish.

Another time when I preached there was a long ladder in the street, standing up against one of the houses. Pointing to it, I asked, "How can I climb that ladder? There is only one way to do so, as there is but one way to heaven – and that is by putting yourself on it and letting it carry you. Many people try various other ways, but in vain. Suppose you were to try to climb the ladder by putting one hand to it while you still remained standing on the ground, would that do?"

"No, no."

"Suppose then you were to put two hands?"

"No."

"Suppose you put one foot, or even both feet on to it, while you are clinging with your hands to something on the ground?"

Mrs Geraldine Dening née Hooper. Small section of full-length engraving, greatly enlarged, in *She Spake of Him* by Mrs Grattan Guinness.

"No, no, that ain't the way. You must put both hands and both feet on it, of course."

"Exactly. That is the way to be a real Christian. It is of little use coming to a service now and then. That is like putting one hand on the ladder. Attending a service regularly is like standing with both feet on it. Making a profession of Christianity is of little use while you are with both hands clutching after this world. You must give your heart and yourself right up to the Lord, and that for ever."

A fashionable lady who happened to be passing at the time heard some of this object lesson about the ladder, and was greatly disgusted that "a clergyman of the Church of England should be preaching in the gutter. He ought to have his gown stripped off his back!"

A few years afterwards I met this lady in London, but she was so changed in her outward appearance that I scarcely recognised her. It was difficult to believe that she was the same person of fashion I had seen in Bath. To my further surprise she came up and offered to shake hands with me.

She said, "Do you remember once preaching in Avon Street about a ladder? I never could escape from the words I heard. I felt that I was the person standing on the ground with one hand only on the ladder. Thank God, the ladder carries me now. How I hated you. You must never mind such things, or be discouraged by them. I am quite sure that my scorn did you less harm at that time than my praises would have done!"

As the work in Avon Street progressed, it pleased God to send us domestic trials. We had seven members of our family ill with scarlet fever, one of whom died.

Georgy was only four years old, and suffered but very slightly from the fever. One day he was permitted to get up and play in the nursery. He was happy but somewhat restless, and kept asking for fresh flowers. These were procured for him, but though they were fresh and bright he was not satisfied. Then he begged to be allowed to wear his white summer coat. This wish was gratified, but still he was not at rest. He asked his friend Miss Hooper to sing hymns to him, and sitting down in his white coat and among his flowers, he looked up into her face and said, "Doi'ee[80] is very ill, and getting worse."

He repeated this two or three times in the course of the afternoon. The doctor was sent for, but was detained till the evening when it was evident that Georgy was passing away. His friend asked if he loved Jesus?

"Oh yes," he replied, "Jesus love me, and died for me. Doi'ee do love Jesus. Mamma, do not cry; Doi'ee is going to be with Jesus."

Soon after he pointed upwards with his little hand and looked steadfastly as if he saw the Lord. Thus his spirit passed away, leaving a happy expression on his face. Now his longing for the bright flowers and white coat was understood, and the cause of his restlessness explained.

It was a time of sorrow, and suspense also on account of the other children. The air of Bath had never suited my dear wife, and this affliction, together with the fatigue of nursing brought her to the conclusion that for her sake and that of the family we should ask the Lord to remove us to some other place. I was rather taken aback, but looking at the matter on all sides I determined that if she asked me again I would do so.

She did ask, and accordingly we knelt down and prayed the Lord to move us. On the morning of the second day after doing this, there came a letter from Sir Thomas Beauchamp offering me a Rectory in Norfolk. Taking this as the Lord's answer to our prayer, we thanked Him and accepted it.

Then Sir Thomas wrote again, to tell me that when the living [first] became vacant he had a wish to give it to me but, fearing it might be his own will and not God's, he had restrained himself. After waiting for four weeks, notwithstanding very numerous applications, Lady Beauchamp said one morning, "Why do you not give Buckenham to Mr Haslam?"

---

80   Haslam says in a footnote that this is the boy's way of
     saying Georgy. See memorial card on page 304.

This was the very sign he had been waiting for. He replied, "I will do so today."

Thus it happened that the very day we were praying at Bath, God through Sir Thomas and Lady Beauchamp was answering in Norfolk.

In this letter Sir Thomas went on to say that the living was worth three hundred pounds a year, with a good house and glebe, and that the population was about twenty people. There was another Rectory attached to it, that of Hassingham, containing eighteen or twenty cottages.

Our hearts sank at this announcement, for God knew that it was not for a pleasant house or money that we prayed, but for another sphere of work for Him.

However, here was the answer to prayer, and we had accepted it "for better for worse." Our reading the same morning was in the eighth chapter of the Acts, where we came upon the words, "Arise, and go unto Gaza, which is desert."

I looked up and found my wife looking at me. Our eyes met. Evidently the words had the same effect on both of us, and from this time we had no more doubts about the matter. I did not even care to go and see the place, for I was sure it would be good and well, and that in some way or other we should have work for the Master. But for business purposes it was necessary that I should make the journey, in order to arrange for the services of the parishes till I could take possession in person.

Sir Thomas received me at Langley Hall most kindly, and the next morning drove me over to my new parish. We crossed the river in a ferry-boat: horses, carriage and all. Then we passed along an avenue of trees with deep ditches on either side, and beautiful green pastures with many cattle upon them. These, I was told, were the marshes.

"Marshes!" I cried. "Why, I have been quietly making up my mind for swamps and all their attendant evils. These look like beautiful fields."

"So they are," said my friend, "and very rich fields too."

Next we passed through a railway station and ascended a hill, at the top of which I observed a gravel pit. "Look, this is a dry gravel soil," said Sir Thomas.

Dry soil, a railway station and green pastures – when I feared a damp flat place buried up in the country. My heart was rising more and more in surprise and thankfulness.

My friend was driving me to the Rectory house, but I begged him to take me to the church first. In order to do this he had to call upon the churchwarden for the keys. We knocked at his door, when his old housekeeper appeared at the window and said that the master had gone out and taken the key of the front door with him, so she could not admit us except at the back.

Sir Thomas said, "Let me introduce the new Rector to you."

"Oh," she replied, turning her face away, "I don't want to see him. I thought Mr C was to have the living. It will be a great disappointment to him, and indeed to us all."

This was my first welcome to Buckenham!

We obtained the keys through the window and proceeded at once to the Norman church with an octagon tower. The interior was fitted up with oak benches and rich stained glass. Here my patron kindly knelt with me in prayer, and was good enough to thank God for inclining me to accept this charge.

From this we went to the Rectory, which we could scarcely see for trees. I said that in Cornwall I built a house in a bare place and planted thousands of young trees, and here God has given me a better house, and trees grown up.

"You will have to cut a great many down," added Sir Thomas.

And so it was. The house was dark and damp for want of light and ventilation, but it was a gem of a place. It had been built at different times after the model of a chateau in Normandy, with a veranda all round. I could scarcely believe that this place was for me, and felt deeply thankful. The garden used to be kept in perfect order, but not having been tended this summer it was overrun with weeds. They were growing in a luxuriant manner as if making the most of their unexpected chance – a warning and a lesson in themselves!

From this we drove through a beautiful lane to Hassingham Church which was even prettier than that at

Buckenham. It had a thatched roof, and a round tower surmounted with an octagon belfry. The inside was beautifully finished with oak carvings, stained glass windows and encaustic tiles. Here again, with thanksgiving, we made prayer for God's blessing.

I said, "The Lord has not forgotten my work and labour of love. I built one church and He has given me two, more beautiful than the one I gave up to Him when with many tears I left Baldhu eight years ago."

I was in a hurry to go home to my family and tell of all the good things the Lord had provided for us. Having completed the necessary arrangements for the parish till September, I returned to Bath to make the most of the three months that remained.

Our open-air services, Temperance meetings, Prayer meetings, Bible-readings, Mothers' meetings and Schools were all in good working order, and so well sustained by those who were responsible for them that my successor would not have much trouble in keeping them on – unless, like some successors, he determined to reorganise everything and overthrow all previous arrangements.

I had been told that it would be useless to begin work at Buckenham till the harvest was over, so I remained in Bath till September, carrying on active operations, especially in the open air. During these last months we lived on Beechen Cliff, from which elevation we looked down upon the city. Sometimes it was enveloped in fog, with towers and spires protruding; and sometimes it looked like a fairy scene, especially on a clear night when the innumerable gas lamps presented a remarkable picture.

My last remembrance of Bath, I must say, was more pleasant than the beginning. I had now many friends, and among them not a few who at first had no sympathy with me.

Early in September 1863 we left this place where I had passed through so many spiritual conflicts and exercises of soul. Taking the train to London, we proceeded by steamer to Great Yarmouth where we landed the next day. Here we remained till the Rectory at Buckenham was ready to receive us.

CHAPTER 28

Norfolk — 1863

AT LENGTH THE DAY arrived for my induction to the Rectory of Buckenham and Hassingham. A neighbouring Vicar who had the commission came to perform the ceremony. He brought me to the church, and setting my hand upon the latch of the door, said, "I induct you as Rector." Then giving me the key, he bade me go in, lock the door on the inside and ring the bell.

I entered, and locking the door knelt down for a few minutes, after which in due time I took hold of the rope and rang the bell in true ringers' style.

When I came out the Vicar said, "What in the world made you so long? Could you not find the bell rope?"

"Yes," I said, "but I knelt down first to thank God, and to ask Him to give me His blessing here for the salvation of many souls."

I am afraid he did not quite understand my meaning, so he wished me goodbye and drove off.

After I was duly installed in this small parish, which consisted of nine cottages only, I began to contrast it with the teeming population I had left. Could it be that God had shelved us in a pleasant country place for asking to be removed?

However, notwithstanding the small population, we had good congregations the first Sunday in both churches, especially in the afternoon at Buckenham which was the larger of the two.

The old gamekeeper, who was a self-righteous kind of man, had been praying to the Almighty, as he said, to send a man who would do them some good. Then, as a matter of course he came to church to see the result of his prayers.

Hassingham Church today.

"Well," he remarked in a deep Norfolk way of speaking, "I think I do like this man pretty well. You see, he ain't like our old "Revarand". The old one put his spectacles on and opened his book, he did, but this here "Revarand" he do take off his spectacles and shut up the book, and move himself about more lively like. Yes, I do think I like the man pretty well; yes, pretty well."

The fact was, some of my words had hit self-righteous and unconverted people rather hard. I was obliged to be very elementary, for upon previous inquiry in the neighbourhood I had ascertained that no one knew anything about conversion.

One woman, after saying "No" to my inquiry on this subject, remembered that when her brother was ill, a man came to see him who prayed very loud with him. When he was dying he shouted and clapped his hands. She ran in to see what was the matter and found him sitting up in the bed rejoicing.

He said, "My sins are pardoned. It's all right, I am going to heaven!"

Thinking he was mad she ran out of the house in a fright. When she came back he was dead, with a happy smile on his countenance.

The Church of Buckenham St Nicholas, redrawn from an original engraving in *Yet Not I*.

Another person to whom we spoke about her soul, said, "Was you always religious like this?"

"Oh dear, no," I replied. "We used to be worldly like other people, but by the grace of God we have been changed – born again."

She said she knew nothing about that – born again! "Have yer been born twice?"

"Yes," I said.

"Well," she continued, "I've lived a number of years in this neighbourhood, and I'm sure people are never born but once about here!"

There was not even a little Primitive chapel within three miles of my church. I found it most difficult to preach to people so entirely dark and ignorant.

After the service at Buckenham church my attention was drawn to a young farmer whom I had also seen at Hassingham in the morning. He was standing with five or six others in the churchyard, and I could tell by their countenances that they were interested, if not awakened. I invited them to come to the Rectory for a meeting in the evening at six o'clock; but as they did not promise to do so, I acceded to the request of a gentleman who asked me to give an address at his coach house three miles off.

I left my dear wife to speak to any anxious ones, should they present themselves. To her surprise upwards of sixty persons came, and filled our unfurnished drawing-room. Many sat on the boxes which were deposited there, and others stood. She gave them an address, and when I came home she told me to my great joy that six had found peace, and that they had asked for another meeting. This was indeed cheering news.

The next evening the drawing-room would not hold all who came, so we opened the windows and let the people stand in the veranda. Again the Lord blessed the Word to the salvation of souls. Finding so great an interest excited, I promised to provide further accommodation for our meetings. To accomplish this I suspended all other business in order to make a large outhouse on the premises available. In a short time this also was too small. Then we removed to a barn we had thought of pulling down, which was capable of holding more than two hundred people. Before long this accommodation proved insufficient, so that some of the men who attended asked permission to repair and enlarge the place at their own expense, which they did.

Here our meetings were continued almost every night for eight months. Great and memorable meetings they were, for seldom an evening passed without blessing to souls. Sometimes as many as ten, and even twenty professed to find peace.[81]

Besides all this spiritual work, we had a great deal to occupy us in setting our house in order. Trees had to be cut down to let light and air into our dwelling, and the dwelling had to be furnished. Also, the garden had to be made tidy for the winter, and above all the pump needed to be repaired.

---

81   Haslam subsequently built a brick pulpit onto the
      outside wall of the Rectory to preach to the crowds,
      and it is still there today.

The old gardener, speaking of this pump, said, "The water is first-rate, and the spring abundant."

He spoke so much of it that I was quite pleased when the machinery was mended, that I might prove it. To my dismay, however, the water was both foul and disagreeable. It was because the water had been stagnant for several weeks; but when the well was in constant use, and the water flowing, it kept fresh and never failed either winter or summer. So, thought I, is it with the well of water within us. If we are not living for others and witnessing for God and His truth, we also become stagnant, and savour of self, or some idiosyncrasy of our own with which we bore everyone who comes near. We cannot be clear, fresh and sparkling unless we draw from the Living Fountain continually, and let the water of life flow out freely to others.

Before our house was in order, a neighbouring clergyman called and found us in our unprepared state. I told him we had been so fully occupied with God's work that it had left us but little time for our own. He kindly took a seat on one of the unpacked boxes, putting his hat on another, and we talked about the work.

I asked him whether he had anything of the same kind in his parish.

"No," he replied; "but I preach the Gospel every Sunday, for all that."

"It cannot be the fault of the Word," I said. "If you have no result, the fault cannot be God's."

"I suppose, then, you mean to say that it is mine!"

"Well," I answered, "I must say that I usually blame myself when there is no blessing in my parish. How people can go on preaching the Gospel, which is 'the power of God unto salvation'[82] and be content without conversions, I cannot tell."

In the course of conversation he told me that a relative of his had warned him against revivals and Dissenters.

82 Romans 1:16

"Oh," I said, "that will easily account for want of blessing. A revival is the work of God Himself – it is no revival if it is not. And Dissenters are not infrequently God's only witnesses in a parish."

He said, "I do not believe in Dissenters."

Finding that he was getting restless, I proposed to have prayer. This he declined, saying, "No, thank you!" and at once rose to go away.

We walked together as he led his horse to the gate. Then stopping abruptly, he said, "I'll have that prayer you proposed."

"Very well," I replied, "so you shall. Come back with me."

We returned and prayed together.

Then he rose up and said, "Will you come and preach in my parish?"

"Certainly, with pleasure."

"My church is very small, you know."

"Never mind; I will come."

He then knelt down of his own accord, and said, "Lord, incline the hearts of the farmers to open their barns for preaching." Then, after promising to write, he took his departure.

I heard the next day that the first farmer he called upon readily assented to his proposal, and that they had fixed for me to go the following Monday.

True to the appointment I appeared and found the place filled to suffocation. Where the people came from I could not tell, for there were very few houses in the neighbourhood. Here we had a great revival of God's work in which the Vicar rejoiced fervently, and in the fullness of his heart went round and shook hands with all the Dissenters in the congregation. It was a most encouraging and happy meeting.

There, and in other places in that parish, I continually held services in alternation with my own. Many remarkable conversions took place, but a publican threatened that he would write to the Bishop and acquaint him that "the Revarands were a-praying with the Primitives." The fact was, he was irritated because his usual customers were better employed than in drinking at his house.

His daughter attended the meetings. One evening she went home rejoicing and told her father that she was converted.

"Don't tell me," he cried, "you're converted! Don't you know that these here people are taking the very bread out of our mouths? Get out of my house with yer!" Striking her on the face he drove her out and slammed the door.

She was much hurt by his violence, but was happy in her soul and crept into the straw shed for the night. Her poor mother had no rest or sleep, and the next morning was too ill to attend to the house. So the father rose early to seek for his daughter, and on finding her ordered her to go in at once and do her work. She willingly returned to her poor mother and was busy all day.

Her father looked at her several times with anger, and in the evening when she ventured to ask him whether she might go to the meeting – having promised to do so – his rage became ungovernable and he threw his cup of hot tea at her. Fortunately he missed his mark.

She picked up the broken pieces and began to wipe the wall and the floor, saying, "Never mind, father, I'll give it up."

At eight o'clock her father came to her, and said, "Thee has been a good girl. Get along to yer meeting."

She burst into tears of disappointment, and said, "It's too late now, father. It will be all over by the time I get there."

"Never mind, girl," he said. "Don't cry. I'll go with thee tomorrow."

On the morrow he did go, and was awakened, and came home penitent and broken-hearted. The second day he found peace, and from that time was a most decided Christian. He used to urge his customers to go to the meetings, telling them what good he himself had received. After a time he determined to give up that business, and I said I must come and preach in his public house before he did so. It must be on a Saturday, for that was the day when most mischief was done.

Accordingly on the appointed Saturday evening I arrived at seven o'clock, and found a few people standing outside the door. I said, "Won't you come in?"

To this they replied, "There is no room inside."

I knocked and the door was opened. On entering I saw the stairs before me were filled with people, as well as a wide passage; also the parlours on my right and left. I was told that every chamber upstairs was crowded, and the back kitchen besides. "The whole house is filled. There are more than two hundred people in it; and though you cannot see them, they will all be able to hear."

I had the doormat for a pulpit, and standing there gave out a familiar hymn. Our singing was very indifferent. The more hearty we tried to make it, the more irregular it became. When we had finished the first verse we could hear that our unseen friends in the various rooms were a long way behind. I gave out a second verse, which was by no means more successful than the first. I may say in Norfolk phraseology, the singing was "very moderate," or "somewhat slight."

I took for my text, "Go ye and learn what that meaneth, I will have mercy, and not sacrifice."[83] I said, "God does not require sacrifices from us for our salvation, but desires to show mercy. If we will let Him, He is ready and willing to save us."

While I was speaking, a smothered voice from one of the chambers was heard saying, "Lord, save me."

As it did not disturb me I went on with my address.

Then another said, "Lord, have mercy upon me." And yet one more in another part of the house.

---

83   Matthew 9:12-13: When Jesus heard that, he said unto them, They that be whole need not a physician, but they that are sick. But go ye and learn what that meaneth, I will have mercy, and not sacrifice: for I am not come to call the righteous, but sinners to repentance.

Still I proceeded, till a man with a loud voice standing near me cried aloud for mercy. This appeared to be a signal for all. On the stairs, in the passages, in the parlours, in the chambers and in the kitchens there were people crying in distress of soul, while others were adding to the noise by their loud Amens and shouts of praise. This for quiet Norfolk was indeed surprising.

With some difficulty I went from room to room, and satisfied myself that the work was general. Soon cries for mercy were exchanged for songs of praise. Some of the people sang one hymn, and some another in the various rooms. This continued until ten o'clock when I thought it was time to break up. We therefore concluded and the company dispersed, continuing to sing as they went along the lanes.

After the people had gone, the thankfulness of the landlord was unbounded. He called his family together and found that they were all rejoicing.

"Now," said the mother, "there's one absent one. Let's pray for him."

This prayer for an absent son was the parting act of that remarkable evening.

I asked "mine host" if he had written to tell this son about his own conversion. "Oh, bless you," he said, "I did that the first thing, and asked him to give his heart to God too."

"Then," I added, "please write and tell him that we have prayed for him."

Letters crossed upon the sea, and the son's letter contained the joyful news that he had given his heart to God and was rejoicing in forgiveness.

Many such incidents were related from time to time, which considerably enhanced the interest of the barn meetings. Truly it was surprising to hear of the conversion of some of the most unlikely people. Farmers, who are generally complained of as hard to catch, were one by one opening their hearts to the Lord – and their barns for His work.

As the meetings increased, excitement prevailed and opposition was stimulated. A clergyman who had attended one of our barn services called to see Sir Thomas

Beauchamp, but not finding him at home told her ladyship of the "sad and dreadful scenes" he had witnessed.[84] He said there were "men standing up with outstretched arms praying in a most extravagant manner, and women almost in hysterics – indeed, there was a frantic noise and confusion everywhere."

"Were the people angry or fighting?" asked her ladyship.

"Oh no, my lady, nothing of that kind. They were more like intoxicated people – quite unmanageable – though I must say they looked very happy."

"Is not that better than the stillness of spiritual death?" asked her ladyship calmly.

The visitor was silent and soon took his departure. He went about after this saying that "the Beauchamps were every bit as bad as Haslam!"

It is true Sir Thomas did rejoice in the work, though at times with some trembling; for there were many complaints, exaggerated of course, and he was much blamed for bringing "such a firebrand into a quiet neighbourhood."

One gentleman, a great friend of his, said to him, "There is sure to be rebellion. The labourers are saying to their masters, 'Are you converted?' There will be rebellion, take my word for it. The people are singing hymns in the lanes all night long. How can they attend to their work?"

Sir Thomas could not see that ruin was so imminent, but he promised to inquire about the things which were said to be taking place the other side of the river.

84   Sir Thomas Beauchamp is the man who had invited
      Haslam to become Rector of the parish.

CHAPTER 29

Geraldine Hooper Again — 1863/64

THE GLORIOUS WORK was now beginning to spread on all sides. If churches were closed against me, they were of but small capacity, while large and commodious barns were opened. One gentleman said, "I never knew before what my grandfather built these large barns for, but the Lord has found good use for them."

Night after night in one place or another, including my own barn, the work went on for seven or eight weeks. Then my strength began to fail and my back to ache, but there was no stopping. Just at this time I received an invitation to go to Dublin. Thinking the work at home could not go on without me, and that my presence was absolutely necessary for its continuance, I declined. Soon, however, the Lord showed me that it was His work, and that He could easily raise up other workers. This He did, and gave me what I so greatly needed: a total rest for three weeks.

One Monday afternoon, feeling unusually weak and tired, I asked the Lord to undertake for me, then lay down on the sofa for two hours' rest. I had scarcely settled on my back when a young converted farmer arrived with his horse and gig, to take me to my evening appointment which was three miles [5km] off.

I said, "Why have you come so long before your time? I want to rest."

"Oh, never mind that," he replied. "I've got business yonder. I'll get you a sofa and some tea. Do come with me now."

I rose up and went with him. The tea and the sofa were provided, it is true, but there was no rest for I had much talking to do. The service in the evening was a happy and very rousing one, so that I forgot all my pains and went on till eleven o'clock.

On putting the horse into the gig to return home, my friend observed that one of the springs was broken. He said, "It is not safe for us to ride in this. You had better stay here for the night."

I could not agree to his proposition, neither could I walk home. At last the Vicar kindly said, "I will drive you back," and at once proceeded with his servant in all haste to harness the pony. This done, we started off at a great rate, when presently the Vicar quietly remarked, "My pony has run away – I cannot manage him."

"Never mind," I replied. "Keep him in the middle of the road and let him go. We shall be home all the sooner!"

I had not said this many moments when the animal began to kick, and continued galloping and kicking as we went. Every time his heels came in contact with the carriage the splinters flew in all directions. Thus we were hurried along, and this is all I remember. I believe the carriage came to pieces and we were thrown out.

My farmer friend who had gone on before, leading his horse with the fractured carriage, heard us coming. He heard also the crashing kicks of the pony, and then saw the creature dashing past him with the shafts and harness hanging at its sides. He turned back, and by the bright moonlight observed broken pieces of the carriage strewn along the road. Then he found me lying unconscious, "in a pool of blood" as he called it, but I was "not quite dead."

A little farther on he perceived the Vicar lying beside the road as if asleep. On being aroused he soon recovered himself and limped forward to my help. While he remained with me bemoaning the sad event, the farmer went to a neighbouring house and roused up the inmates to borrow a carriage. Then putting his own horse into it they lifted me up and carefully drove home. It was after two o'clock when we arrived. Having laid me in bed they started off five miles [8km] farther to fetch the doctor. On examining me he pronounced that there was not much the matter, beyond a scalp wound from which he believed I should soon recover – if I was kept very quiet and was not allowed to read or talk.

Thus I was laid down for a fortnight. God was resting me. It might appear to some a strange way to rest, but rest it truly was, and I scarcely know how I could have had it in any other way. I had suffered no pain; and the loss of blood, the doctor said, was rather in my favour than otherwise. I had therefore abundant reason to thank God not only for myself but for the work's sake also.

During the time I was laid aside I was astonished to find what general interest was awakened in my behalf. Most unlikely people called at the house to inquire after me, and their numerous acts of kindness and consideration quite moved me. I had no idea that God had given me such acceptance in the neighbourhood; for judging from reports I had come to the conclusion that everyone was against me, and that there would have been but little regret had I remained insensible altogether!

When able to get out again I rejoiced to see the progress of the work, and to find how the Lord had raised up and brought out other workers.

Among the number was a clergyman who came to see me when he heard I was laid aside, and kindly offered his help. He said that he had never preached in another man's parish without leave, but for love of me he would do anything I wished. I took him at his word and sent him to conduct a barn meeting. He received great blessing from the Lord in that place, and returned home rejoicing. After this experience he took courage and worked more freely.

Besides him, there were three or four farmers who became preachers, and many others were raised up to help in different ways.

Thus I found that the Lord had given me the rest I wanted, and had provided the fellow-labourers who were needful for the progress of the work. In addition He taught me that He could do without me, and that the work was not mine, but His.

Refreshed with rest, and glad to hear of the progress of the work in all directions, I longed to get out again into the thick of the battle. The atmosphere was full of the sound of revival, and everyone was talking of it. Whether in the house, on the road or in the train, this was the one theme of conversation.

Opposition also was rife.

One doctor went about saying, "We shall want to build a new wing to the lunatic asylum, for I am sure that many will be driven out of their minds by this excitement."

It is true that one dear and happy old man was apprehended by a magistrate's order, and sent away in a cart to the asylum. All the way there he protested that he was not mad.

"Yes," said the keeper, who had charge of him, "that is what they all say."

However, in two or three days he was liberated, and before his discharge he had the joy of conveying a message of peace and salvation to one or two desponding ones who were shut up in that place.

Some of my neighbours, the "Revarands" as the Rectors and Vicars of Norfolk are called, made no secret of their thoughts about me. They considered that I was fanatical, disorderly and irregular, to say nothing worse. At the same time they did not mind letting their people remain in spiritual death. Some of them employed their time shooting, fishing or farming – anything, everything but the all-important occupation of winning souls for which they had been solemnly set apart.

Not a few of these sent complaints to the Bishop about me and my intrusions; but his lordship wisely remained silent, though he kept their letters stowed up in a drawer – and brought them out on a future occasion!

It was bad enough when I went out preaching in all directions, but far worse when Mrs Haslam began to speak and find general acceptance among the people. This was ten times more distasteful!

A Rector's wife wrote to me, as a "brother in the Lord," to say that she and her husband had been praying for a revival in Norfolk for years but, "If this is a revival, it has come in such away that I cannot thank God for it." She then went on to implore me to "let our dear good Bishop arbitrate. Let us leave the question of women's preaching to his grave decision."

I feared the "grave decision" far too much, and would not risk having such a useful instrument, so owned and blessed of the Lord as my wife, buried out of existence. Nor did I care to involve the Bishop in any responsibility as to our doings.

At this critical time who should offer us a visit but Miss Geraldine Hooper from Bath. This young lady, it will be remembered, was a great help to me in Avon Street where she went about with Mrs Haslam to other meetings. After we left Bath she took up our mantle and went forward with a double portion of our spirit, and with much more result.

I need not say we welcomed her with much joy. Her striking appearance at our little country church, and the clear ring of her voice in the hymns during the service, attracted considerable attention. When it was known that she would speak at the barn meeting in the evening the people came out in crowds, and the place was filled in every corner.

Her address was like kindling a fresh fire, and a very bright and warm one it was. The people became wild with admiration, and their eagerness to hear her was intense. Her fame spread so rapidly that the Norwich papers took up the subject. The editor of one of these papers began a series of tirades against Buckenham and the work. Week by week fierce and long articles were published, which of course did not stamp out the fire but rather added fuel to it.

Just at that time the record of a dreadful event was going the round of the newspapers. It told about three thousand people who were burnt alive in St Jago [in Jamaica] in a building from which they could not obtain egress. This was contrasted with our proceedings. "There," it was said, "only bodies were burnt; but here souls were being destroyed every night – and till two o'clock in the morning."

One evening while the reporter was busy taking notes in the barn, his horse managed to kick his carriage to pieces. I was kind and lent him mine. Not withstanding this consideration, in the next issue of the paper there appeared a very exaggerated and spiteful account of that meeting. It stated, among other things which it is needless to rehearse, that I was "sitting quietly in the barn while the ladies were speaking; but then I was only the Rector!"

I must say it was quite true that I was there, and was delighted to hear the two ladies. They both spoke wonderfully well and with great power. I do not wonder at the devil being angry, as he certainly was.

While the ladies were in such demand at home, I was again urged by my good friend Mr Bewley[85] to visit Dublin. I accepted his invitation and arranged to go.

The voyage across the sea was unusually rough, and consequently we were much behind time. Added to this I was very ill, and felt the motion of the vessel long after landing. I was nevertheless hurried along to Merrion Hall. On arriving there I was urged to go on the platform, if it were only for a few minutes, to show myself to the large assembly and tell them I was too ill to speak.

I could scarcely stand steady without holding the rail, and was very exhausted. However, the Lord gave me a message and I spoke for nearly an hour, and by the end of the address I felt wonderfully well. I then conducted an after-meeting to which fully a third of the congregation remained. A most memorable meeting it was, the first of many. Out of utter weakness came strength, and out of helplessness great help. The omnipotent Helper manifested His presence and many souls received blessing.

Mr Bewley was delighted, and in the joy of his heart went forward to arrange other meetings – no less than thirty-two in eight days. With such abundant provision, and a people ready to hear, I prolonged my stay and then returned to my work at home.

I feel that I must insert here one incident that occurred during my visit, for it was so characteristic of dear Mr Bewley and the Lord's way with him. One morning I received a letter from my dear wife, reminding me that the expenses of moving and doing up the Rectory at Buckenham had brought us into debt a hundred pounds. She felt that if I told Mr Bewley my circumstances he would gladly help us. I

---

85   Mr Bewley (Henry Bewley of Dublin built Merrion Hall in 1863) has not been mentioned previously in Haslam's two books abridged here.

did not see my way to this, having already put the matter into the Lord's hands.

She wrote back to say it was all pride and shame; that I was afraid to ask; that she felt sure Mr Bewley would help – and had a great mind to write herself. I was considering this letter upstairs in my room, and waiting upon the Lord about it, when Mr Bewley called me down.

As soon as we were seated in his study, he said, "I am going to ask you a very impertinent question. How much is your living worth?"

I replied, "Three hundred pounds a year."

"Is that enough for you and your large family? Do you want help?"

I said, "Here is a letter come from my wife today. I was considering it upstairs when you called me. Now that you ask, I do not mind telling you."

He said the Lord had that morning bid him give me a hundred pounds. "There it is," he added, handing me a cheque for that amount. This he had written before calling me down. He said, "I have much gratification and thankfulness in giving it. God bless you, and yours."

With tears in his eyes, the dear man shook my hand warmly. Tears were in mine too.

CHAPTER 30

Not Women's Work! — 1863/64

ON MY RETURN HOME I found that the ladies were invited to large barns in other parishes, and to the theatres in Yarmouth and Norwich. One clergyman seriously objected to women's preaching, saying, "The Scripture teaches that they should mind their children at home."

But this did not apply to Miss Hooper, as she had none to mind! Having once heard her, however, his mind was so changed that he declared he would "go through fire and water to hear her again."

"You shall hear her again," I said. "She is to preach in your neighbourhood in two days' time. I cannot be there, so you go and be her chaplain."

He assented.

It so happened that he had to go through drenching rain – that was the water. When he arrived, to his amazement he found that, as the barn would not hold the people, they had gone preacher and all into the Primitive Methodist Chapel. He followed and went in too, but did not hear the last of it for a long time – that was the fire! So actually he did go through both fire and water; but not without reward, for he was converted, and afterwards became a zealous and useful man.

Miss Hooper's popularity attracted hundreds of people to the barn meetings. One evening at the end of January, as I was returning home on a clear frosty night, I could hear singing, though I was nearly a mile from my house. On approaching nearer I distinguished the tune, and thought I could hear Miss Hooper's voice. Hastening forwards I was astonished at the scene before me. It was a bright moonlight night, with snow on the ground and a cold north-east wind. In spite of this, there was a very large crowd standing in rapt attention listening to the preaching.

Miss Hooper, in company with Mrs Haslam, was standing in a cart round which were suspended from the trees my drawing-room and dining-room oil lamps, besides other lights. I was told that the barn was full of people, and also the adjoining classroom. Standing among the crowd I heard the best part of the address. In her characteristic way she told a humorous story, but one which I have no doubt is well remembered by many to this day. It made the audience smile, but the application of it was very solemn and pointed.

She said that a gentleman once went to visit a friend in a lunatic asylum. While he was standing at the balcony a strong man suddenly caught hold of him with a tight grasp, and said, "Jump down! Jump down!"[86] With much presence of mind he calmly replied, "Why, any fool can do that. Come with me, I will show you a far better trick."

The man followed him down the stairs into the garden. "Now," said the gentleman, pointing to the same balcony, "you jump up there – that's the thing for a man to do."

The poor man tried, but I need not tell with what result. "Any fool," she continued, "can go to hell. But come with me, I can show you the way to heaven. You cannot get there by your own efforts, but Christ can lift you in."

The effect was marvellous, and the result great. At the end of the address she dismissed the congregation, inviting the anxious ones to come into the barn.

Besides her winning influence, this young lady was able by her readiness and wit to control the largest and roughest meetings. It not infrequently happened that the people in their eagerness to enter and obtain good places jostled one another, so that angry feeling and altercations arose. But a word from her soon brought the dispute to an end.

---

86 On page 37 of the biography of Geraldine Hooper, *She Spake of Him*, there is a fuller version of this memorable but very non-PC story, where it is stated that this man is an inmate – "a great strong man with a whip in his hand." (See next footnote for book details.)

One evening there was likely to be a serious disturbance. This was caused by a man sitting in a front row keeping on his tall hat. The people behind called to him to take it off. He rudely refused to do so, whereupon another man threatened to knock it off. He defied him, saying, "Come up and do it, that's all!"

Miss Hooper instantly rose, and said quietly, "Let the gentleman wear his hat, by all means. Perhaps he has something the matter with his head."

"I hain't!" cried the man, hastily taking off the obnoxious appendage. There was a shout of laughter, but that was as quickly silenced, and the proceedings of the evening went on smoothly.

Miss Hooper's power was irresistible. People were spellbound, as if obliged to do as she bid them; nevertheless, they were willing also.

Miss Hooper's last meeting at Buckenham was held on Sunday evening, February 16 1864. It was a bright moonlight night, and although very cold she stood out in the open air in a wagon, her usual pulpit on such occasions. At the conclusion of her address she most solemnly warned the people that "there would come a last day of grace, and a last day of life, to each one there," and affectionately urged all those who had not hitherto done so, to come to the Saviour.

Dear Mr Bewley in Dublin had generously given me forty thousand tracts and little books for distribution in Norfolk, and being anxious to know how many people were present that night I brought out forty packets, each containing fifty books. Placing men at the three gates, I bid them give one to each person as they passed. In this way I ascertained that more than eighteen hundred persons were present.

The gratitude and esteem of the people for miles round were very great, and they would not let Miss Hooper go without a testimonial of their regard and affection. They made among themselves a subscription for a handsome gold watch, which was duly purchased and presented to her, with a suitable inscription.

From this place she went forward to London and Bath, and many other places, and continued speaking incessantly as she had done in Norfolk. She died August 12 1872, at the early age of thirty-one. On her monument in Bath is inscribed the following testimony:

During the last years of her brief life she proclaimed the glorious Gospel of the Grace of God not less than four thousand times to large assemblies in Bath and other parts of England.

Hundreds of souls will bless God to all eternity for the good they received through the instrumentality of this wonderful young lady.[87]

87 It is important not to underestimate the vast amount
of effective preaching carried out by Geraldine
Hooper. Geraldine married Henry Dening in 1868,
had one child, a girl in 1870, and died in August 1872
at the age of thirty-one. The official diagnosis was
erysipelas, a bacterial skin infection generally caused
by group A streptococci. If this was the correct
diagnosis, it took a very severe form, causing
blindness, mental confusion and death within just a
few days. The opinion of Geraldine's doctor and
friends was that she had worked too hard for many
years, with insufficient rest. For her funeral in Bath,
6,000 people were allowed into Locksbrook cemetery,
and many thousand more had to wait outside, such
was her fame. The story of her short life is told in *She
Spake of Him* by a close friend, Mrs Grattan Guinness.
Published by W Mack, Bristol and The Bible Society,
London c1873, it tells of an interesting life in a book
with extracts from many letters and talks, nine
excellent line illustrations of Bath, and an engraving
of Geraldine with a sample of her handwriting.
Unfortunately, most modern readers would consider
Mrs Grattan Guinness' writing over-sentimental and
heavy going.

CHAPTER 31

Great Yarmouth — 1864

MISS HOOPER'S FAME, together with the newspaper reports, brought out hundreds of people from Norwich to our barn meetings, though the distance was eight or nine miles. The frequent trains to and from Norwich which stopped at Buckenham helped some of them, but the greater number marched in companies, singing along the road, particularly when they were going back at night.

On the whole I do not think that we gained anything by this large influx. Formerly the people came with desire as the Lord bid them, but afterwards too many did so from curiosity to see what was going on. Consequently there was more distraction and dryness in the meetings.

A gentleman who was tired of waiting for the clergy to invite me to Norwich – especially as one of them boasted that "there are nearly fifty churches in Norwich, and Mr Haslam is shut out of all!" – hired the Lecture Hall and invited me to preach there.

These services became part of the regular institution of the city and were announced accordingly. Indeed, they were proverbial. If any were anxious about their souls, it was said, "Oh, you must go to the Lecture Hall!" Or if anyone was venturesome enough to propose going, he or she was warned, "Take care, you're sure to be converted if you go there!"

Only in eternity will all the good that was done in these meetings be known, and not only in this city but in many towns in the county. Town Halls and Corn Halls were made available when churches could not be had, and God provided preachers to carry on the work. Several ladies as well as gentlemen were forthcoming, whose labours were then blessed. In many instances they still continue to be, after a lapse of fifteen years. In some of these places the work has subsided, but in others it has increased tenfold. Thus we can see that the Lord is willing to work whenever His people are willing to offer themselves.

In this work I steadily maintained my purpose not to form a church or society in connection with the Hall services. I would not even have a Bible-reading for the converts in Norwich, but urged them to go to their respective pastors. There were already churches and organizations enough in the city. Even if they were not perfect I did not care to add to them. My object was to teach the lessons that while in the world we need not be of it, and that under a dead ministry we may still trust in Christ. Leaving one church to make another implies that we can make a better one, or do better than our neighbours.

For instance a chapel, or room, was built by some converted people not far from Norwich, which the Rector of the place [cynically] named St Haslam's Chapel. This was a great honour to put upon me, but I could not help feeling that if this Rector had preached the Gospel to his people, they would never have gone to the expense of making such provision for themselves.

As the summer advanced, our barn congregations diminished on the weekday evenings, the people being busy in their gardens and fields. Having received various invitations from the coast of Norfolk, I accepted one from Great Yarmouth. Here I commenced operations by preaching on the beach, and at the close of the address we retired to the Seamen's Chapel to draw in the net.

At the close of the meeting a gentleman came forward and invited me to his house. He took great interest in the services, and he, his wife and daughter were kind friends who entertained me and other evangelists. He arranged the meetings, took the Corn Hall and the Town Hall, and made himself responsible for all the expenses.

The Corn Hall was continually so crowded, and the air often so oppressive, that we longed for the use of the theatre. On making application for it we were refused and told that "the regular performers" were coming, as if we were only irregular performers. However, on one occasion we gained our point and obtained admission to this dark, dirty, dingy place. Bills were displayed all over the town to announce the fact that Rev W Haslam would preach at the theatre: "no collection."

This commodious place was thronged to excess with persons of all classes. It was a novel thing in that far off eastern county to have preaching in a theatre, and it created a great sensation. Some of the people said that they had heard of "actors becoming clergymen, but never before of a clergyman going on the stage!"

I preached to the dense crowd that filled the place above, below and around, also on the stage where I stood, from the text, "How shall we escape, if we neglect so great salvation?"[88] I afterwards published this address in a tract called *The Great Salvation,* which remains as a memento of that one occasion on which I was permitted to be "a performer" in the theatre.[89]

The Yarmouth meetings were not without fruitful results. Souls were saved, backsliders restored and believers encouraged to devote themselves to the Lord's service.

One clergyman from the country, who had been there, wrote soon after to offer me a visit for a week, that he might see the work for himself. I gladly welcomed him and took him with me to a Corn Hall meeting in Yarmouth, where I was engaged to preach that evening.

He happened to know the Vicar of the place and therefore, as he said, sat in misery all the time for fear the door should open and the Vicar would walk in and find him there. This quite spoiled that meeting for him. The next evening I took him to a barn meeting where he was not disturbed by such fears, but he complained that he had not received the benefit he expected there. I told him that in order to experience the power of a stream he should be in it, and not on the bank – that he should take part in the proceedings.

88   Hebrews 2:3
89   This tract is not included in *Building From The Top.*

The following evening I asked him to pray, which he did very well. Then I called upon him to say a few words to the people. He complied with this request and came back better satisfied, but had not yet worked in the after-meeting.

On the fourth evening he learned by experience how to lead a soul to Christ to receive forgiveness of sins, and the next day he worked with interest as well as energy. He returned home on Saturday rejoicing on the mountain-top, and told his wife that he felt as if he had never been converted before. From this time he began to work in earnest to win souls, and wondered how he could ever have been satisfied to go on so long without manifest result.

He was abused for his efforts of course, and all the more so when he invited me to come over and help him. Now he was not dismayed by opposition, and in his quiet way continued working for several years.

From this place I went to the capital town of Suffolk, Ipswich. Here I had the honour of a church to preach in, and found a dear brother who was counted as black a sheep as myself. Ever since, and up to the present time, the Lord has continued to give me fruit in Ipswich and its neighbourhood.

CHAPTER 32

The New Lodger — 1864

HASSINGHAM WITH ITS PRETTY thatched-roofed church is a small place, and passing by you would think nothing ever happens there. Moreover, you have to go out of the way to pass it at all through narrow lanes bordering on the marshes. Even here some eventful things did occur, for God is no respecter of persons or places. Anywhere, if there is a soul to pray, there is God to answer; and everywhere where the Gospel is preached it is the savour of life unto life, or the savour of death unto death.

At the time of which I am writing, a family in the neighbourhood was severely afflicted with scarlet fever. The children were taken ill one after another. One little one died, and two others [A and M] were so dangerously ill that it was uncertain which would go first. The parents were in great trouble about them, and the more so because they were not sure of their eternal safety. They prayed earnestly that the girls might be saved, if they were not; or if they were, that they might give some testimony to that effect.

At midnight when the parents entered the chamber of [M] the eldest daughter, she said of her own accord, "Oh, mother, I have been thinking that I ought to have told you and father that I am converted. Don't be afraid if I die."

What joy this was to them. The mother eagerly asked her when she was saved.

"Don't you remember that Sunday afternoon when you spoke to me and A in the garden? She is converted too."

This was the other daughter, who was lying ill in the next room. After a time the parents went to A, but finding her asleep they returned to M. It was not long before they saw that she was dying. She was quite aware of the fact, and very happy, rejoicing in the Lord. Thus she departed, leaving good and cheering testimony behind.

Having closed her eyes, the sorrowing yet grateful parents went to watch by the bedside of the other sick one. Presently she awoke, and seeing her mother was there, she said, "Oh, dear mother, I do not know why I never told you that M and I are converted. That Sunday when you spoke to us about Jesus we both found peace. I am not afraid to die. I do so want to go away to heaven."

Her father gently suggested that she should wait the Lord's time.

But she replied, "What if He does not take me now? I do want to go now."

He answered, "You must not be so wilful or impatient about it. I wish you were more submissive to God's will."

She said no more and soon fell asleep again. In an hour or two she woke up with a start, and said, "Oh, mother, what do you think? I have seen M." She had not yet been told that her sister was dead. "I thought I was dying and just going into heaven. The bright gate was open, and who do you think came out of it to meet me? It was M, looking so bright and happy, and dressed in a beautiful white robe with a lovely wreath on her head. She came running up to me, and said, 'Oh, A, I am so sorry. You must go back. You are so wilful, you cannot come yet.'"

This dear child did not die, but recovered from that time and is still pressing on her way to the celestial gate, taking all she can with her. After this the father himself was taken ill, and during his illness, which was very severe, he also had a wonderful vision which had a good and rousing effect upon his soul. The affliction passed, but not without leaving a lasting blessing upon the family.

People used readily to come to Hassingham Church, although the service commenced as early as ten o'clock in the morning. Some of them liked the "Revarand", and some did not care much for him, for they had heard "far better than he," and so on. My object, however, was not to gain their approval, but themselves.

Among others there came a lively, chatty woman who was much occupied all the week with her family, her house and her business. After listening to my preaching for several Sundays she arrived at the conclusion that I intended to "upset everything," and said she could see with half an eye that things were not to go on as they used to be. "No," she added; "if I take his meaning, we must be downright saints all ready for heaven at any moment, or else perish." She thought there should be "moderation in everything, particularly in religion."

One day she surprised us by coming to the afternoon service on Sunday, and more so by attending several meetings on the weekday evenings. I began to hope she would be saved. But to my sorrow she became more and more irregular, even on Sundays, and then ceased coming altogether. She always justified her absence as if her conscience was not easy. This is how people go back, in spite of good impressions and resolutions, if they do not definitely yield themselves to God.

It so happened that while she was in this state of mind a governess was selected for our little school. I went to this woman to ask whether she could accommodate her until I had arranged permanent lodgings. To this she readily assented and went to the station to meet her lodger on the Saturday.

In course of conversation she found out that the new governess was what she called "quite innicent," and "did not know nothing about 'convarsion'."

"You will see," she said. "He'll take and cut you up and turn yer inside out. You'll hear about hell and damnation, and woe betide ye if ye don't give in. You'll have to be converted, right off."

The poor young woman was much frightened at the prospect, for she could not imagine what was to happen or what was to be done to her. She said she had "never heard about conversion for church people."

"It is time ye did then," answered the woman. "Don't ye know that it's impossible for anyone to get to heaven without it, or even to be a Christian without it?"

The governess said she had "been made a Christian when she was baptised, and that she had been confirmed too."

"Oh, you are an innicent!" exclaimed the woman.

"Well," the girl replied, "I do not know of anything more. I am a regular communicant."

"Why, poor child, he'll take and hang yer up over the fire of hell, and make yer cry out and promise to be converted. You'll have to do that, be sure you will."

"Mr Haslam did not look to me a man like that. He was so cheerful and kind. I can scarcely believe all this about him."

"Oh," replied the woman, "you don't know."

What with the strange place and such tremendous horrors awaiting her, the poor schoolmistress did not sleep much that night. In the morning her courage had well nigh failed, and she was disposed to stay away from church.

"What, not go to church!" exclaimed the woman. "Why, the Revarand will be down here after you in a crack, and find me in all this 'ere mess. No, you far better go with good pluck. He can't kill you, ye know. He will expect you at the school at half-past nine."

During the sermon the little heart of the governess began to tremble, yet she could not tell why. There was nothing terrible in the discourse, or in the manner of the preacher. The sermon was about pardon for the sinner through Jesus Christ. The conclusion was a solemn appeal to all present to accept the terms offered, together with a warning to those who neglected to do so. In order to obtain pardon and life, individuals were urged to yield themselves to God, as rebels under sentence of death. It was announced that the subject of justification, as distinct from pardon, though connected with it, would be considered in the afternoon.

The schoolmistress cried very much, and remained a long time on her knees after the sermon. She said that she did not know how she felt. The Gospel plan of salvation was all new to her; she had never heard it before.

She returned to her lodging an hour after time, rejoicing in the forgiveness of her sins. When she arrived, the woman of the house said, "There you are! Did not I tell ye that ye would be converted – turned inside out – upside down – or 'right side up' they call it at the Rectory?"

The woman was much agitated, and the more so when the governess responded, "Whatever they call it, I thank God that I went to church this morning. My sins are pardoned."

"Ha, ha," laughed the woman, "that is what they tell you. I don't belave a word on't. It's all moonshine, my dear. Don't you belave it. I thought you had more sense than that!" Her children were crying, which made her testy and sharp. Hastening the dinner, she said, "It's time you were gone again. The other church is a mile off."

The governess asked her if she would not go too.

"I go? Dear no!" she replied. "I've quite given up going this long time. That Revarand makes me feel so uncomfortable. I don't know what to make of him. I've not yet got over what I heard last."

Thus this woman continued to refuse the Gospel, or even to hear it.

Time passed on till one bright summer Sunday in June we were all assembled in church, when suddenly the heavens were darkened with clouds and a loud clap of thunder announced a storm of no small energy. It lasted for more than an hour, pouring out a deluge of rain in large drops. While the congregation was detained in church we sang hymns, looking out now and then to see whether the clouds were breaking.

As I was standing at the door I heard the step of someone in pattens clamping along.[90] It was our friend coming in her weekday clothes with a large umbrella to fetch her two children. When she re-passed, carrying her two girls in her arms and holding the umbrella over them, I said, "There you are. I wish you cared as much for your soul as you do for the children's clothes."

"Ah, well," she replied, "don't say any more. I'll come next Sunday, that I will."

Two days after this I was called up in haste in the middle of the night to go to a dying person. I went immediately and found it was this same woman, doubled up with pain. She threw herself about with great violence as she writhed in agony. Upon seeing me she evidently was reminded of prayer, and at once began to plead for mercy for her soul. Her prayer was distracted, and what with fear for her soul and groaning

90   Pattens can be either a type of clog, or metal frames
      that fit under shoes or boots to keep them out of the
      mud when walking in the road.

in her bodily distress, she was like one beside herself. It took no less than six women to hold her down. Crying, struggling and praying by turns, she passed away. It was a most awful thing to witness that fight for life, and that unavailing effort to escape. She was dying without hope, and what aggravated her distress was that she knew it. It was a solemn case of refusing God and being refused by Him.

Before sunrise on the Wednesday she was gone, and her poor body laid out for its last resting place. Her face looked so calm and placid that it was difficult to realise the frantic and terrible scene we had witnessed an hour or two before. Neighbours came that day, and said, "She looks so peaceful and happy. Surely she must be in heaven."

When it comes to this touching point, how many there are who side with men rather than with God. They would sooner believe that unconverted people go to heaven than that God's Word is true. Notwithstanding this, her death for the time at least struck a blow to many careless ones, and her funeral was expected to be one of great interest.

Her friends asked me to allow it to take place on Sunday, and one person suggested, "Do not say she is lost. It cannot do any good."

"On the other hand," I replied, "can it do any good to the unsaved to let them suppose that such an open and determined rejecter of the Gospel has gone to heaven?"

At the service I was reminded forcibly of her words, "Don't say any more. I'll be here next Sunday." I told the people of it, and said, "Here she is, to be sure, but it is only her poor body. If her soul could send you a message now, it would be, 'Do not come to this place of torment.'"

There was a little angry feeling at first, but afterwards there came a melting power of the Spirit, and many wept. It is useless to rebel against God, for He willeth not the death of the sinners, but would far rather that they should yield themselves to Him and be saved.[91]

91   See 2 Peter 3:9

CHAPTER 33

A Tedious Sermon Becomes Interesting — 1865

BESIDES JOURNEYS to Lowestoft, Ipswich, Yarmouth and various other places in England, Scotland and Ireland, I went by urgent invitation to Hythe in Kent. The Lord had put it into the heart of a good man there to engage the Town Hall for evangelistic services. He possessed marvellous faculty for organization, and for marshalling forces and people.

My friend had much encouragement, but it was not without opposition and its accompanying unpleasantness. I was in the thick of similar troubles at home, and therefore was able to sympathise with him – and cheer him also.

One summer evening when the windows of the hall were open, not only for air but to give stray listeners in the street an opportunity to hear, we were greatly disturbed by noise. A heavy cart, called in Norfolk by the expressive name *tumbril*, was drawn backwards and forwards slowly over the stones for half an hour in front of the hall. The driver shouted to his horse all the time, especially when he was turning round. It was very distracting, as doubtless it was intended to be, even more so than the organ grinder who had been paid on previous occasions to serenade the meetings, or the brass band either.

I could not help taking encouragement from this interruption. It was so manifestly of the devil that I urged the assembly to bear it patiently, and said, "You may now and then lose a few words of my address, but never mind that. You will surely see great things here for your good, and for the glory of God. Do not fear. The devil knows that a great door is opened, or he would not trouble himself to be such an adversary."

My friend, however, had to struggle single-handed for a long time against these difficulties. The Evangelists only came and went, but my friend had to abide and bear the brunt of the battle. It was hot and sharp every now and then, and came up like a tempest against the wind – that is, from most unexpected quarters.

Times are changed since those days, and the Gospel has more acceptance than it had. I do not suppose, however, that human nature is changed, or that the offence of the Cross has ceased; but it would appear that the devil has changed his tactics. Now, when Gospel preaching is more general and light is spreading, Satan uses other means to hinder its acceptance. He says to many people, "It is quite true, you must be born again; you must be converted or you will be lost; you must be pardoned before you die; there is no repentance or forgiveness in the grave." But he adds, "Do not be troubled, you will not die today; do not hurry – wisely take time to consider – procrastinate – wait to feel something – live in hope of being saved hereafter." Such are a few of his devices, and everyone who is working for souls knows how sadly effective they are.

Here, as in too many places at that time, the Vicar was opposed to the work. Instead of co-operating with it and thanking God for it, he preached against the service in the Town Hall and in every way used his influence to hinder people from attending. My friend was so disheartened by this, and with the false doctrine that was taught, that he was disposed to give up going to church. I thought this a great pity and urged him to continue his attendance at the parish church.

I said, "You will hear several chapters read from the Bible, besides three or four psalms, and some good prayers which were written by holy men many years ago and have been in constant use ever since. My advice to you is go and worship God, and endure patiently what you hear from man. Even this last may turn to profit."

I recommended him to take notes of the sermon, and then compare the statements of the preacher with the words and teaching of Scripture.

He afterwards told me that he was much surprised how quickly the time passed while he took notes, and the otherwise tedious sermon became interesting. This was especially the case when some dogmas were propounded, which were very startling and diametrically opposed to the inspired Word.

One Monday my friend showed me two parallel columns of statements, the Vicar's and St Paul's, which I must say presented a remarkable contrast – the traditions of the Fathers in contradiction to the Bible.

I said, "You should take that to the Vicar, or send it to him. He is an earnest man and never hears anyone but himself, and never sees any side of teaching but his own. It would be a real kindness to show him the other side. I am sure he is an honest man and does not intentionally obscure the truth."

My friend wrote, but I am sorry to say the Vicar did not take the letter in so good part as I had supposed!

The exercise of comparing bad theology with good Scripture teaching is certainly more profitable than complaining of bad sermons. But some of the converts who had neither patience to take notes nor intelligence enough to compare them with the Bible, collected money and came to ask my advice about building a chapel.

"Oh, pray do not," I said somewhat hastily, evidently to their great disappointment, for they thought they were doing a very laudable and self-denying thing and had intended asking me to lay the foundation-stone. "There are churches and chapels enough at present. Fill them first, and work amongst the various congregations. You will do yourselves more good by carrying life to them, than by separating from them."

They were scarcely persuaded, but said they would try. Soon after, I heard that a number of them had joined the Independent Chapel, and being a majority they had voted the old minister out, giving him ten pounds to go. They then called a converted man to preach to them, for the edification of believers and the conversion of sinners. This was a novel idea which I must say had never entered my mind.

From this place I was taken to Sandgate to speak at the Soldiers' Home, where an interesting work had been going on for some years. From Sandgate the work spread to Folkestone. There, as at Hythe, the Town Hall was the scene of continued operations by means of several evangelists.

From thence the work spread on further still to Dover, and even to Walmer, where the Lord made His word to prosper abundantly.

CHAPTER 34

Up Before the Bishop — 1865

MY PARISH OF BUCKENHAM was but a small one. I accepted it in the hope that I might be the more free to do good in the county at large, or rather in the two counties of Norfolk and Suffolk. My hope was not disappointed, for I received letters from all parts inviting me to come and preach the Gospel.

Besides the invitations I also received letters from Bishops and clergy taking me painfully to task. As to these complaints I must say that I never intended or desired to make myself obnoxious to the ecclesiastical powers. For all that, I could not refuse the appeals which were continually sent me. It was not pleasant to be reproved, nor can I say that my heart did not beat with some agitation when I read these letters. Bishops one after another reprimanded me, and sometimes two or more at the same time.

My brethren the clergy were even fiercer in their denunciations, and in less guarded terms gave me the benefit of their thoughts concerning my doings, or misdoings.

One I will mention here, and willingly let the others pass, the more so because times are changed and there is now increasing sympathy with evangelistic effort.

While I was away on my visit to Kent I preached at the Town Hall in Folkestone. The Vicar there would not condescend to write to me, but sent his complaints to the rural Dean. This dignitary consulted a lawyer and with his help, as I suppose, drew up a grave charge against me for intruding into that parish. It was something to the following effect:

"Whereas a person entitled Rev William Haslam, clerk in holy orders, Rector of the Rectory of Buckenham in the county of Norfolk and diocese of Norwich, did in the afternoon of such a day, in such a month, and such a day of the month, enter into the town of Folkestone, and then and there proceeded to the Town Hall of the aforesaid town of Folkestone; and did there, in the presence of witnesses – and they were not a few – deliver a religious address, or lecture, or sermon, without the permission of the Vicar of the parish, in which the said Town Hall is situate," etc.

This paper, in full official character and in due legal phraseology, was forwarded to the Archbishop of Canterbury as diocesan of the parish in which the offence complained of was perpetrated. His Grace enclosed the curious document to me, with a note demanding why I intruded myself into his diocese without his permission. And how dare I preach in another man's parish without his invitation? Upon what authority did I do so?

There was some delay in the delivery of this letter with its great seal, owing to my absence from home. In the meantime a friend of mine in London heard that the Archbishop had "got hold of Mr Haslam, and was about to stop him." He immediately called upon the Earl of Shaftsbury, who promptly took occasion to remind his Grace of the Act of Parliament which legalises such preachings. His lordship was good enough to say that he thought the clergy of the Church of England ought to be as free to preach the Gospel anywhere as other people, if not more so.

In reply to his Grace I acknowledged that I had been to Folkestone more than once, and that the Lord had given blessing to His Word in that place. As to my authority for doing so, I could only plead with all deference that I was constrained by the love of God inside, and by the Word of God outside. I begged to say respectfully yet firmly that I had full liberty to do so according to law.

His Grace sent my letter, together with a complaint, to my Bishop. He immediately summoned me to his presence.

On the appointed day and time I put in my appearance and was asked to take a seat. Then this methodical prelate went to a drawer and took out a large bundle of letters. Proceeding to another drawer, as if the one devoted to my parish was not enough, he took out more letters and deposited the heap on the table in silence.

Looking at me, the Bishop said, "It would appear that you have the care of all the churches!"

I made no reply.

Selecting one letter from the pile, his lordship asked me whether I had been preaching in Kent.

"Yes," I said, "I have, at several places: Hythe and Folkestone among the number."

"Pray, upon what authority did you do this?"

I replied, "I have already answered that question in a letter to the Archbishop."

However, I had to go over the old story of many years: Bishops and clergy could not – or it appeared would not – see that Gospel preaching is not an official or ministerial act. I claimed the liberty to preach the Gospel wherever I was invited. The Bishop asked me how I divested myself so easily of my ministerial character.

"Why, my lord," I replied, "this is one of the easiest things possible. In this county the clergy do not go out shooting and fishing ministerially. The rural Dean himself shot me the other day as I was passing along the road, because some partridges happened to rise. Fortunately they were spent shots and pattered on my waistcoat, but they might have struck my face and put out my eyes!"

His lordship said no more on that subject.

Among other questions the Bishop asked me was whether I had forbidden a young lady to go to confirmation.

"Certainly not," I answered. "I remember once preaching for a clergyman, and after the sermon a lady came into the vestry, and said, 'If your sermon is right, this book is all wrong.'

"I asked 'What is the book?'

"She replied, 'It is one upon Confirmation.'

"I then put the question to her whether she wished to be confirmed. She answered in the affirmative. I said, 'Are you going to be confirmed in your sins, or in the forgiveness of your sins?'"

The Bishop interrupted me somewhat sharply, and said, "Why did you say that?"

"Because," I replied, "that you, as the Bishop, present the candidates for confirmation to God as persons who have received forgiveness of their sins."

Then that subject dropped. For nearly two hours I was closeted with his lordship, and must say that I was grieved and disappointed with the result of my interview. I should have counted it an honour to be browbeaten by some of the Bishops, but under this good prelate I felt discouraged and hurt in mind that he did not understand me better; that such as he, for the sake of legal and ecclesiastical technicalities, should take part with some unconverted men who neglected their parishes and the souls of their people. It was as if parish boundaries were of more consequence than the salvation of souls. He was not responsible for my going about, and he might have been glad that the Gospel was taken into parishes where it was never preached; and more particularly where sacramental errors were taught in place of spiritual truth.

From many of my brethren the clergy I did not expect much, and I must say received less. There were, however, honourable exceptions. Some entirely sympathised with the work, and were as fearless and free as I was about preaching. Others, within judicious and prudent bounds, rejoiced in spiritual work.

One brother wrote to say, "Thank God for directing your steps to my parish. May God's blessing come with you. Kindly honour me by staying in my house for the night."

Another wrote, "I hear you are coming to my parish. As you are a priest of God, I cannot bear the thought that you should preach anywhere but in God's house. We will defer Evensong to any hour you name, and then you shall preach in the pulpit of the parish church."

Dear well-meaning man, I hope that he obtained a blessing to his soul, but it was hard, dead work to preach in that church, for most effectually did the ceremonials strangle evangelistic effort.

These instances were by no means the rule, but rather the exception. Preaching in other men's parishes without their leave was a thing not to be tolerated, even though souls were perishing. I received rude letters calling me "ungentlemanly", letters threatening me with the terrors of the Bishop, and letters of remonstrance. These things were hard to bear, but I must confess that I would rather have had them over and over again than no work for God, and no souls saved. Woe was me if I did not preach the Gospel, and woe was me if I did!

As years advanced it was found that the prejudice and fear entertained as to the effect of my preachings were groundless. It was observed that the dreaded gatherings stirred up the people beneficially, and in many cases brought them to church more frequently. An influential clergyman stated at a clerical meeting that as far as he knew or could ascertain, congregations had been doubled and communicants increased. This being the case, the animosity which had prevailed against me began to melt away, and I was invited to come and preach – even by clergymen, in churches!

CHAPTER 35

Old-World Commentaries — 1864/71

THE REVIVING and quickening influence of the Holy Spirit was not by any means confined to the working classes. It included under its blessing many persons in the higher ranks of society. For such as these we devised meetings for Bible-readings. Here we sat together at the feet of Jesus, to learn of Him by anyone through whom He pleased to speak. Besides this we sang hymns, and as a clergyman observed to his amazement, we "actually knelt down on the drawing-room carpet, and prayed extempore prayers."

Sir Thomas and Lady Beauchamp were pleased to open their rooms at Langley Hall, and our friends at Burlingham House in the opposite direction did the same. These two houses, with ours, made three centres of operation at which we were enabled week by week to gather believers and their friends. I had the advantage of a railway station near mine, which enabled me to invite people from Norwich, Yarmouth and other places along the line. My wealthier friends had a numerous acquaintance of carriage people who thought nothing of driving six or even eight miles to these gatherings.

Some of the neighbouring clergymen joined us with the laudable intention of putting us right, and brought their old-world [Bible] commentaries. These books used to be esteemed when they themselves were young. We were not sorry to have the opportunity of testing them by the Word of God. Our meetings were effectual, not only for enlightening and encouraging us, but also for brushing off cobwebs of mistakes and false impressions obtained from traditional teaching. We began for obvious reasons by considering elementary truths.

For instance, at an early occasion we took for our subject, "The Forgiveness of Sins." After a short exposition of a passage of Scripture we opened the meeting for questions or conversation. By some it was counted great presumption to say our sins are pardoned. By others it was contended that it would be far greater presumption to doubt the efficacy of the Blood of the Lamb of God, which had been shed once for all for the remission of sins.[92]

In the year 1864, after the first winter's work in the barn at Buckenham – dignified by the name of Haslam's Cathedral – I invited those who professed to have received blessing to come for tickets, that we might have a tea-meeting on Whit Monday. Upwards of six hundred and seventy persons applied. Though all this number could not come to tea, they promised to attend the meeting and bring others with them.

It happened to be a bright and warm summer afternoon, so we had the tables spread in the orchard where the apple blossom was in full bloom. The barn in its whole length was before us as a boundary of the orchard. Upon this I had a long strip of calico extended, with the words, *What Hath God Wrought* written upon it in large letters. After tea, bidding the guests a hearty welcome in the name of the Lord, I said I would call their attention to those words, first as a question.

I asked the people to testify individually as to the blessing he or she had received. One after another then stood up, and in a few words bore witness of salvation. The first hour thus quickly and rapidly passed away. By this time, other guests having arrived, we arranged ourselves for the general meeting.

After a hymn and prayer I took the same words as an exclamation, *What Hath God Wrought!* Our hearts were very full, and with much joy we thanked God again and again. I said I had come there about eight months before, almost alone, and now behold what the Lord has done in these few months! We had indeed something to praise God for. Here

92   See Matthew 26:28 and Revelation 7:14—and of course Exodus 12: 21-23.

was a large and visible result of the Gospel preachings, which had been maintained under many difficulties. Before we separated that evening it came to my mind to invite all present to come again on the Whit Monday of the following year.

Whit Monday gathering at Buckenham, redrawn
from an original engraving in *Yet Not I*.

"Come," I said, "and meet others whom the Lord may give us between this time and then."

We met again the next year under even happier circumstances, and so continued our gatherings for eight successive years until I left the neighbourhood. I may add that the Lord was pleased to give us fine weather upon every occasion. Sometimes it rained the day before, sometimes the day after, and sometimes even before and after, but on the Whit Monday itself we had no rain. On one occasion the clouds were threatening and not a few feared that we should have a downpour, but it did not come. One woman thought she felt a drop of rain and put up her umbrella, when a brother from the wagon platform cried out, "Sister, where is your faith?" Instantly the umbrella disappeared amidst loud laughter. She, as well as the rest of the company numbering at that time more than fifteen hundred persons, remained dry. It did rain in torrents that night, but not till all the people had gone home.

Year by year increasing hundreds came to tea and to the general meeting afterwards. One Whit Monday, as I was speaking about the day of Pentecost as described in the second chapter of the Act, I remarked that the Holy Ghost came upon the people who were assembled with one accord in one place; that they were all filled with the Holy Ghost, and began to speak as the Spirit gave them utterance; that the multitude were amazed and in doubt, saying one to another, "What meaneth this?" Others mocking, said, "These men are full of new wine," and others were pricked in their hearts, and said to Peter and the rest of the Apostles, "Men and brethren, what shall we do?"

I said, "The Holy Ghost is not changed. He can fall on us and fill us now."

While I was yet speaking, as if by a preconcerted signal – which of course had not been made – as least fifty or sixty persons fell simultaneously to the ground, and perhaps three times that number praised God with loud voices. One did not catch it from another, but all were under the influence of the same Spirit. From the platform the scene was one of extraordinary confusion.

From time to time, one after another, those who had been seeking mercy found it and began to rejoice. This made others who had not found peace more terribly in earnest. Thus we continued for two hours till it was time to go to the trains. Those who were still anxious were led between two persons, and in most cases they were crying as they went along. The trains being late we continued our meeting at the station.

If I could have produced this wonderful result, as I was subsequently charged with doing, I should certainly have done so and on a much larger scale in succeeding years. Indeed, I do not think I should have waited twelve months. It pleased the Lord on that occasion to give abundant blessing in this remarkable manner, but on subsequent occasions it pleased Him to work in other ways. We had various manifestations of Divine Power and Presence which were equally reassuring, though not so openly blest.

About eight years after my appointment to Buckenham, while preparing for the Whit Monday gathering of 1871, it came to my mind that we were to move away from Norfolk; but I had no idea whither, or under what circumstances. I had nevertheless a vivid impression that this was to be the last time of meeting. I could only say, "Yes, Lord," and leave myself in His hand.

We had lived in this pleasant home longer than in any other place since we left Baldhu in 1855. I could not help feeling some regret, but this was only a cry of nature to which I did not consent.

A few days after this I received a note from Lord and Lady Howe, with an invitation for me to visit them at Gopsal, in Leicestershire. I went there and had services and meetings in the churches and villages about.

During my stay his lordship said, "You ought to have a church without a parish to it. I have one in London, and when it is vacant you shall have it."

I returned home from this visit with a pretty clear idea that we were to move away from Buckenham that year. However, I did not mention it to anyone, but proceeded with the arrangements for our annual gathering. It so happened that a much larger number of persons than usual notified their intention to be present.

We had a fine sunny day and plenty of fruit blossoms and flowers to adorn the scene, together with many flags. Besides these things we had the unexpected pleasure of welcoming several distinguished friends: Lord and Lady Kintore; Lady Howe; Sir Thomas and Lady Beauchamp; Mr Dening, and his wife who was none other than our dear young friend Geraldine Hooper; Mr Brownlow North who was the special speaker of the occasion, and many others.

The singing and addresses were more hearty and earnest than ever. Mr Dening spoke briefly, and then modestly made way for his wife Geraldine. He designated her as "the express" while he himself was as an ordinary train. After a most telling and powerful word from this gifted lady, Mr Brownlow North stood up in his heavy fur coat as if it were the depth of winter. His address was good, and worthy of himself. Many precious souls date their blessing from that eventful day.

It was said, "All this excitement will cease when Haslam is gone." But thank God I am happy to say the work has survived. In many places it has gone on with unabated zeal, and my successor in the Rectory of Buckenham is one who is a faithful witness for the truth.[93]

93   These words were written in 1882, eleven years later.

CHAPTER 36

Little Missenden — 1871/72

DURING THE SUMMER of 1871 I accepted Lord Howe's offer of Curzon Chapel in Mayfair, and my successor at Buckenham was duly appointed. There being some delay about institution to the church in London, his lordship kindly gave me the living of Little Missenden, a small country parish in Buckinghamshire.

On looking over the Vicarage I found that it was but a cottage which could not possibly contain my family. His lordship desired me to enlarge it at his expense, so I commenced operations without delay. I reversed the house, making the back the front and the front the back. By rearranging the rooms, adding new ones, and strengthening the whole with a strong veranda, the little Vicarage was soon transformed into a comfortable house.

The whole appearance of the place was so altered in a short time that Lord and Lady Howe could not imagine what we had done to it. There was a huge elm near the house which not only overshadowed it, but made it very damp and unhealthy. It was quite a sight to see the fall of this majestic tree.

While the builder was at hand I took him into the church which was close by, to see what we could do to improve it. It was a quaint old building. Some parts were very ancient and rude in their Saxon antiquity, and other parts more rude still with what were modern improvements. The pulpit, with its capacious reading-desk below, was an unsightly erection and a great deal too large for the place.

We fell to work at once to demolish the whole structure. To our surprise we found that the props under the pulpit were completely eaten away with dry rot. How it stood I do not know, for with a very little shake it fell to the ground with its own weight. By the following Sunday a strong and more suitable pulpit was set up, and a convenient prayer-desk. The church was thoroughly cleaned out. Nearly a cartload of rubbish was taken away from the tower, and dry sticks in abundance from the crows' nests in the belfry.

Externally the church was a picturesque edifice, with a little turreted tower prettily situated. Somehow I could not settle there, for my prayers were dry and my hopes accordingly very small. Nevertheless I worked on, hoping against hope. I know it is not by might or by power that God's work is to be done, but by His Spirit only. Therefore, in simple dependence I trusted Him to lead me in a way that I knew not.

Little Missenden Church today.

During my ministry I laboured to rouse up the drowsy people, and endeavoured to build up those who had been quickened. Some of the neighbours thought my preaching was "too exciting."

"Exciting!" I cried. "I only wish I could see a little excitement, or any sign of awakening amongst the congregation!"

I have, however, gone before my story and put second things first. Before I commenced the alterations at the Vicarage and the improvements in the church, I made it my business to inquire into the spiritual condition of the people. In order to do this I went from house to house, beginning with the cottages near the church. I first endeavoured to ascertain the names of the occupants, the number of the family, whether they went to church or chapel – or neither – and last but not least I asked, "Are you converted?"

The answers I received to this last question would make one smile, but for the solemn consequences of the unconverted state. Some had been christened, some registered, some confirmed, many vaccinated – but whatever conversion could be they did not know. At the Baptist chapel they heard about Election, and at the church they had heard about Baptismal Regeneration, but this new Vicar meant something else.

After a whole day's trudge I at last came to a little shop where the name of the occupant[94] was over the door. I wrote that down, and entering in, said, "I know your name; now let me ask you, Do you go to church?"

"Yes."

"Are you a communicant?"

"Yes."

"Are you converted?"

She made no reply.

I continued, "People here do not appear to know anything about conversion. Do you?"

Still she did not speak.

"What do you say? Are you converted?"

"I dare not say I am not."

94   Haslam does not give the woman's name
     immediately, and when he does he puts it in quotes
     as "Lydia". So this may not be her real name, but a
     light-hearted reference to a New Testament vendor –
     "Lydia, a seller of purple." Acts 16:14.

"Very well, thank God for that. Suppose I say you are. I will put C against your name. Now, can you tell me anything about it? How were you converted?"

"I never told anyone in my life."

"Then it is time you did. I should like to hear your history."

She said, "When I was a little girl there came to the opposite house a man who preached on Sunday afternoons. Whatever his subject was, he always said one thing: 'Whether you are a Churchman or Dissenter, Christ is the door by which you must enter.' He made us understand that we must enter in at the door to be saved, or else we should be lost for ever."

Lydia continued, "Shortly after this time I was taken ill with a fever. My illness was so dangerous that the doctor thought I should die. One evening I overheard him say to my mother, 'Do not be surprised if the child dies in the night. She is very bad.'

"This frightened me so much that I cried to the Lord to take me inside the door and save my soul. All at once while I was praying I felt sure that my sins were pardoned and my soul saved. At three o'clock in the morning I was so happy that I called my mother. I said, 'O mother, what do you think? Jesus has pardoned my sins and saved my soul. I am not afraid to die now.'"

The poor woman began to cry and bade her be quiet and go to sleep again. In the morning the doctor came to see her. He shook his head saying, "She is quite delirious, poor thing. Out of her mind. She will not live much longer."

The Vicar was then sent for because her mother thought her end was so near. He came, and when he heard the child say her sins were pardoned and her soul saved, he too thought she was out of her mind, and recommended a wet towel to be applied to her head immediately.

She did not die, nor go out of her mind, but remained happy and recovered from her illness. Not meeting with sympathy in this experience she kept it to herself, and in course of time her happy feelings faded away. For fifty years she had not told anyone of her conversion. No wonder she was dejected and often felt unhappy.

While she was speaking to me I observed her face lighting up with animation. She declared that once more she was happy. Bearing this testimony was like a new conversion to her, and this time she determined to let everyone know what the Lord had done for her soul. She had many opportunities of telling her story to the various customers who frequented her shop.

She had a very conspicuous advertisement in her shop, which attracted attention directly you entered. It was printed in red, blue, green and gold letters, gorgeously framed and glazed. It announced that she was "sole agent" in that part of the country for Messrs Huntley & Palmer. She did not sit down and cry because no one else sold biscuits for that great firm. On the contrary, she counted it a privilege that everyone who wanted them must come to her. I have often quoted this old lady when people have told me that they had no privileges, that they stood alone in their parish. Sole agents for Christ should let their light shine, and all the brighter if the place is dark.

At Christmas time we had a public tea. At the meeting afterwards I told the people that I had been preaching to them for many months, and now it was their turn to speak to me and tell what the Lord had done for them during that time.

Our friend "Lydia" of the shop spoke well. She said that as far as she knew she had been "sole agent" for the Lord in that village for many years, but had never given her testimony before, and she was thankful for the opportunity. I was also thankful to add that she was no longer a sole witness for God, as there were others who could tell of the Lord's goodness to them – if they would. Several persons did so, and gave clear testimony of their salvation.

Our church services were well attended, but some of the leading people in the place did not sympathise with me or my efforts. Consequently, the poorer people did not listen with as much interest as they might have done. In spite of this drawback we had cases of conversion now and then, and the Lord did not leave me without encouragement.

There was one sick man in the village who was more like a corpse than any living person I have ever seen. He was blind, speechless and so paralysed as to be unable to move either hand or foot. He had been in this condition for nine years. Though he could not speak or see, yet he could hear and understand what was said to him. This avenue to his soul being open, I told him of God's love in giving His Son to die for him, and of salvation through the blood of Jesus by the power of the Holy Spirit. I believe that poor man was saved. His wife, who interpreted his signs, assured me of the change in his soul.

If I had come to Little Missenden for the salvation of this one poor sufferer alone, it was worth the coming.

Very different was another case I will mention: that of a young man who was full of life and vigour. He was leading a useless and aimless life, riding about the place and smoking all day long. He lounged into church sometimes in the afternoons. He may have done so regularly, but if so I had not observed or noticed him. One Monday morning he came to my study, and throwing his hat carelessly down took a seat. With a long, deep sigh, he said, "I am very miserable."

I asked, "What is it about? What can I do for you?"

He said, "I don't know. You seem to know all about me. I cannot guess who has informed you. I would give a good deal to find out. Some of the things you mentioned happened years ago, and some only lately."

I said, "God knows all about you. He tells me what to say."

"How you must despise me! You might just as well have called out my name in church yesterday, for everyone seemed to know who you meant. Some even turned round and looked at me while you were speaking."

"Now," I said, "I think it is time for us to go to business. My instructions are to open your eyes, to turn you from darkness to light, and to bring you from the power of Satan to God – that you may receive forgiveness of sins. When a man's eyes are opened he sees and knows that he is lost, and that there is nothing between him and hell. If you were to die as you are, where would you go?"

"Ah," he replied, "I know only too well. I have known this for nearly three weeks."

"Why did you not come to me before?"

"I have been to your gate three or four times, but could not sum up courage to come in. I thought it would be so foolish to tell you my fears. You would think I had committed murder, or gone out of my mind. I have prayed, and read the Bible, but it makes me feel worse and worse. I have been trying to live a better life, and this does not satisfy me. On Sunday I heard what you said about the house that was built on sand."

I interrupted him, saying, "Do you understand now about building on the Rock?"

"Yes," he said with a smile; "I think I see that instead of doing my best, I ought to rest on the finished work of Christ."

"Have you done this?"

"I have tried, but do not feel any better."

"Waiting to feel," I said, "is a device of the devil to keep you from salvation. It is surprising how he tries everyone with that device, and hinders many. If you believe that Christ died for you, you should thank Him for it."

"How can I thank Him, if I do not feel saved? "

"My dear man," I said, "I do not want you to thank Him for what you feel, but for what He did. Did He die for you, or did He not? If He did, then thank Him. Tell Him, if you like, how unworthy you are to do so. But thank Him nevertheless."

He muttered, "He will see what a hypocrite I am, and send me away."

"No," I replied, "a hypocrite is a person who thanks when he does not mean it; but you mean it, and yet do not give thanks. Thank Him as well as you can, till you can thank Him better. The wall is salvation, but the gate is praise. Praying is like knocking at a door, and thanking God is like going in when it is opened. Come, let us thank Him for His love in giving His Son to die for you."

As we did so, the young man looked up and said, "I feel better."

"Oh, never mind your feelings," I replied. "Thank and praise God. Say, 'Glory be to God, Jesus died for me.'"

Soon he came into joy and liberty, and exclaimed, "It is wonderful, wonderful! I am saved! I am sure I am!"

After this we took a walk together; and as we mounted the high ground he looked back into the valley where stood the church and vicarage. "Ah," he said, "I little knew why I was brought here. I thought it the dullest place in creation. Now I thank God for directing my steps thither."

This gentleman made it his business to visit the cottages, and talk to the people about their souls. My short sojourn in this place was not for nought, though I only went there till the church in London was vacant.

CHAPTER 37

A Madman in Mayfair — 1872

WHEN I HAD BEEN at Little Missenden about twelve months I received a letter from Earl Howe to say that Curzon Chapel in London would be vacant at Michaelmas, and in the course of October 1872 I commenced my ministrations there. It was a day to be remembered, and one which made a lasting impression in my memory. There were fifty to sixty people present, in a church which could accommodate a thousand. Some of this number were personal friends who had come that morning to welcome me to London. Indeed, I needed all the welcome – and a good deal of cheer.

After the service, a lady and gentleman dressed in deep mourning came into the vestry and thanked me for my sermon. Then the lady told me that her late daughter had received blessing under my preaching in Paris,[95] and just before her death this daughter had made the mother promise that she would hear Mr Haslam as soon as she had the opportunity. She and her son-in-law, the husband of the deceased daughter, had accordingly come to hear me on this the first day of my ministry.

---

95 This is Haslam's only mention of Paris in the two books abridged here. In the *Sword and Trowel* dated June 1888, page 294, the famous Baptist preacher CH Spurgeon recalls "rides" with Haslam in Menton in the south of France. Spurgeon honeymooned there in 1856 and took many breaks in Menton from 1871 onwards, dying there in 1892. Haslam may have combined his visit(s) to Menton with a preaching break in Paris either connected with Geraldine Hooper who was born there, or with the unnamed person in Paris who released him of a debt of 300 pounds when at Baldhu.

I was interested in these persons, without knowing who they were. After a few questions, I said, "I suppose your dear daughter did not intend you merely to be hearers of the Word, but doers?"

Neither of them made a reply.

I continued, "Perhaps you are both believers in the Lord Jesus?"

The lady hesitated. Perhaps like too many she had never before been asked a direct question on the subject of her soul's salvation. After a few words of explanation about the character of living faith I prayed with them. They thanked me warmly and went away, though not for long. In the afternoon they came again to the church, and in the course of the week took four or five pews for themselves and their household. They remained with me to the last.

Curzon Chapel, Mayfair, redrawn from an
original engraving. The whole Chapel was built of brick.

The same good effect and result was by no means produced on another personage who had been accustomed to "sit in that chapel." He had been as one of the pillars of it, and his daughter took much interest in the singing. He was very much disturbed by the doctrine he heard, and did not come again that day.

The following Sunday morning he put in an appearance as usual. This time he was even more disturbed and went away with the determination to leave the church, which he did. Not content with going himself and taking away his family, he influenced six other personages to resign their pews. Shortly afterwards he was observed by some friends of his at another church. They were surprised, for he had often urged them to attend Curzon Chapel. They desired to know why he had left.

"Oh," he replied, "there is a madman there now. I cannot listen to him. I heard him for two Sundays and have had enough of it. He is quite mad. He says his sins are pardoned!"

His friends, not being satisfied with the ministry they were attending, and having their curiosity sufficiently aroused, ventured to Curzon Chapel the very next Sunday. It happened they agreed with this madman so fully that they determined to leave the other church and settle in this one. One after another they in like manner became "mad": the father, mother, sons and daughters. They remain a consistent and happy family, rejoicing in the Lord and losing no opportunity of doing good.

A few Sundays after, another family of position and influence found their way to Curzon Chapel. There, I believe, the Lord blessed them. They also remained to the last, and were a great help to me in many ways. The younger members of these two families took a room near the church, for the benefit of some of the neglected hundreds who lived in the back streets of this wealthy neighbourhood. In this room they convened meetings for singing and speaking, and were much encouraged in their efforts.

These tokens of blessing were no small support to me in the beginning of my ministry, for which I was deeply grateful. Still, for all this, I was very cheerless and unsatisfied. It was a desolate time of year too in Mayfair. The streets were silent and empty, and the days getting darker and shorter, as well as damp and foggy. The great houses were shut up. I was informed that if any of the owners were at home they lived in the back parts, for fear it should be supposed they were so unfashionable as to be in town at such a time. Housekeepers and housemaids were for the most part in sole possession of the mansions which looked so lonely with shutters shut and blinds drawn down.

I struggled on as well as I could till after Christmas, when I began to think of improving the appearance of the Chapel. There was indeed room for some improvement. I cannot well describe the general dingy appearance of this place of worship. The pews were high, and stained with a very dark colour – as were also the heavy gallery, the pulpit and the reading-desk.

Lord Howe, who manifested a lively interest in the matter, took me to see St George's Church, Hanover Square, where the pews had been cut down. He desired that those at Curzon Chapel might be treated in the same way, and undertook to bear the expense.

The carpenters were soon set to work to lower the high pews, and while they were thus employed, painters and gilders were busy painting and decorating the galleries in a lighter colour. On examining the old pulpit, which had been set up when the church was built in Queen Anne's time, we found it was made of oak with inlaid panels. Instead of painting it, we had it scraped and varnished. Before the middle of February the church presented a very different appearance, and was as attractive now as it had been dismal before.

In February the Houses of Parliament are opened and the members come to town, bringing many others with them. We were in readiness to receive such of the great folks among them as belonged to our congregation.

Interior of Curzon Chapel, Mayfair,
redrawn from a photograph dated 1900 in
the Westminster City Archives..

Some discovered that eleven o'clock was too early to begin the service, though I had made no alteration. To please them I changed the time to half-past eleven.

Then came a great lord, who said, "You give us a very bad character before the public. It would appear as if we were all late on Sunday mornings. I breakfast at eight o'clock and much prefer the service at eleven."

As this lord was a great man and one who had always sat in this church, and his father before him, we deferred to him and again reverted to the original time which was really more convenient.

Then the service was too long. Would I omit the Litany and have it in the afternoon? This was a reasonable request, to which I complied. Then I received a message to say that Lady So-and-so and her sister, who had worshipped in Curzon Chapel all their lives without finding any fault, were obliged to read the Litany at home to themselves. "It was a great grievance! Intolerable! They must go elsewhere!"

At last we came to the real cause of all these troubles – the sermons. They were "so exciting," – I only wish they had been – they were "too personal," "too simple," "too long," and so on.

One day a nobleman called to have his name taken off the book, and give up his pew. The clerk in attendance asked whether he wished to take sittings. "Oh dear, no," he replied; "the people are all leaving, are they not?"

"Not at all, sir," said the clerk. "Some are going, but others are coming. The fact is, sir, we are going to work in earnest now, and must clear out the rubbish."

The nobleman laughed exceedingly, and said, "Oh then, take me out; I am rubbish."

The clerk looked at the number of his pew, and seeing his name and who he was, said, "Oh no, my lord, I did not mean you. I cannot take your lordship's name off. You are not rubbish."

He was amused, and consented to let his name remain. What is more he came to church and ultimately received blessing.

Notwithstanding this, and some other exceptions, certainly the coronets were making off one by one. People were expected to take a side either for God or the world. If the latter, they were told it was all the heaven they would ever have. The warning was given plainly enough, and was evidently well understood.

One gentleman left because his daughters declared they "could not bear that man." The daughter of another gentleman was not permitted to come, because her father did not approve of my teaching. I look back upon this time and think it was much honour to have been so estimated of men, though I feel that I did not speak half so clearly as I should have done. It was a mistake, for I tried in my wisdom to do something with my congregation instead of wholly trusting God.

I could not resist going after some of my runaways to see the places and hear the persons of their choice. Some went to high church, more to broad church, but most to the so-called evangelical or low. In the first we heard nothing but the theology of "doing". You were to do this, observe that and abstain from the other. Prayer was recommended, as if religion and devotion consisted in saying prayers so many times a day. Blind Bartimaeus prayed by the wayside because he was blind. But when according to his faith he received eyesight, he followed Jesus, glorifying God. This is the character of Christian life. A Christian is not a begging, but a praising soul.

As to the broad churchman, he made some startling statements which certainly kept us awake wondering what was coming next. "The Bible is not inspired." "It is not a book to be relied upon." "There are many assertions in it which modern science has proved to be false." "Nothing should be believed which is not understood."

This was indeed bringing down the wisdom of God to the mind of man, instead of bringing up the mind of man to the wisdom of God. The fact is, we must believe the Word of God before we can understand it. We must do His will before we can know His doctrine.

As to the low or evangelical preacher, he was very wordy and equally dead. He pleased his hearers and they pleased him – though they remained unconverted. There was a great deal of the word of the Spirit, but nothing about the work. His congregation might truthfully say, "We have not so much as heard whether there be any Holy Ghost!"[96]

96   Acts 19:2

CHAPTER 38

Moody and Sankey — 1873/75

I BEGAN MY MINISTRATION at Curzon Chapel in the midst of gloom, fog and damp – as to the atmosphere outside – and in dreariness and desolation with regard to the congregation inside. In spite of these obstacles and others I have mentioned, such as the withdrawal of old seat holders, the Lord gave me His blessing together with His presence. Some were gathering round me who appreciated the Gospel message which I delivered week by week, and their number was increasing.

In due course the spring advanced. The days became brighter and longer, and the mansions which had been closed all the winter were once more opened. The neighbourhood of Mayfair which had been so lonely, now presented a more lively appearance, but I cannot say we had as yet a corresponding reviving at Curzon Chapel.

After Easter it was even more manifest that this part of London was filling. The whole place was alive and in a state of excitement and whirl – pretty well, I thought, for people who profess to "hate excitement." This whirl and rush continued increasing as the season advanced, all day and all night, often more in the night than in the day. This kept up a continual furore in the place. The contrast between the season and the time before the season was as great as that between the blaze of summer and the depth of winter.

And then the long-expected London season was over and I had scarcely said half my say. A fashionable church, as they call it, is as great a sham as the fashionable world, if not a greater, and far more trying. The fact is, the people who come up to London at this time really live and exercise their influence in other places. Their time and thoughts are thus fully occupied, and too often their minds are quite distracted with the multiplicity of their engagements.

What had I been sent here for? I had been among the poorest and most degraded in Bath, now I had come to the neighbourhood of the greatest and richest people in the world. The one were eager to get money, ever so little of it – the other to spend it, ever so much, sometimes to squander more than they had. As far as their souls were concerned, or eternity, these were matters of no consideration, although there were of course exceptions in both places.

There was some talk of a Mission in London, to which five hundred Missioners were to be invited. I thought this would do very well, but unhappily for me it was fixed to take place early in February. However, it was better than nothing, and I availed myself as much as possible of the opportunity, determining besides to have a proper Mission at my church in "the season".

By way of preparation for the forthcoming effort, the Friday previous to its commencement was set apart for intercession and instruction on Mission work. The clergy and their Missioners were invited to meet at St Paul's Cathedral that day, and I was asked with a few others to address them. The subject entrusted to me was Faith, and it was arranged that I should preach immediately after the regular afternoon service.

On my arrival at the Cathedral I saw many of the clergy walking about in cassock and girdle; some with birettas and some with capes. They appeared to be very pleased with themselves and the Catholic or Romish appearance they presented. Doubtless they desired to look like real sacrificing priests, though they were ministers of a Church which has repudiated such priests, with their sacrifices and altars too.

Obviously these gentlemen had it in their hearts to utilize the London Mission for promoting the Catholic revival, and by its means to recommend confession and absolution as necessary to salvation. I, on the other hand, regarded the Mission as an opportunity given by God for reviving the real spiritual work of the Reformation – an opportunity for making our Church a more living protest against the Christ-denying legality of the Romish communion.

I thought to myself, "You shall hear something about this when I am up in that pulpit!"

It was not a pleasant prospect, nor was it a cheerful time when it came. However, at the proper moment I found myself sailing along in the white-robed procession from the vestry, and was conducted to the great pulpit in the nave with all due honour.

I gave out the hymn which was well sung, and then repeated some collects in which I emphatically prayed for the true Catholic Church, and all who professed and called themselves Christians, that they might be led into the way of truth. After another hymn I announced my text, which I took from Hebrews 11:1, "Now faith is the substance of things hoped for, the evidence of things not seen."

I commenced by saying that without faith it is impossible to please God. Then, referring to the words of the previous preacher, I said, "I quite agree with what we have just heard – that unless we have been reconciled to God ourselves, we cannot properly or effectually be ministers of reconciliation to others. We should be witnesses, as well as ministers, of God's truth."

I reminded them that our martyrs sealed their testimony with their blood. Why were our Reformers burnt? Why did Ridley, the Bishop of this Cathedral, suffer martyrdom? Was it not because he testified that salvation is by simple faith – that is, by direct and personal transaction with God, without the intervention of priest or sacrament? Was it not because he declared boldly that Christ is not on the Romish altar, but in the believer's heart?

At this point a man in a cassock prostrated himself before the "high altar" as he would call it. Not a few went down on their knees, and putting their hands together prayed of their charity, as I suppose, for the soul of the heretic in the pulpit. At the same time at least fifty or sixty others rose up from their seats and walked away – not very noiselessly – into the transept beyond hearing. The sounds reverberated in the dome a long way overhead so that I was obliged to wait till silence was restored before I could proceed with my instruction.

Then I repeated what I had just been saying, and continued my address. When the time was up I gave out a hymn, and then closed with an extempore prayer and the benediction. Descending from the pulpit I was conducted to the vestry in due form.

On arriving there, the ground was strewn with surplices, hoods and stoles thrown down in haste. The vergers regarded me with amazement, as if I were some uncouth monster from the country. Probably they had never had such a scene in that orderly place before. I came forth into the crowd alone and had to bear the gaze of many, and the contemptuous looks of not a few.

One high churchman in costume came up to me, and said, "I respect you for faithfulness to your views, but I do not agree with them."

I longed to show him that his Church doctrine in many cases is not Bible truth, but he was not disposed to talk. [97]

One Evangelical clergyman, a friend of mine, looked dissatisfied. I said to him, "Well, did it do?"

"Do!" he rejoined. "It has done for you. You will never be asked to preach here any more!"

"That may be," I replied; "but I would not have lost this opportunity for anything."

Another friend who happened to be present greeted me cordially and thanked the Lord for my testimony. There were others also who congratulated me.

The London Mission proceeded as was arranged, and I took my part in it, preaching at three different churches.

I have reason to think that my congregation at Curzon Chapel benefited, though we had no regular mission there at this time. Previous to this I used to be regarded as a singular man and unlike anyone else. Now, missions were so openly

---

97   There are more details of this service in *Yet Not I*
     which are further developed in a paper subsequently
     published by Haslam, *Notes of an Address on Faith at
     St Paul's Cathedral, February 6 1874*, London, Morgan
     and Scott.

recognised and conversions so commonly spoken about that my hearers were reassured.

Knowing what to expect the following year, I thought I would devise something novel and attractive in the way of special services. By this means I hoped to reach some of the worldly ones, for I did not believe in their alleged dislike of excitement.

As the season of 1874 advanced I called attention to the subject of a coming Mission I had planned for June. Prayer was asked, preparation made and notices given, so that expectation was stirred. I invited my friend Rev WHMH Aitken[98] to conduct the Mission. He was not so well known then as he is now, nor were such efforts as well understood. Notwithstanding, it pleased God to send us a large congregation the first Sunday. We had a royal duke, and noblemen of every degree with their families and servants. On one occasion Mr Disraeli and Mr Gladstone were present, though at different ends of the church.

The next season Mr Aitken returned and preached with unabated earnestness and zeal. By this time the congregation was more conversant with spiritual subjects, and consequently the results were greater. Another circumstance, too, which greatly helped us to arrive at this very desirable state was the visit of two American evangelists to the West End.

Messrs Moody and Sankey who had been working in the provinces during the winter months came to London in the early spring. During the season of 1875 they held meetings in the Opera House at the Haymarket. On their arrival I commended them, and announced from my pulpit that if any of the congregation required tickets I should have much pleasure in procuring the same for them. The vestry was besieged, and the messages and letters I received kept me busy for several weeks. I distributed more than three hundred cards of admission weekly, chiefly for the reserved seats.

98   William Hay Aitken, the son of Rev Robert Aitken
      who had earlier helped Haslam in Cornwall. (See
      page 50ff)

I had the satisfaction of seeing many of my people, and others with them, regular in their attendance at these meetings. Their eagerness to come again and again, and the rapt attention with which they followed the speaker, showed that God was speaking to them.

One nobleman remarked to another in the house, "I have been to hear that fellow Moody."

"Indeed," was the reply, "how do you like him?"

"Oh, very well, very well. What is more, I am reconciled to Haslam now. I understand him better. I believe the man means well. I mean to stick to him."

By one means and another it pleased God to give me a hearing in Mayfair; and He also gave blessing with His Word, though the effect was not so manifest as in the lower orders of society.

It takes at least three years to gather a permanent congregation in London. We sometimes hear of a crowd coming together the first season, which is too often dispersed in the second. It is always better in this, as in other things, to begin low and rise high, than to begin high and descend gradually to the less and less.

Before the beginning of the fourth London season I found myself supported by a good, steady congregation. For all this, some said, "Nobody goes there!" Others remarked, "I can tell by the appearance and walk of the people as they pass whether they are going to Curzon Chapel or elsewhere." It was becoming quite a settled matter what, and who, the people were that attended my ministry.

One Sunday morning I had been preaching about the will of God. I said there was too often a mistake in the minds of Christians upon the subject. They thought it was their duty to resign themselves with as much cheerfulness as possible to circumstances pressed on them by the Providence of God; that they ought, whether prostrated by affliction or otherwise, to still appear content and submissive. Instead of this, I explained to them that true resignation consists in rising up into the will of God with thankfulness, instead of bowing under it with submission.

How many stop at Calvary, as if there was nothing more for them than to remain there till they are taken to heaven.

This theology, of going from Calvary to heaven direct, is far too generally taught and accepted. It is true that the Saviour died, and a most important part of truth it is – as important as a foundation is to a house. Obviously, however, the foundation is not the house, any more than the unseen though vital root of a tree is the tree itself which bears blossom and fruit.

I endeavoured to press home this teaching in order that the Foundation Stone, laid once for all, might not be confused with the cleft Rock of Ages – the believer's hiding-place. Truly the blessed Saviour died to save us, but it is equally true that He rose from the dead. Moreover, He ascended up on high and is coming again in His glory.

When we believe in His death, our souls are quickened into spiritual vitality, just as the body of the Lord was quickened in the grave. When as saved ones we believe in the Risen Saviour, we are raised to newness of life in Him. When we believe in the Ascended Saviour we sit in heavenly places in Him, and mind those things which are above – where Christ sits at the right hand of God.

CHAPTER 39

Gold, Silver and Precious Stones — 1876/78

I THOUGHT THAT I had found at Curzon Chapel a resting place where I was to labour to the end of my days. It suited me exactly, for besides having a promising congregation I had much spare time and freedom for Evangelistic work all over the country. Still I cannot say that I was fully satisfied with the result of this desultory labour, or that I did not often long and desire to be bringing more souls to Christ.

It is true that the Lord from time to time gave me the joy of leading sinners to Himself, and I had many opportunities for building up believers. Nevertheless, I could not help looking now and then at the vast harvest-field outside my own little sphere. This made me restless to reach and win more souls for Jesus.

The generosity of the congregation, as to pecuniary matters, was not the object of my ministry; but for all that it was a good indication that they were satisfied, and that their hearts were open to show their thankfulness in something more than words. At two of the special missions which were held at Curzon Chapel, upwards of two hundred and seventy pounds were freely offered in the boxes at the doors. Out of this amount two hundred pounds were appropriated to the organ, which is now in the chapel. My appeals for public charities were liberally responded to.

For instance, when I asked for a contribution for hospitals, one hundred and fifty pounds were forthcoming at one service. When I pleaded for the Church Missionary Society, one hundred pounds were given; for the Indian famine, eighty pounds; and so on. Besides the pew-rents, six pounds a week on an average were collected for the current expenses of the chapel. These were contributions to public charities and for necessary expenses, but there were others of a private nature which were even more freely given. Those connected with myself I feel bound to mention.

One Christmas time, while I was in domestic affliction and distress,[99] it came into the minds of two housekeepers who attended my ministry to collect a small sum in order to give me a "little" Christmas present. They had not the remotest suspicion that I had any want at that particular time, for as a rule I do not tell my troubles to neighbours and friends – who have enough of their own – but to God. He has invited, yea even commanded, us to call upon Him in the day of trouble – see Psalm 1:15 – and bids us cast all our care upon Him, for He careth for us. 1 Peter 5:7.

It so happened that I was in need, and had told my trouble at the Throne of Grace. This is how and why it came into the minds of my humble friends to "give me something." They hoped to collect about twenty pounds, but before many days one had already obtained over fifty, and the other almost as much. Each of them said that although they were collecting secretly, people ran after them with money.

On a set day I observed an unusually large attendance at the Bible-reading, and wondered why it was. While the last verse of the hymn was being sung I saw the clerk coming up the aisle with a large silver salver. On beholding it, I earnestly hoped they were not going to present me with that thing. "Is it come to this?" I thought. "A silver salver in place of the orthodox teapot, as a testimonial of respect and esteem?"

However, I was not kept long in suspense. A gentleman came forward and took from the ample surface of that conspicuous plate, which had been borrowed for the occasion, a purse which he handed to me, saying, "It contains one hundred guineas."

I was taken by surprise indeed, and could not help telling the kind donors that though they did not know my present

99   Haslam's wife Frances died in May 1877. He later
      married again, to Eliza Stone. See Appendix 3.

need, the Lord did. I said, "I feel sure that God put it into your hearts to give me this seasonable help."

Many of the friends assembled were moved to tears, as I testified of this personal instance of the loving-kindness of the Lord. I thanked them heartily and begged they would join with me in thanking and praising the Lord also. After this I exhorted them to trust God, as I had done, under all circumstances. I believe He sends or permits troubles, not to trouble us, but to bring us to Himself – that He might melt us more and more with His love.

A lady who was in town at the time happened to be at church that night. Hearing that this present had originated from servants, she immediately set on foot a subscription from the masters, and in a short time sent me the handsome sum of two hundred and fifty pounds more.

Various other tokens of love and thankfulness I could record, which I continue to remember with deep gratitude. I have learned what a blessed thing it is to have an empty purse, which nevertheless has money in it when it is needed. For many years I have experienced the happiness of trusting my Heavenly Father for all things.

I had laboured hard and diligently to gather my congregation together, and was in the midst of happy and prosperous work when the sad news reached me that my friend and patron, Lord Howe, had been bereaved of his only child. This event was a great blow to his lordship. Doubtless he felt it all the more from being himself in an enfeebled state of health. Not many months after, he too was called away, and in less than twelve months Lady Howe followed.

Another succeeded to the earldom, who apparently cared nothing for spiritual matters or spiritual people. In a short time his lordship dismissed the various Scripture-readers and Bible-women who had been employed on the estate by his predecessor. Supposing that I, the incumbent of Curzon Chapel, was something of the same grain – that is to say, of the same genus as a Bible-woman – he proposed to dismiss me likewise.

It had somehow come to his mind, and could not be eradicated, that my appointment ceased at the death of the late Lord. I protested that this was a real incumbency under the Bishop's institution, and that on this consideration I had given up a permanent living, which was as good as four hundred pounds a year, to take Curzon Chapel. Besides that, I had spent several hundred pounds – which my late patron said I might put into my own pocket – to improve the chapel and make it more acceptable to the congregation.

His lordship could not see it. He had dismissed Bible-women, and Mr Haslam must go too. In kind consideration he would give me three months' notice, or if I preferred it I might give him three months. I declined this offer and held on to my work.

The following year it came to this: the chapel is private property and his lordship can turn the key of it, or take off the roof, or turn it into a skating-rink. Then came a message to say that great improvement of property was in contemplation in Curzon Street which would be for his lordship's monetary benefit. Curzon Chapel is to be pulled down, but my lord is so unwilling to injure Mr Haslam that he will defer his own benefit for another year.

I did not accept this notice to quit, and in reply sent a vigorous remonstrance to his lordship about pulling down the chapel for the sake of monetary gain. To this I received no answer or even acknowledgment.

Shortly afterwards I announced to my congregation that I had heard the chapel was to be pulled down. This intimation did not appear to touch them in the least – perhaps they did not believe it. As the time drew near I was blamed for contemplating such a step. I do not think I should have entertained the idea if the congregation had been more alive to the real state of the case.

Three months before the time named for the destruction of the building I gave notice again to the seat-holders, as I was in duty bound. But this also was passed by without any remark or expression of regret.

Such being the case, I accepted an invitation from my friend Mr Aitken to join him in a Mission Society which he had recently formed in memory of his father, the late Rev R Aitken. Having settled this, I announced to the patron that I would vacate Curzon Chapel at Midsummer 1878.

When it was really apprehended that I was going to leave, the congregation appeared to awake as from a sleep. They at once drew up a letter to Lord Howe, which was signed by three hundred and eighty-four persons in a few days. This was sent to his lordship, and a deputation of twelve lords offered to wait upon him to receive his answer. But the plea was returned and the deputation declined. So at the stated time I ceased to officiate at Curzon Chapel, and the congregation dispersed.[100]

It is impossible to think of that happy time, and the many generous friends, without much regret. At the same time I cannot do otherwise than thank God for bringing me out into a wider and more important sphere of usefulness.

When I left Curzon Chapel I entered at once into the work of Parochial Missions, and have been incessantly labouring in this field for the last four years.[101] I did not seek or make this opening for myself. If anything, I much regretted being disturbed from Mayfair and my work there. However, I can see now that it was the right thing, though I did not do so at the time.

It is another instance of the Lord leading me in a way that I knew not. He has not forsaken His servant nor ceased to direct his steps. What is more, He has given me another helpmeet in my second wife,[102] who is in full sympathy, and as thoroughly devoted to the work as myself.

100 Curzon Chapel remained in use for a number of years after Haslam's departure. He was succeeded the following year by Robert James Simpson, who was Perpetual Curate from 1879 to 1886. Did the new lord have a change of mind about selling so soon, or was he merely anxious to get rid of Haslam? In 1899-1900 plans were filed for a "Proposed erection of a mansion for the Duke of Marlborough on the site of the Curzon Chapel." A photograph of the intact exterior, and another of the intact interior, both dated 1900, are in the Westminster City Archives Centre, refs: C.131.1 (2) and C.131.1 (3) respectively.

101 Writing in 1882.

102 Eliza Stone. See Appendix 3.

We go from parish to parish as we are invited, and from one place to another proclaiming the two-fold message to the saved and the unsaved. To the former that they may be stirred up to become workers for the Lord, and to the latter that they may be saved.

It is so important to their own well-being and joy that believers should understand that they were not created or redeemed to be saved. Rather, they were created, redeemed and saved that they should be witnesses in themselves of the love of God, and testify about His willingness to save others.

In every place in our mission journeys we find some believers like stranded vessels. They did run well, but somehow their peace ebbed away and the joy of their salvation passed from them. Therefore I urge them to launch out again and never more trust to their own prayers or resolutions, but in a Risen and Living Christ. He is able to keep them, even as a shepherd keeps his sheep.

Twenty years ago laymen were doubtful whether they ought to preach, and the general public thought it an absurd thing for anyone to say his sins were pardoned. Now, everywhere we find forgiven ones praising God, and this in spite of increasing infidelity and wickedness.

It is a great mistake to ask God to help us to work. We should rather give up ourselves to Him that He may use us. Therefore, instead of our asking Him to help us, we should understand that He is asking us to help Him. The work is not ours but His. It matters little how unworthy the instrument – the great Lord can accomplish His purpose with it. The weaker the tool, the greater is the glory of Him who can produce successful results.

Our work, however earnestly, zealously and conscientiously done is but wood, hay, stubble – and as such will all be burned. God's work on the other hand is as gold, silver and precious stones – which will stand the fiery test which is to try everyone's work of what sort it is.[103]

---

103 Haslam's interpretation of I Corinthians 3:11-13.

Epilogue

William Haslam, the parson who was converted by his own sermon, died in 1905, twenty-three very active years after completing *Yet Not I*. As we have seen, his early understanding of the Christian faith, that God's approval can be earned by living a decent moral life and following the 'right' form of church worship, gave way to his experience of conversion: sin is mankind's essential problem, while forgiveness has been secured for us by Jesus on the cross and is offered free to any who will repent and believe the Good News. This is summed up in a well-known verse from the New Testament. "For God so loved the world, that He gave His only begotten Son, that whosoever believeth in Him should not perish, but have everlasting life."[104]

Haslam ends *Yet Not I* with this thought: "It is a great mistake to ask God to help us to work." He expands on this in a later book *Leaves From My Note-book,* in a chapter entitled *Haslam's Pen,* part of which is reproduced below.

> One day, in the course of an address I was giving to young believers, I was telling how I began to work in my first zeal. I said, "I used to sit down and plan what I would say, and how I would say it. I consulted men and books to confirm me in my work, and of course asked the Lord to help me carry it out to the best of my ability. I knew of no other way, therefore I went on, thinking it was my duty to persevere through many discouragements, both within and without.
>
> "In the midst of these manifold undertakings God awakened me to see that I was doing my own will instead of His. During all this time I was under the delusion that I was serving my Master in heaven.
>
> "Imagine a pen getting up to write your letters, or asking you to hold it up while it went on writing its own thoughts. You could not trust such a pen as that, and

104 John 3:16

would be afraid to use it. In like manner, God cannot trust believers who go about to do their own will, neither can He use them to carry out His purposes."

What a number of earnest people there are just like that pen. They are working their own will, and verily think they are doing God's service.

It is noticeable how in spite of having doubts from time to time about his calling, Haslam was used by God to be a great blessing to others – because he made himself constantly available. The story of his pen is so simple yet so powerful. It was God who wrote with the pen, and Haslam was prepared to be nothing more than the writing instrument. "Yet not I, but the grace of God which was with me." (1 Corinthians 15:10). How else could he have achieved so much for God?

I am not entirely sure where Haslam saw himself in regards to the various Christian churches and chapels. Soon after his conversion at Baldhu, he writes, "I, who was still in my grave clothes though out of the grave, was sorely offended at people praying and praising God so heartily and so loudly in the church." These reservations quickly pass as he sees the blessings that the noisy worshippers gain, and he adds, "I was by this time not afraid of noise, so long as the power of the Lord's presence was evident." Even so, throughout Haslam's writing there are occasional hints that he would prefer things to be a little quieter, although he could write: "I had, however, discovered … that the people who most objected to noise had nothing yet to make a noise about. When they had, they generally made as much or more noise than others."

Some time after Haslam's conversion one Vicar accused him of being a Jesuit, and another of being a Bryanite – a member of the Bible Christians. Haslam would have seen these labels as representing two extremes, although he welcomed Bible Christian Billy Bray to teach in his schoolroom, something he would almost certainly never have trusted a High Churchman to do. He would surely be happy to see charismatic renewal at work in the Church of England as well as evangelical scholarship and cooperation in missionary endeavours throughout every land.

In the Courtney Library in Truro there is a letter in Sigvald Muller's file (see Appendix 2), from John Enys of Penryn, dated 29 January 1895.

> Dear Mr Muller,
>
> Thanks for your card as I should not have seen your interesting letter, not seeing the *West Briton* regularly. Haslam after his <u>Conversion</u> [underlined sic] lost his head I think, and any thing he wrote must be taken with reservation. I remember him years ago. [The letter then goes on to the weather].

All this about a man who was befriended and sought by eminent people, and eventually given the living of the prestigious Curzon Chapel in Mayfair! Whenever I read heated criticism of Haslam's Christian faith I am reminded of the words of St Paul in 1 Corinthians 1:23-24: 'But we preach Christ crucified, unto the Jews a stumbling block, and unto the Greeks foolishness. But unto them which are called, both Jews and Greeks, Christ the power of God, and the wisdom of God.'

It is not easy to single out just one of Haslam's thoughts for special mention from the many told here, but I would like to repeat the following from page 230 of this book:

> Now, when Gospel preaching is more general and light is spreading, Satan uses other means to hinder its acceptance. He says to many people, "It is quite true, you must be born again; you must be converted or you will be lost; you must be pardoned before you die; there is no repentance or forgiveness in the grave." But he adds, "Do not be troubled, you will not die today; do not hurry – wisely take time to consider – procrastinate – wait to feel something – live in hope of being saved hereafter." Such are a few of his devices, and everyone who is working for souls knows how sadly effective they are.

The thought that strikes me particularly forcibly is this. We may be sure of our own eternal salvation, but are we applying Haslam's words to our family, friends, neighbours and work colleagues? Are we thinking that somehow all will work out right for them in the end? Or are we, as comes over time and time again in this book, like the newly converted, excited to tell others just what the Lord means to us, and that He loves them too?

Maybe my final quote from this book will help make this sharing easier. It is from page 170, where Haslam says the religion of four letters is better than that of two!

> I asked another man, "What was finished on the cross?" Not receiving any answer I went on to say, "Our salvation was finished there. That being so, there is no need for you to be 'doing' in order to obtain salvation. The religion of four letters is better than that of two. That is to say, the religion which rests on what Christ has done is better than that which depends on what you can do."

Appendix 1

Haslam on the Way of Salvation

William Haslam is at his most readable when he is recounting first-hand experiences and conversations. He held back some incidents from the two books abridged here, and subsequently put them into two further books: *Gleanings From the Harvest* and *Leaves From My Note-book*. These books contain fascinating stories, but for reasons of confidentiality he has gone to some length to conceal names and locations.

Haslam has frequently stated God's way to forgiveness and new life in Jesus. For any readers still unsure of his meaning, I am reproducing part of a chapter from *Gleanings from the Harvest*. Haslam receives a letter from a clergyman who has read *From Death Into Life*. The letter says, "It is an extraordinary book, and you seem to live in an atmosphere I do not know. I would give much for an hour's talk with you." So a time is arranged, to follow a meeting where Haslam has been speaking.

> We had not walked many steps when he remarked, "I agree with every word you said in your address. Indeed, I enjoyed it very much. You kept to the Word of God with a simplicity which was charming, and gave illustrations that were very telling. Some of them were rather humorous to be sure, and I couldn't help smiling."
>
> "I am glad you liked the subject," I said.
>
> "Yes, indeed I did," he replied. "But do you mean to say that every man may know about his salvation and be assured of it?"
>
> "Why not, if our salvation depends upon the finished work of Christ for us, and if our assurance depends upon the truthfulness of God?"
>
> He did not answer, so I continued. "If the blood of Jesus was shed for me, and I plead it, then the destroying angel cannot touch me. And if God says, 'When I see the blood I

will pass over you,'[105] how can I entertain a doubt about it? We do not believe about the blood, but in it. That is to say, we have a personal interest therein. We ought to know whether we are pleading the blood, and be sure that we have no other plea for acceptance. The blood was shed to take our sins away. How can we believe that our sins are taken away, and not believe that we have a personal interest in the blood?"

My friend went on assenting in a general way, but still raising fresh questions.

As we walked along, I ventured to ask him whether he had passed from death into life. "Are you saved?" I said.

"What a question," he exclaimed, "to put to a clergyman! You are a strange man!"

"My dear friend," was my reply, "if you are a guide to others, there is a greater need for this question."

"Is it not an insult," he said "to ask a clergyman such a question?"

"Far from that," I replied. "If you are saved, it gives you an opportunity to testify to God's goodness."

"You certainly put things in a strange way. Do I look like an unsaved man? My father-in-law is the Rev Dr –." He looked as confident as assurance itself. "Well, you are a strange man," he repeated again, continuing to walk forward. "Stranger than your book, though you are very like it – very like!"

"Come, friend," I said, "why not give me a plain answer to a plain question?"

"What do you want me to say? I preach the doctrines of the Reformation as much as you do."

I said, "It is well to preach these doctrines, but do you preach Christ?"

By this time he began to wax warm, and said rather impatiently, "I wish to be saved as much as you do."

"But, my friend," I replied, "I do not wish to be saved, for I am saved. When a man wishes for a thing, it is because he has not yet obtained it."

105 Exodus 12:13

By this time we had reached the Rectory, and going into the drawing-room continued our discussion.

We had already talked for more than an hour, and as yet I had not received a definite answer to the simple question "Are you saved?" to which "Yes" or "No" would have sufficed.

At length, interrupting the course of the argument, I could not help telling my visitor that when believers come together they do not argue about believing or not believing, but they rather have communion one with another and rejoice together.

At last I suggested that he should do a little thing, which he characterised as a novelty.

I said, "Here is paper, pen and ink. Now will you write down in black and white the words 'I wish to be saved'?"

"Yes," he said; "I know a great many good men who would do that. I have no objection."

"Well, then, do so," I said.

Whereupon he took the pen in hand, and wrote the words, "I wish to be saved."

This done, I asked, "Have you any objection to sign your name to that?"

"None whatever," he replied, and signed his name in full with a flourish.

I took up the paper and looking at him, said, "I could no more do that than I could deny God. If I wrote that, it would imply that God had not saved me. You have committed yourself now."

He looked somewhat confused, so I continued, "I can show you a way out of your trouble. It is of no use arguing about these things. Will you write just one word more over what you have already written?"

"What is it?" he inquired.

"Write the word 'Lord' at the head of the paper; that will turn it into a prayer, and then God can give you an answer. 'Wishing' is like writing a letter and sending it without any address."

After a little more contention he took up the pen again and wrote the word "Lord".

"Now," I said, "the writing stands thus, 'Lord, I wish to be saved,'" Putting the paper down on the table, I said,

"Lord, save him. Do save him for Jesus' sake!" Then we knelt down.

The very attitude of kneeling seemed to melt his heart. It is surprising how people argue while they are sitting, and more vigorously still when they are on their feet, but once down upon their knees Satan's influence seems broken.

My friend wept in prayer and sought salvation. Better still, he found it, and we praised God together.

What a wondrous change there was in that man now that he was rejoicing. Before this he knew the Word of God intellectually, but when he believed it in his heart he could not help thanking God with gladness. The water of the Word was changed into the wine of the kingdom.

This is what Jesus does over and over again when sinners are united with Himself in an everlasting union. "Water" stands for the inspired Word of God, and by it our dark minds are enlightened and made wise unto salvation. But salvation itself, with the joy of it, is by faith in the Lord Jesus Christ.

I could scarcely believe that this happy rejoicing man was the same person who only a short time before had been disputing and contending with me. I invited him to come to luncheon, but this he declined, saying, "I have already had a good luncheon today. I have a friend in town who thinks I am a Christian. I must go after him and see if he is one. I will go and tell him what the Lord has done for my soul."

In the evening I saw these two gentlemen come into the church and sit together. At the conclusion of the service he introduced his friend to me, as one who could praise God with him.

This clergyman returned to his church and people a changed man. His words and views were the same, but now they had a power and a purpose in them which they had not previously. His congregation could see that he was not so much preaching about a subject, as speaking to them personally about their salvation, with a joy they had never observed before.

Appendix 2

Haslam's Archaeology

Some people have accused Haslam of two separate offences: arrogance, and deliberate dishonesty. The first allegation comes from a quick reading of a few passages in the originals of the two books abridged here, particularly his apparent boast that at his first parish of Perranzabuloe he was the busiest man alive. In fact, he says he was accounted the busiest man alive. He wrote these words in connection with the time he spent racing around the countryside and pleasing the Bishop of Exeter, so that: 'It was said that the Bishop's best living would be given to me in due time.' The irony of this, as Haslam saw it, was that this same Bishop eventually tricked him out of his living. To understand Haslam's wry style of humour, and his ability to laugh at himself, it is necessary to read more of his writing than the occasional sentence.

The charge of dishonesty, and even vandalism, focuses solely on his account of various archaeological excavations at St Piran's Oratory, within the boundary of his first parish. These accusations, if true, would reflect badly on the integrity of Haslam's other writing, so it is important to deal with them fully.

Haslam's accounts, and the written accounts of others, show that the Oratory was severely vandalised by the locals immediately after a previous excavation by a Cornishman from Truro called William Michell, eight years before Haslam arrived in Perranzabuloe. Sigvald Muller from Newquay wrote an article for the *West Briton* about the Oratory many years later, in 1894, and says on page 36 of the draft for this article in his notebook (held in a small file by the Courtney Library in Truro) that after Michell's excavation: 'The altar was destroyed by gravediggers, who searched for treasure...' So Haslam could only find wreckage in 1843. He rebuilt the altar, but critics claim he got the orientation wrong. At the same time some stones were removed behind what Michell had thought was a niche in the east wall, to reveal what Haslam decided was a small window. Considering the whole archway to the south entrance, and much of the east wall, was destroyed within two weeks of Michell uncovering the Oratory in 1835, removing a few stones to reveal what may or not have been a window seems a minor offence. Haslam set out to write a record of his own excavation in 1843/44, and tell something of the earlier (unpublished) 1835 excavation by William Michell. It is not the purpose of this Appendix to add to the controversy of dating St Piran's Oratory, but to sort out exactly who said and did what – and when.

The earliest published record connecting Haslam with the Oratory comes from his lecture on The Old Church of Perranzabuloe, as it appeared in the *West Briton* on Thursday December 8 1843:

> *Royal Institution of Cornwall*
>
> The ordinary meeting of the society, on Friday evening last, was very numerously attended, in consequence of notice having been given that the Rev W Haslam, of St Perranzabuloe, would communicate to the meeting an account of his researches at the old church, which was for so long a period buried amid the sandhills.

The *West Briton* newspaper gives a brief summary of Haslam's address, which appears to concentrate on Michell's earlier work. The reporter ends his article with the promise that '…this most interesting paper would very shortly be printed.' Perhaps Haslam had not finished his own investigations, for he waited a whole year before publishing his book *Perran-Zabuloe* in December 1844.

In the Journal of the Royal Institution of Cornwall, XVIII 1910-1911, pp 294-296, there is an account of the Annual Meeting of the Institution held at the Museum Building Truro, on Tuesday December 20 1910. The following extract about the 'sham' altar stone is of interest:

> Rev W Iago said that when Mr Haslam was alive he had some correspondence with him regarding the altar at St Piran oratory, and that gentleman told him that the

present altar stone, with the inscription, + S Piranus + was placed there on his instruction by a mason ... He had Mr Haslam's plain statement as to what he did, and he said it just before his death [in 1905] ... Mr J H Collins hoped this sham altar stone would be taken out and thrown over the cliff (applause) ... Rev W Iago said they might at any rate obliterate the false legend. Even if they kept the stone it was in the wrong position and the corners were cut out in the wrong place ... Mr Earthy (secretary of the restoration committee) said they had decided not to allow the stone to remain there, and to obliterate the inscription.

This report of apparent deception understandably causes concern today, but in his 1844 book Perran-Zabuloe [106] written sixty-one years before his death, Haslam says:

[The altar] has since been carefully rebuilt with the same stones; a solid block of granite, nearly a ton in weight, cut to the exact peculiar shape and dimensions of the original altar, has been placed over it; and as the altar is now, and is likely always to be, more a tomb than an altar, the name of St Piran has been deeply cut in the granite, in early Roman characters.

When writing *From Death Into Life* in 1880, Haslam again makes it clear that: '...we made up the deficiency with a heavy granite slab.' He goes on to explain in detail how the inscription was subsequently cut on his instructions. An openly acknowledged action, and hardly a deathbed revelation!

Lodenek Press, Padstow, published a book in 1982 that has also been responsible for unwarranted condemnation of Haslam. In *Search of St Piran* by EWF Tomlin, 44 pages, contains many excellent photographs, maps and diagrams, covering 'the past and present state of the Oratory, and its history as understood in the late twentieth century.' Tomlin was the nephew of Cornish antiquarian Dr TFG Dexter, 1860-1933. However, Tomlin makes some unfortunate errors on pages 15 and 16, which imply Haslam was

106   page 74 of the original – page 22 of the 1998
       Oakmagic reprint.

untrustworthy. Having briefly discussed William Michell's excavation in 1835, Tomlin continues:

> This spoliation [plunder or pillage – of 1835] was followed by the well-meaning but not always beneficent attentions of two clergymen, the Rev'd CTC Trelawny and the Rev'd William Haslam, who began to undertake on their own account a certain amount of amateur excavation and even restoration. In 1843, Trelawny, a retired rector who had been a Fellow of Balliol, wrote a book called *Perranzabuloe, the Lost Church Found.* …William Haslam, resident curate at Perranzabuloe, and responsible for the fake altar with its anomalous inscription, published his book the following year. …It [Haslam's] was a meandering book, facts being interspersed with homilies, and it consisted largely of a history of the Celtic Church followed by an account of the Oratory-chapel "as it was when first recovered from the sands in the year 1835." It relied chiefly upon Michell's findings …Haslam's conclusion was that the Oratory-chapel had been built either "by St Piran himself in the fifth (sic) century or soon after by his successors." Many years later, however, in a book called *From Death Unto Life, or Twenty Years of My Ministry* [1880], Haslam sought to convey the impression that he had personally "discovered" the Oratory-chapel. This claim, reiterated in the *Dictionary of National Biography*, received spurious reinforcement from his inaccurate translation of Camden's "in sabulo positum" as "buried in the sand", and by his implied suggestion that it had remained so for fifteen centuries. (Tomlin *In Search of St Piran* pages 15-16.)

The reference to CTC Trelawny writing his book in 1843 is nonsense. The Rev Trelawny Collins (or Collins Trelawny as he later became known – see below) wrote *Perranzabuloe* in 1836, long before Haslam came on the scene. Collins Trelawny does not appear to have done any excavation himself, and maybe did not even visit the site until a year after Michell's exploration was complete, using Michell[107] as his source. Haslam carried out his own excavations of the Oratory eight years later after it had once again become filled with sand. Although he refers freely to Michell's work in his 1844 book *Perran-Zabuloe*, Haslam also reports his own discoveries. As we will see, Haslam makes no claim that he discovered the Oratory.

As for Haslam's *Perran-Zabuloe* being a meandering book, I have read it several times and cannot agree with this comment. It is not particularly interesting, but I have yet to spot the homilies unless Tomlin is referring to a short section where Haslam laments the fact that people are staying away from church, and the very occasional Bible reference, comparing Old and New Testament worship to later Christian practice, to reinforce his argument of an early date for the Oratory. Tomlin says he consulted the copy in the British Library, and some of his criticism could be the result of a rather cursory read. A reference to Haslam and Perranzabuloe may be in some dictionary of biography seen by Tomlin, but I can find no entry in the electronic (Oxford) *Dictionary of National Biography*, or in the original volumes published before the Oxford University Press took over the project in 1917.

As part of his attack on Haslam, on page 16 Tomlin says Haslam claimed that the faith was brought here in person by St Paul. Wrong. Haslam's exact words are: 'We readily admit that St Paul *or his companions from Rome* [italics mine] ...planted Christianity in this island'.[108] He is just reflecting a belief held reasonably widely at the time.

---

107 *"To whom the author is indebted for many of the particulars here related, and also for the drawings which accompany the volume."* Collins Trelawny
Perranzabuloe, Rivington London, fourth edition 1839, page 25. Mitchell's notebook, homemade from sheets of paper, is in the Courtney Library, Truro. The original drawings, apart from a plan view of the Oratory are now missing.

108 *Perran-Zabuloe* p.4

Whether or not this is historically correct, it hardly destroys confidence in Haslam's writing. More importantly, Tomlin tries to discredit Haslam by claiming that the 'lost church' was never lost at all, and only covered in sand for relatively short periods.

Why does Haslam say that 'in sabulo positum', in Camden's 1607 Britannia, means that the Oratory of St Piran was buried in the sand, and not situated in the sand, as Tomlin believes is the correct translation? *Positum* from which we get our English word positioned can be translated in several ways. It is a matter of choice whether the Latin *in* means in or on or onto. Haslam's understanding seems to be that the Latin means literally in the sand. He would have been extremely conversant with Latin, and his translation was probably a deliberate one. It's not an important point anyway, and other writers quoted by Tomlin say it was buried or lost. But even if a historian says the Oratory was there, is not proof that it was exposed to view, unless specifically stated. After all, it is 'there' today, but at the time of writing deliberately covered in sand for protection.

The Rev Collins Trelawny, 1792-1878, was one-time rector of Timsbury, Somerset and Fellow of Balliol College Oxford. His name causes some confusion today, for in early editions of his book *Perranzabuloe* he uses the name C Trelawny Collins, and in later ones C T Collins Trelawny. Charles Trelawny Collins took the additional surname Trelawny in November 1838, and became Charles Trelawny Collins Trelawny. This later name is the one I am using here. He wrote *Perranzabuloe, The Lost Church Found* in 1836, and this book went to several editions over more than fifty years. It describes Michell's excavation of the Oratory in 1835, but was primarily an anti-Roman Catholic polemic arguing that the Church of Britain was fully established before the Church of Rome.[109]

William Haslam's book on the excavations of the Oratory was published in December 1844. *Perran-Zabuloe* was also

109 Collins Trelawny *Perranzabuloe*, fourth edition 1839, Appendix 4, page 270.

not specifically on archaeology, but aimed at demonstrating that the early Cornish churches: '…differ from those of the Saxons and Normans. … If it be shown that they do not belong to either of these periods or people, they necessarily belong to an earlier.' [110]

A long article by Sigvald Muller from Newquay, in the *West Briton* dated January 24 1895, is a detailed condemnation of Haslam, also without substance. Muller argues that Haslam was either a liar or an exaggerator, on four main grounds. The first we can dismiss quickly. Haslam writes that some of the interior of the Oratory was plastered in a mix of china clay and sand. Sigvald Muller says that Michell wrote that the plaster was lime and sand. Well, one has to say, so what? Haslam was new to Cornwall and not an authority on local plaster and mortar, and particles of china clay are often found in building sand. Possibly china clay had been mixed with lime as a wash, to give the brilliant white finish noted by some writers, and Haslam – who, we will see later, wrote a letter saying Michell had told him it was china clay – failed to realise it was only a surface coating.

Three other criticisms deserve serious consideration. Muller's main objection is that Haslam seems to have invented the orientation of the altar, pretending St Piran, his mother and a friend were found buried underneath. The thrust of Muller's argument is that Michell in his notes never identified the three skeletons. Thurstan Peter of the Royal Institution of Cornwall reproduced the contents of Michell's 1835 notebook (probably using Muller's transcription) in 1904 in the RIC Journal volume XVI (pages 133-143). But not all of it. On page 135 Thurstan Peter writes: 'The following is a complete copy of his [Muller's] notes, except the introductory portion as to the history of the saint, which, as of no value, I omit.' This is an unfortunate omission, as on page 9 of his notebook Michell wrote:

---

110 Haslam *Perran-Zabuloe*, page 140 – page 53 of the 1998 Oakmagic reprint

This holy man resigned his soul into the hands of his Creator and his remains to his devoted parishioners, who *interred them beneath the altar* of the Church which he himself had created in honour of the Deity – about the year 480. [Italics mine]

In 1836 Collins Trelawny wrote:

On removing the altar, three skeletons were discovered; one of gigantic dimensions, the second of moderate size, and the third apparently of a female. No doubt the former is that of the old saint Piranus himself, and the latter his aged mother Wingela.[111]

A quick reading of page 8 of Michell's notebook where he writes about Wingela, and his words on page 9: 'who interred them beneath the altar' could lead someone to believe that Michell was claiming that Wingela was also buried there, although this is clearly not what he meant. Since the legend was well known, and Collins Trelawny wrote that Michell was the person 'to whom the author is largely indebted for many of the particulars here related,'[112] it was reasonable for Haslam to believe that this was a definite identification.

What about Muller's claim that: 'This altar is a pure invention of Mr Haslam?' The problem is that although Haslam agreed that the altar was against the east (front) wall, he thought it was originally aligned east-west (down the length of the church) rather than in the traditional sideways position. Collins Trelawny writes that:

On visiting the ancient church of Perranzabuloe, soon after the first edition was sent to the press [1836], the writer was grieved to find...the interior of the sanctuary

111 Collins Trelawny *Perranzabuloe*, fourth edition 1839, page 29.

112 Collins Trelawny *Perranzabuloe*, fourth edition 1839, footnote on p. 25.

itself has been desecrated by many acts of wanton profanation.[113]

When Haslam re-excavated the Oratory in 1843 he noted[114] that, 'Modern research has torn down the altar-tomb which once stood over St Piran's remains.' In 1880 he wrote that 'the altar...was fallen, but enough remained to show the original shape and height of it.' Haslam certainly had nothing to prove from falsifying the orientation, so why does Muller make such an issue of it being a pure invention of Mr Haslam? There must have been something that led Haslam to deduce – rightly or wrongly – that the altar had originally been constructed east-west.

Michell himself seems to have been confused over the dimensions of the altar, calling it 4 feet long, 2½ feet wide and 3 feet high – instead of the 5 feet 3 inches long, 2 feet 3 inches wide and 4 feet high in his notebook – in a letter dated September 1835 written to Mr Budd, the editor of the *West Briton* announcing his discovery. A large sheet of paper dated 1903 in Muller's file shows Muller's attempts at working out the size of the altar to fit in with the measurements Michell gives on page 13 of his notebook. He explains how he interprets Michell's rather strange sketch, by assuming (probably correctly) that the altar 'front' in Michell's drawing is actually made up of the front and both sides. In that way he comes close to Muller's 5 foot 3 inches. Given this uncertainly, why should Haslam be pilloried for his interpretation of what Sigvald Muller and Thurstan Peter admit is a confusing state of affairs?

Maybe someone rebuilt the altar east-west after Michell's work, when clearing up the chaos left by people robbing the Oratory for souvenirs. Tombs in churches are traditionally east-west, and if the altar was also a tomb, as Haslam maintained, the conventional orientation may have been an overriding factor in its original design. If I wanted a bookcase to fit along a wall, I would ask how wide it was,

113 ibid, appendix 9 p. 279.
114 *Perran-Zabuloe*, p. 39.

not how long it was. A draftsman and engineer I have discussed this with says that if the altar was sideways-on at the front of the church like a conventional altar, he would give the dimensions as 5 feet 3 inches wide, 2 feet 3 inches deep and 4 feet high. Realistically, I think we have to conclude that Haslam made a mistake, but was his confusion simply caused by his misunderstanding of Michell's use of the word length? As we will see below, no one at the time seems to have said, "Excuse me, Vicar, but you've got it wrong!" Possibly the onlookers kept quiet because they thought Haslam was deliberately reburying the skeleton in an east-west tomb, rather than rebuilding the original altar.

Muller's final major attack on Haslam is the drawing of the doorway of the Oratory on page 70 of Haslam's *Perran-Zabuloe*[115]. Like Trelawny, Haslam says it was made from: 'a rough sketch by W Michell Esq' (*Perran-Zabuloe* p. 69). Muller insists Haslam copied it incorrectly, because there is a very different picture of the same doorway at the start of Chapter One in the early editions of Collins Trelawny's *Perranzabuloe*. Drawings at that date, of course, could not be reproduced photographically but had to be copied as an etching or engraving, so accuracy depended on the skill of the engraver and the quality of the image he was given to copy. There is in Collins Trelawny's *Perranzabuloe* a ridiculously inaccurate reproduction of the Perranzabuloe church font, so it looks as though the sketches he gave the engraver were far from accurate.[116] Significantly, by the 1868 edition of Collins Trelawny's work, the picture of the Oratory doorway is replaced with one that is very similar to Haslam's, presumably authorised by Collins Trelawny (ten years before his death) who must have acknowledged it as more accurate, maybe after re-examining Michell's sketches

---

115 pp 69-70 become pp 18f in the Oakmagic reprint.

116 The reference to illustrations is to Rivington's London editions. I have a Stanford & Swords New York edition of 1846 (reprinted from Rivington's 5th edition) but it contains very few illustrations.

(which are now missing). In the same 1868 edition there is also a plan of the Oratory, with the altar east-west, copied from Haslam's *Perran-Zabuloe*, as though Haslam's orientation was at that time still considered to be correct.

We are left with the problem of what the Oratory really looked like in the first half of the nineteenth century. My 1839 copy of Trelawny's *Perranzabuloe* has an engraving in the frontispiece that is generally similar to that in the front of Haslam's *Perran-Zabuloe*. Both may have been engraved from a sketch or sketches made by Mitchell immediately after his excavation of 1835. Whether these engravings are accurate or not, it is impossible to say. In Trelawny's eighth edition of *Perranzabuloe* dated 1884 there is an engraving of a perfect building, complete with a wooden door on the south side, but no roof. (Trelawny wondered if there had ever been a roof.) Since the Oratory is shown on the top of a small hill, we can quickly dismiss this whole picture as an excess of artistic licence. Facing page 107 in *The Age of the Saints* by William Copeland Borlase, 1893 Joseph Pollard Truro, is a heavily retouched photograph of the Oratory, where the artist has redrawn the stones on the west side of the south doorway, making them into horizontal layers, while none of the stones in the other walls matches those in contemporary photographs. The only reliable pictures we have are photographs dating from the late nineteenth century, by which time the Oratory had become a ruin. There is no way to test anyone's pictorial or verbal description of the Oratory in the 1830s and '40s. Everything we see and read has to be taken on trust – even the details in Michell's notebook. Although the remains of the Oratory have been deliberately covered in sand to save it from further harm, there are plans by the St Piran Trust to reveal it again.

At the AGM of the Royal Institution of Cornwall in December 1910, mentioned earlier, there was another attack on Haslam by Morley Collins, whose paper on the Oratory was read by Thurstan Peter to the Institute on 20 December. Collins mentions the 'niche' above the altar, and wrote,

> I have examined this aperture carefully, with regard to its construction, and although it now shows that it has been

> tampered with, it is my opinion that originally it was a
> niche and not a window as now exists.

Haslam seems to have identified the 'niche' or 'recess', as Michell called it, as a window by examining the outside of the wall and excavating inwards, although he does not actually claim to be the one who opened it up. Since the exterior evidence would have been removed in order to expose the 'window', Morley Collins' examination could not have been conclusive, especially, as we can see from existing photographs, much of the original stonework on the east wall had fallen by 1910. Morley Collins died a few weeks after his paper was read, at the age of twenty-six, about the same age as Haslam when he 'revealed' the window in 1843, so we have the opinion of one young man against another.

In a speech a few months earlier, Thurstan Peter from the RIC had been particularly critical of Haslam, and a newspaper report of this on 22 August 1910 brought a spate of letters, both for and against Haslam. Thurstan Peter was one of the trustees responsible for the inept attempt at preservation of the Oratory in 1910, a cause of far more damage than Haslam's possibly mistaken restoration of the altar and window/niche.

In the Journal of the Royal Institution of Cornwall, in 1904, (volume XVI, part 1, pages 133-143) Thurstan Peter reproduces what he says are all Michell's notes on the excavation of the Oratory, including Muller's drawing of his understanding of the shape of the (long broken) top slab of the altar, interpreted from Michell's hard-to-decipher drawings. So far so good. However, Thurstan Peter is unable to stop at that, and rehashes the old criticisms of Haslam. He takes sides with Michell and Muller where they differ from Haslam's accounts, but adds nothing new except to write, "[Haslam's] whole account seems to be the product of an hysterical and vain man." Who or what could have persuaded the respected Royal Institution of Cornwall to sanction such personal invective, especially during Haslam's lifetime? In 1854 Haslam observed that, "The idea of preaching to awaken souls was considered very strange and fanatical" (see page 108 of this book). Maybe some of the twenty-five clergy listed as RIC Members and Council for

1904 were keen to belittle a man who had disturbed their millponds years before, and caused such an 'offence'.

And vanity? In the same 1904 paper, Thurstan Peter accuses Haslam of, 'claiming to be the discoverer of the church.' If Haslam had claimed this, it would indeed be a sign of vanity. But as we will see, this is a misreading of Haslam's text. Indeed Haslam's was careful to acknowledge the work done by Michell in 1835, and the small amount of 'reconstruction' he did in 1843, so that the accusations of dishonesty are not convincing.

A refreshingly uncomplicated and carefully researched recent book is *In the Shadow of St Piran* by Eileen Carter,[117] who has done a huge amount of work to bring us a detailed and illustrated history of St Piran and the Oratory. There is a slight anti-Haslam bias in a couple of places, caused by some of the sources and reports dealt with here, but the book is far more carefully written than Tomlin's publication by the same publisher, contains some good photographs, and is extremely readable.

My time-line below shows the major events at Perranzabuloe. The first two places of worship on the coast were overcome by drifting sand. The third, built nearly three miles (4.5km) away, and well inland, where Haslam became curate in 1843 still stands as the Parish Church of Perranzabuloe. The dates are those given by Haslam and Trelawny, and are not always in agreement with current thinking.

450-600 AD St Piran's Oratory first built. (Not impossible, but nowadays a date of 800 or later is considered more likely, although there may be the remains of a much older building under the Oratory).

c900 Second church built close by, when the Oratory is overcome by sand.

c1100 This church demolished and rebuilt on its same site.

117 92 pages, published by Lodenek Press, Wadebridge, 2001.

1420	The church demolished yet again and rebuilt on its same site, in Perpendicular style.
1752 on	Several attempts at clearing sand from the Oratory, all unsuccessful.
c1789	A labourer reports finding walls, after a natural event cleared some of the sand. (Haslam 1844 *Perran-Zabuloe.*)
1803	Second church finally demolished for good, due to constant inundation by sand.
1803/4	Third church built in its present position in Perranzabuloe, using stone and timber from the second church.
1805	Third (present) church dedicated.
1814	Some of Oratory visible, according to Lysons Brothers' Magna Britannia.
1835	William Michell from Truro excavates the Oratory.
1835	Excavations immediately plundered by visitors. (Sources, Collins Trelawny and Sigvald Muller.)
1837	Excavations already disappearing under sand. (Source, Collins Trelawny.)
1843	William Haslam re-excavates the Oratory. He lectures about it in December.
1844	Haslam publishes his book *Perran-Zabuloe* a year later in December, possibly after carrying out a further examination.

According to an inventory taken in 1281 by the canons of Exeter, St Piran's second church contained the saint's head, and a hearse in which his body was placed for processions. The remains were still there in 1433 when Sir John Arundel bequeathed money to enclose the head of the Saint in the best and most honourable way they could. Haslam thought the remains of St Piran were buried in the Oratory for protection at the Reformation, but it is possible he made a mistake in the identification of the skeletons, and unearthed the remains of other people. In his 1835 notebook, Michell says, 'There were many bodies interred, both in the Chancel and the Nave of the Church.'

We now come to the words of Haslam that have caused the greatest controversy. Writing in 1880, thirty-six years later, he says in chapter 4 of *From Death Into Life* (page 25 in this book):

This was enough. I got men, and set to work to dig it up. After some days' labour we came to the floor, where we discovered the stone seats, and on the plaster of the wall the greasy marks of the heads and shoulders of persons who had sat there many centuries ago. We found the chancel step, and also the altar tomb – which was built east and west, not north and south. It was fallen, but enough remained to show the original shape and height of it.

I put a notice in the newspapers, inviting people to come and see the old church which had been buried for fifteen hundred years! In the presence of many visitors, clerical and lay, we removed the stones of the altar, and found the skeleton of St Piran, which was identified in three ways.

We have already seen how Haslam obtained his identification of the skeletons from Collins Trelawny's 1836 book, but we can find fault with his advert that the Oratory had been buried for fifteen hundred years. However, I think Haslam is laughing at his enthusiastic naievity in 1843, which is why he puts the exclamation mark. In his book *Perran-Zabuloe* page 62[118] he is more circumspect: 'It is by no means impossible that the despoiled ruin in the sands was erected in the sixth century, and overwhelmed about the ninth.' On page 56, Haslam wonders if the Oratory was built before St Piran's death in 480. So by 1844 Haslam believed the Oratory could only have been in existence for thirteen or fourteen hundred years, and buried for just part of that time. Haslam may have been too uncritical in accepting Trelawny's arguments for an early date.

By the phrase 'The hill under which it was buried was easily known by the bones and teeth which covered it,' Haslam may mean the Oratory had become buried in sand again after 1835 – a possibility in view of Collins Trelawny's observation in 1837 – but more likely that the Oratory had been buried in the past, and because of the bones and teeth on the surface, the locals always knew where it was.

118 p 62 = 1998 Oakmagic reprint: p10 // p56 =reprint p4).

The controversial word in *From Death Into Life* is *'discovered'*. A careless reading, applying it to mean that Haslam is claiming to have discovered the whole Oratory, has perhaps brought him the most criticism. But Haslam says, *"We discovered the stone seats* etc." No mention here, or anywhere, of discovering the Oratory. I might explore Truro and say I'd discovered a maze of narrow streets, or discovered a superb restaurant tucked away in Penzance, or a great art gallery in St Ives, but people would be foolish to think I meant no one had discovered these places before. So, here, Haslam is telling us the various things he discovered inside the Oratory. Note that he says *the* stone seats, *the* plaster of *the* wall, *the* greasy marks, *the* chancel step, and *the* altar tomb. Michell had already written in his notebook about most of these, but made no mention of the greasy marks, indicating Haslam's ability to pick up on small but significant details (see footnote 6 on page 25 of this book).

I would expect someone pretending to have found these things for the first time to be more careful with their wording and say *some* stone seats, *some* plaster on *a* wall, *a* chancel step, *an* altar tomb. Haslam sounds as though he is happy to acknowledge that he knew in advance what he would find there. Indeed, on page 71 of *Perran-Zabuloe* (page 19 of the 1998 Oakmagic reprint) Haslam writes that in 1843 the sand was 'again cleared with very great difficulty, in order to make exact measurements of the church, and to rebuild the altar-tomb of St Piran.' So he must have heard what was inside the Oratory, and knew that the altar had been wrecked since Michell's excavation – and maybe wanted to see why Michell had given contradictory dimensions for the size of the altar.

Incidentally, both Muller and Peter mention some pencil notes on the back of Michell's notebook, and took this to indicate that Michell returned in Haslam's time to check these dimensions. There is nothing to support this theory, and it is more likely that Michell returned in 1835 or 1836 after publishing the incorrect measurements of the altar in the *West Briton*. The pencil notes are scribbled and have many crossings-out. The only legible measurement today is 'chancel 9 feet six inches.' There are also some words that may read: 'correctly ascertained the…walls…And

…showing the precise points where woodwork had been fixed for the purpose of separating it from the nave.' So this definitely seems to be the result of an undated return visit to confirm a few details. There are no pencil marks on page 13 where Michell gives the 5 foot 3 inch etc size of the altar, so treasure hunters may already have demolished it when he returned - assuming he had rebuilt it.

And the legend? That St Piran was buried in the Oratory (but not necessarily under the altar) was indeed a legend, and as far back as 1607 Camden wrote that St Piran was buried in the chapel at Perranzabuloe. Even if Michell had already found the skeleton of St Piran in 1835, it does not alter the fact that the saint's burial within the Oratory was a legend. It is of course possible that Haslam is using legend to mean word of mouth – from the time of Michell's excavation.

Haslam's claim to fame, surely, is that he brought the excavations to a much wider public by advertising his findings, to draw in 'many visitors, clerical and lay.' He also seems to have roused the Royal Institution of Cornwall to take a greater interest in the Oratory than Michell had managed, as well as publishing a book on the subject.

Haslam says he reburied the three skeletons, placing a heavy granite block weighing nearly one ton on the altar, perhaps to deter further desecration of the graves underneath. He makes no secret of having done this, even if he got the orientation wrong. A fascinating reference to a later excavation comes from a sheet of paper in Muller's file in the Courtney Library, copied by Muller from a note written by Sir Paul Molesworth in 1863. It says:

> The bones were taken by me, out of the altar tomb in the East end of the old Oratory of St Piran… when the stone erected by the Rev Mr Haslam formerly curate there had been overthrown, about the time of the visit of the Cambrian archaeological society in 1862. I restored the stone to its place and finding certain bones in the tomb, buried them on the North side in the angle of the 'X' in enclosed plan, extracting only those in this bottle, which may be St Piran's relics.

Not surprisingly, in view of the looted relics, Muller has written on the document that it must not be referred to in print! The 'X' on the drawing is shown in the north-east corner of 'Haslam's' altar, where it joins the east wall.

So there must have been further vandalism after 1844, in spite of Haslam's heavy altar stone. Molesworth says he replaced the stone, thereby allowing the members of the Royal Institution of Cornwall to attack it with such glee in 1911.

The Rev W Iago (pronounced Jago in Cornwall) held several senior posts in the Royal Institution of Cornwall over the years, and was quite a leading light when it came to St Piran. He is the man who said at the RIC meeting in 1910 that… 'when Mr Haslam was alive he had some correspondence with him regarding the altar at St Piran oratory.' But he seems to have forgotten a letter he received from William Haslam in 1895, defending his work on the altar in 1843. Iago's letter to Muller, in Muller's file in the Courtney Library, is dated 31 January 1895 and is in response to Muller's critical article in the *West Briton* on 24 January. I quote is as written, including the underscores and brackets:

Dear Mr Muller,

Many thanks for your letter. Mr Haslam has written to me acknowledging the paper I sent to him. He says that, "In *'Death to Life'* there is a footnote which sufficiently explains that he did not mean to say that he was the first to discover and dig up the old church. He merely states that he did dig it up, in the presence of many representative people from Truro." He adds, that "He is not sure but that Mr Michell was there and helped the visitors to understand the arrangement of the place, which he (Mr Michell) first uncovered."

With regard to the altar, Mr Haslam states that "its shape and position he received from Mr Michell. And the large skeleton was laid bare before the assembled people." He (Mr Haslam) measured it himself. He did not analyse the china clay, but Mr Michell told him it was clay as well as he can remember. He adds that "Mr Michell saw his MSS and the proof sheets before they were finally passed for the press and never suggested any alteration."

He remembers <u>Mr Hingeston-Randolph</u> as a youth, and says he saw and knew what he (Haslam) was describing, and never pointed out anything as incorrect at that time.

He says that "Collins never saw the Church till he (Mr Haslam) took him to see it in 1845." (I notice that Collin's book is dated 1835!!)

Most of his information was received from Mr Michell. "It was ruinous when he came, and he (Haslam) made his sketches at Easter 1843, and had it partly cleared out and took internal measurements."

He says "he did not make the altar according to his own imagination. Mr Michell saw it restored and said it was right."

I find it most unfortunate that this letter has not been published before. It does not automatically put Haslam in the clear, but it is important to bear in mind that William Michell died two months after the publication of Haslam's *Perran-Zabuloe*, and may have been either too ill to argue with Haslam, or was suffering from forgetfulness. Of course, a charge of poor memory could possibly be levelled against Haslam, for he was seventy-seven when he wrote to Iago, and his excavation had taken place more than fifty years earlier.

However, Haslam was publishing *Praise* magazine from 1897-1899, so his mind must have been pretty sharp in 1894/5. One thing I find especially interesting is Haslam's mention that Collins (Trelawny) never saw the 'Church' – presumably he means the Oratory – until 1845. When first reading Collins Trelawny's *Perranzabuloe* I decided he had not seen inside the Oratory when he wrote his book in 1836 (not 1835 as Iago says) because sand had once again filled the interior, and probably he could only see the exterior of the walls when writing his book, using Michell's notes. So it is likely that Haslam is right, and 1845 was the first time Trelawny was able to inspect the inside. If this is so, it is evidence of the reliability of Haslam's memory on the other details. The explanatory footnote Haslam says is in *From Death Into Life* is not in any edition I have been able to examine, but may be in a late one.

Quite honestly, I've been disappointed by the careless approach by those who seem to have set out to destroy Haslam's reputation. Were these attacks made because he was 'an outsider' thought to be meddling in Cornish history, or did his evangelical church views upset too many clergy and other establishment figures at the time? Michell seems to have been guilty of inaccurate recording, as well as laying the site of the Oratory open to desecration, but he came from Truro and was viewed as a hero!

Several of Haslam's ideas on the past, in common with the ideas of those who wrote much more learned books even fifty or sixty years later, would no longer be supported – nor would the digging techniques he and others employed. Haslam notes that the east wall of the Oratory fell during Michell's excavation, although clearly not all of it. We have to realise there were no archaeological standards in those days. Mortimer Wheeler's *Archaeology from the Earth*, Clarendon Press Oxford 1954, was the first technical and popular book to be published – after which there was no excuse for professionals and those on the fringes. But it came more than a hundred years too late for Haslam and his contemporaries.

Of course Haslam made mistakes about the Oratory. He was not carrying out a professional archaeological dig. He had the parish of Perranzabuloe to run at the time and, to quote his tongue-in-cheek words, he rode all over the county from north to west, restoring churches and designing schools, and was accounted the busiest man alive! The deeper we dig, the more we can see that just about every person mentioned here, writing before 1983, has been careless or mistaken from time to time – some especially so – but there is no evidence that any of them were deliberately deceitful, even though some important material seems to have been suppressed. The lesson from all this is that it is important to examine original sources if we are not to believe uninformed criticism.

APPENDIX 3

Key Dates in Haslam's Life

Mostly supplied by members of the Haslam family

- 1818 January 5, William Haslam born to Thomas Haslam (1790-1832) and Eliza (née Pyefinch) in Sumatra. Thomas Haslam was a Captain in the East India Company's 25th Regt Bengal Native Infantry. WH was one of seven known children.
- 1819 baptised December 1, Fort Marlborough, Sumatra.
- 1823 (if not slightly earlier), WH's father is transferred to Barrackpore (near Calcutta), West Bengal, India.
- 1841, completes Bachelor of Arts degree at University College, Durham.
- 1843 March, becomes Perpetual Curate at Perranzabuloe Church, Cornwall.
- 1843 December 1, gives a lecture at the Royal Institution of Cornwall, Truro, about the old church at Perranzabuloe.
- 1844 December, publishes his book Perran-Zabuloe. (See Appendix 4 for publication dates of other books.)
- 1846 November 10, marries Frances Ann Taunton of Totnes, Devon. Married by Rev Thomas Phillpotts, Vicar of St. Feock and nephew of Bishop Henry Phillpotts.
- In the same year becomes Perpetual Curate of Baldhu church, Cornwall.
- 1847 July 20, foundation stone laid for Baldhu Church.
- 1848, living with his new wife, Frances Ann in Tresithick, Feock, Cornwall.
- 1848 April 5, first child, Wilhelmina Fanny, born at Tresithick.
- 1848 July 20, Baldhu Church consecrated by the Lord Bishop of Exeter (Bishop Phillpotts) and dedicated in honour of St. Michael the Archangel.

- 1849 December 25, birth of first son, John Horsley.
- 1851 February 25, birth of son, William Doidge.
- 1851 October 19, converted by his own sermon while preaching at Baldhu.
- 1852, birth of son, Thomas Aitken.
- 1853, birth of son, Robert Taunton.
- 1855, birth of daughter, Margaret.
- 1855, feels God's calling to move on from Baldhu. Invited to take charge of a new parish in Plymouth, but Bishop Phillpotts after accepting his resignation of Baldhu refuses to allow him to take up the Plymouth post.
- 1856, Bishop Phillpotts allows him to become Perpetual Curate at Carnmenellis, Cornwall, probably after helping out on the retirement of the Vicar. (See church baptism register.)
- 1857, birth of son, James William Barnabas.
- 1857, takes up a new post at St John's church in the town of Hayle, Cornwall, being promised a new church by the Rector. Works among the dockers and factory workers.
- 1858, birth of daughter, Caroline Charlotte.
- 1859, February 25 son, George Fenton christened at Phillack, Cornwall.
- 1859/60, dismissed from Hayle by the unsympathetic rector.
- 1860 very early January, moves to Bath, in charge of the district of St Paul's in the parish of Holy Trinity in Bath.
- 1861, birth of daughter, Georgina, at Hayle. She may have died in very early childhood: It is not known why Frances Haslam was back in Hayle.
- 1861, known to have ten children. Seven of his children ill with scarlet fever, one of whom, Georgy, dies at Bath in 1863. (See memorial card below.)
- 1862 January, living at 4 Stanhope Place, Bath.
- 1862 January 18, birth of daughter, christened Maria, but known as Mary Frances Ann, and later signs her name as Fanny A.
- 1863, under the patronage of Sir Thomas Beauchamp becomes Rector of the parish of Buckenham with Hassingham, Norfolk.
- 1865 April 18, his mother Eliza dies aged 70 in Dehra, India.

- 1871, appointed to Little Missenden, Buckinghamshire, prior to taking up appointment in Mayfair at the suggestion of Earl Howe.
- 1872, becomes incumbent of Curzon Chapel, Mayfair, London.
- 1875, officiates at the marriage of his eldest son, Rev John Horsley Haslam to Ellen Marianne Gorham at Tunbridge.
- 1876, Earl Howe dies. His heir wishes to demolish Curzon Chapel to make way for something more profitable.
- 1877 May 18, his wife Frances Ann dies at Jesmond Lodge, Redhill, Surrey aged 57.
- 1877, speaks at the Keswick Convention, at which he will become a regular speaker.
- 1878 June 25, marries Eliza Stone at St Mary, Hornsey. Eliza is 21 years his junior. Eliza's father is Charles Stone a warehouseman. Living at 42 Curzon Street, London.
- 1878, leaves Curzon Chapel to join up with Rev W Hay Aitken, the son of his old friend Robert Aitken and continues his evangelistic ministry with the Church Parochial Mission Society until 1893.
- 1880, living at 19 King's Road, Brownswood Park, North London (the house of his first child Wilhelmina).
- 1880, speaks at the request of Charles Haddon Spurgeon at the Metropolitan Tabernacle, Newington, London.
- 1882, receives an MA from Durham University.
- Travels extensively, especially after leaving Mayfair, preaching in many parts of the world, often visiting such countries as India and Canada where some of his children were living.
- 1890, latter part of the year travels to India. On the last night of his tour he preaches to a packed Bombay church where he 'seemed to be full of the love of God and the joy of His service.' (Bombay Guardian March 21.)
- 1893, living at 66 Marina, St Leonards on Sea. His health is not good, but he continues his regular Sunday afternoon evangelistic services in the Pier Pavilion.
- 1897, living at 19 King's Rd, Brownswood Park, North London (Wilhelmina's house).
- 1897 until the end of 1899, produces a magazine called *Praise*.

- 1901 living at 11, Grosvenor Gardens, St Leonards-on-Sea, East Sussex with his wife Eliza, and two servants.
- 1904, eldest son, John Horsley dies 27 August, aged 54, at Lucerne, Switzerland.
- 1905, dies 26 January at 11 Grosvenor Gardens, St Leonards-on-Sea, East Sussex of heart failure and pneumonia, aged 87. His coffin is laid to rest with a large floral Cornish cross at Reigate Cemetery, Surrey.
- 1905 June 22, wife Eliza dies at Camberwell House, Peckham Road, Surrey.

A fuller biography of William Haslam can be found on the author's website www.williamhaslam.com.

This obituary from the *Hastings and St Leonards Advertiser* for 2 February 1905 is a fitting summary. The only known error is William Haslam's place of birth, which was Sumatra, not India, although he spent much of his childhood in India.

DEATH OF A NOTED EVANGELIST - We regret to record the death of the Rev William Haslam, of 11 Grosvenor Gardens, St Leonards, which took place on Thursday at the age of 87 years from heart failure. The late Mr Haslam was born in India. He came to England and graduated at Durham University. The early years of his ministry were spent in Cornwall, when his antiquarian researches in regard to churches and Druidical remains caused him to be recognised as an authority on the subject. Mr Haslam was subsequently in Norfolk and at Curzon Chapel, Mayfair.

Some 50 years ago he conducted mission services in conjunction with the late Rev W Aitken, father of Canon Hay Aitken, of Norwich, and he worked with Canon Hay Aitken on the staff of the Church Parochial Mission Society for many years. He has held Evangelistic mission services in all parts of the country, and also in Scotland and Ireland, and has visited India, Canada, the United States, North Africa, etc. He is perhaps most widely known as the author of *From Death unto Life* which describes his early ministry; also of five other books and of numerous tracts which have had a very wide circulation.

Mr Haslam had lived in St Leonards for nearly twenty years, and in spite of blindness and increasing feebleness had until recently held services at St Leonards Pier on Sunday evenings. Devotional meetings at his own house were continued up till the last few months. The death of his eldest son, the Rev J H Haslam, vicar of St Saviour's, Denmark Park, S.E., in August last was a blow from which he never recovered. The funeral took place at Reigate Cemetery on Tuesday.

In Memory of
GEORGE FENTON HASLAM,
Aged 4 Years.

BATH, APRIL 29TH, 1863.—JESUS CALLED A LITTLE CHILD UNTO HIM.

"Is it well with the Child? It is well."—2 Kings iv. 26.

Georgy's memorial card – see page 194.

Appendix 4

Websites and Bibliography

This writer's website is www.williamhaslam.com, where there will be updated details of this book while it is still in print, and links to many sites of interest, including those below, which were all active at the time of publication.

A key link is: www.williamhaslam.org. On this independent website there are discussion groups, and a place for people to pose questions and share their views and discoveries with other Haslam enthusiasts. A real goldmine including OCRs of many works. Be prepared to put time aside to follow all the threads!

The St Piran Trust: www.st-piran.com "The St Piran Trust is a non-profit-making charitable Trust which is committed to the development, protection and good administration of the historic sites on Gear Sands connected with St Piran." (Quote from the Trust's site.)

Copies of second-hand books relating to this period can be found through such sites as:
www.usedbooksearch.co.uk, www.abebooks.co.uk and www.abebooks.com.

> [Hint: I have found that using the advanced search mode on booksellers' sites and typing in variations of "Rev William Haslam" "Haslam William" and so on, plus just one keyword, often produces more results than typing the title. Some searches allow synonyms.]

The opening chapters of the original text of *From Death Into Life*, plus an order form for the whole book on CD: www.revival-library.org

A full copy of the original text of *From Death Into Life*: www.gutenberg.org/etext/14578

Books by William Haslam in the British Library

This list shows only the earliest edition, and the library reference, of each title held by the British Library, in date order of publication.

- Perran-Zabuloe; with an account of the past and present state of the Oratory of St Piran…1844 {796.c.51.}
- The Heavenly Jerusalem. A sermon on Heb. xii. 22 to the Cornish… (The Letter of King Charles the martyr…) 1845 {4474.aa.92.(7.)}
- The Cross and the Serpent being a brief history of the triumph of the Cross ... in prophecy… 1849 {3185.c.34.}
- A Letter to the Archdeacon of Cornwall, on the occasion of a lecture (on Conversion) delivered…1853 {4107.dd.1.(21.)}
- Conversion. A lecture, etc.1853 {4107.dd.1.(23.)}
- LYNE, Charles, A correspondence with ... W. Haslam ... (on the public statement made by him "that the neighbour…") 1854 {4107.dd.2.(14.)}
- Notes of an address on Faith, at St Paul's Cathedral,etc. 1874 {4473.aa.4.(21.)}
- The Threefold Gift of God; or, Christ Jesus, the object of faith, hope and love.1876 {4226.bbb.19.}
- Personal Experience; being lectures on Bunyan's *Pilgrim's Progress*.1877 {4414.de.18.}
- A Personal Christ. [With a prefatory note, signed H. F. B.] Second thousand. 1878 {4372.de.11.(13.)}
- Building from the Top; and other readings. [A series of religious narratives.] {4422.i.11.}
- *From Death into Life*: or, *Twenty Years of my Ministry*.1880 {4766.c.9.}
- *Yet Not I*: or, *More Years of My Ministry*. {4907.bb.11.}
- "Full Salvation" as seen in Bunyan's *Pilgrim's Progress*.1884 {4419.dd.15.}
- The Lord is coming: a plain narrative of prophetic events in their order ... Fourth Thousand.1885 {MIC.A.7638.(7.)}
- Gleanings from the Harvest. [A tale.] {4412.ccc.24.}
- Leaves from my Note-book. 1889 {4401.l.37.}
- Notes from Keswick.1890 {4422.c.26.}

Index

Ecclesiastical matters